Channel of Blessing

A Spiritual Journey into Identifying and Understanding Your Spiritual Gift

Bobby Mullins

Channel of Blessing
ISBN 1-930285-03-5

Library of Congress Control Number: 2001087943

Copyright © 2001 by Robert T Mullins
Cover Photo by Elizabeth Olson
Published by The Master Design
   in cooperation with Master Design Ministries
PO Box 17865
Memphis, TN 38187-0865
bookinfo@masterdesign.org
www.masterdesign.org

Additional copies of this book may be purchased from:
        Cherokee Baptist Church
        5340 Quince Road
        Memphis, TN 38119
        901-683-7344

Unless otherwise noted, Scripture quotations are from the KING JAMES VERSION as translated in 1611.

Printed in the USA by Bethany Press International.

JJ

Contents

Preface

Introducing Spiritual Gifts
    As It Hath Pleased Him 1

Identifying Spiritual Gifts
  The Spiritual Gift of Prophecy
    A More Sure Word 20
  The Gift of Serving
    Naturally Caring 42
  The Gift of Teaching
    Knowing with Certainty 71
  The Gift of Exhorting
    As a Father Does His Children 92
  The Gift of Giving
    Living to Give 116
  The Gift of Organizing
    Able to Endure 144
  The Gift of Mercy
    In Deed and in Truth 177

Understanding Spiritual Gifts
    For the Profit of All 205

Endnotes 243

Spiritual Gifts Inventory 245

This book is dedicated

To Wanda, my wife, best friend, and helpmeet (Gen. 2:18) in all areas of life, whose gift of mercy balances my gift of prophecy;

To the members of Dixie Lee Baptist Church, Lenoir City, Tennessee, where the sermons which formed the foundation of Channel of Blessing *were first preached;*

To the members of Cherokee Baptist Church, Memphis, Tennessee, who put into practice and proved the content of Channel of Blessing.

Preface

Upon the writing of this Preface, I had thirty books in my personal library that dealt solely with the subject of spiritual gifts. I am adding to this number as I become aware of books I do not have on the subject. Only three of those books are in full agreement on the number of spiritual gifts and how they are classified and divided. Even conservative Bible scholars disagree on such basics as the number of spiritual gifts with some believing the Bible designates anywhere from 18 to 32 different spiritual gifts. Some even believe that the spiritual gifts listings in the Bible are not comprehensive, but representative, and that it is possible to have spiritual gifts besides those listed in the Bible. When it comes to the differing ways of dividing spiritual gifts, most of the books favor dividing spiritual gifts into three groups, based on the three main listings of spiritual gifts in the Bible. Some of the ways various authors have divided the gifts into three groups are miraculous gifts, enabling gifts, and team gifts; speaking gifts, ministering/serving gifts, and signifying gifts; enabling gifts, serving gifts, and sign gifts; Godhead gifts coinciding with the Father, Son, and Holy Spirit; and, motivational, ministry, and manifestation gifts.

Four major references in the Bible address the subject of spiritual gifts: Romans 12:6-8; 1 Corinthians 12:8-11,28-30; Ephesians 4:11; and 1 Peter 4:10. The biblical and theological basis for *Channel of Blessing* has been drawn from those passages. I mentioned in the previous paragraph that three books on spiritual gifts in my personal library are in full agreement in their approach to the subject. Those books are: *Discover Your God-Given Gifts* by Don and Katie Fortune (Chosen Books, 1989); *You Have a Grace Gift* by James H. Smith (Brotherhood Commission, SBC, 1987); and, a booklet published by Bill Gothard's ministry, The

Institute in Basic Life Principles, titled, *How to Understand Spiritual Gifts*. *Channel of Blessing* is in accord with those books in believing that spiritual gifts are classified as motivational (Rom. 12:6-8), ministry (1 Cor. 12:28), and manifestation gifts (1 Cor. 12:8-11), and that the key to an understanding and effective use of spiritual gifts within the church is through the motivational gifts. Every Christian has one of seven possibilities as his/her major motivational spiritual gift. The purpose of this book is to help Christians to identify and exercise their major motivational spiritual gift and to know the characteristics of the other motivational gifts so that we can better understand and accept why other Christians think, act, react, and respond differently from us.

I sought to write this book in such a way that a pastor can preach through the material in sermon form, a teacher can teach through the material in a classroom setting, and an individual will find it easy to follow in private reading and study. I have purposely written this book with the intent of avoiding controversy. There are theological differences between Charismatic believers and non-Charismatic believers on such issues as speaking in tongues, miracles, faith healing, and determining what is meant by the "word of wisdom" or "word of knowledge." Other books can deal with the differences. The main theme of *Channel of Blessing* deals with the motivational gifts. The basic characteristics of the motivational gifts, and how one determines his/her major motivational spiritual gift, are common to all Christians, regardless of how they "split hairs" on other doctrinal issues. In *Channel of Blessing*, I wanted to stay within those areas where we are alike.

My prayer for you is that *Channel of Blessing* will be a spiritual journey in helping you to identify and apply your main motivational spiritual gift. If you believe you already know your spiritual gift, then I pray that *Channel of Blessing* will help to reaffirm your gift as well as give you insight how your spiritual gift relates to the other motivational gifts. May each of us as we have "received the gift, even so minister the same one to another, as good stewards of the manifold grace of God" (1 Peter 4:10).

Bobby Mullins
February, 2001

Introducing Spiritual Gifts

1

Introducing Spiritual Gifts

"As It Hath Pleased Him"

This book is about spiritual gifts. The subject of spiritual gifts either draws a quick, favorable reaction from those who have an understanding of the subject, or receives little or negative reaction from those who have never been taught the concept properly. Varied views have been taught regarding spiritual gifts and how they are manifested in each of our lives. In this book, I take a different approach from what you may have been taught previously about spiritual gifts. I believe it is the most biblical way to teach spiritual gifts.

There are varying interpretations regarding Bible passages that deal with spiritual gifts. Although this book's approach in applying the verses contained in those passages is not the norm, it is not a newly discovered teaching technique. It is as old as the Bible. It centers on the idea that there are seven major motivational spiritual gifts, and one of these represents your dominant spiritual gift.

Many are taught that there are anywhere from 16 to 19 spiritual gifts listed in the Bible. Depending on what book you study or who your teacher is, the total number of different spiritual gifts may vary even more, according to how an author or a teacher interprets biblical passages addressing spiritual gifts. Some believe that the list of spiritual gifts is endless and the ones listed in the Bible are just some examples of possible spiritual gifts. There are also those who believe that you can have multiple spiritual gifts. But I believe God is more detailed and concise than that.

The emphasis of this book is for us to develop qualities of all the spiritual gifts, but each of us has only one major motivational gift. And, oh, the joy you experience in your life when you gain an understanding of your spiritual gift; allowing God to use it to work through you. This book is intended to be a guide in your spiritual journey to identify your spiritual gift and apply it in your daily walk of faith.

As you permit this book to teach you about spiritual gifts, it will be done in a way that has worked in a variety of settings by preachers and teachers, some of whom may even differ theologically on various issues. If you will read this book in its entirety, you will have a good idea of what your spiritual gift is, and you will have a knowledge and understanding of the other gifts. The apostle Paul teaches in the twelfth chapter of 1 Corinthians that, **as it hath pleased Him** (v.18), God has given to each of us one of the major motivational gifts, which we are to use where He has placed us in service in the body of Christ, His church (Eph. 4:7, 12; Col. 1:18).

If I were to choose one of the great hymns of the faith to be a theme song for this book, it would be *"Make Me A Channel Of Blessing."* Your spiritual gift is a blessing that God has given to you to be used as a channel of blessing to the other members of the body of the church. Individually, none of us can do all that is necessary for the church of Christ to affect this world the way our Lord wants us to. But if each of us will faithfully fulfill God's will for our life, in the way He has motivated us to do it (your spiritual gift), then the church, and especially the local church to which God has led you, will make a difference for Jesus in this world. Your special gift will not only be a blessing from God to you, but it will be a channel of blessing to others whom you serve alongside in the work of God. Likewise, their special gift will be a blessing to you as their gift is a help to you where you are not specifically gifted.

Do you see why an understanding of spiritual gifts and the proper application of them is imperative to the effective functioning of the body of believers? I hope that you will take this spiritual journey to find your special gift for blessing, and gain an understanding of the other gifts, so that all of the members of the body of Christ will flow together as a channel of blessing within the world.

Design Of Spiritual Gifts

Several components make up God's design for spiritual gifts. A familiarity with the following components is necessary to properly understand God's purpose in giving spiritual gifts and how we are to use them.

Definition of a Spiritual Gift

First, consider the **definition** of a spiritual gift. This book defines a spiritual gift as:

> *A grace gift from God, manifested by the Holy Spirit, which is exemplified and expressed by what motivates us to do God's will in ministering to one another for the common good, that each of us might fulfill God's will for our life in order to help achieve His ultimate will for all mankind.*

Distribution of Spiritual Gifts

Second, who is given a spiritual gift? Every biblical passage on spiritual gifts speaks to Christians. First Peter 4:10 says: "As every man hath received the gift, even so minister the same one to another, as good stewards of the manifold grace of God." Ephesians 4:7 states, "But every one of us is given grace according to the measure of the gift of Christ." Both of these verses address Christians. Therefore, every Christian is given a spiritual gift.

Your spiritual gift is activated the moment you are saved, when the

Holy Spirit unites with your spirit (Rom. 8:16-17). Just as we are born with natural abilities, when we are born again spiritually, God takes our natural and unnatural abilities, and turns them into means by which He can work through us divinely, providentially, and supernaturally.

Designation of Spiritual Gifts

How many gifts does a Christian receive? In 1 Peter 4:10 and Ephesians 4:7, the emphasis is on *gift*, singular, not *gifts*, plural. In the Bible, the Greek word, *charisma*, means *gift*.

The way the Greek word has carried over into English gives added dimensions to the word, *charisma*, than what it actually meant in its original Greek form. But Christians who are part of the charismatic movement do not have any more spiritual gifts than any other Christians. One Christian does not have more *charisma* from God than another Christian. You have one major motivational spiritual gift, but there are multiple ways to express it. I will discuss the various ways by which you can express your gift later in this chapter.

Development of Spiritual Gifts

And so, each Christian receives one main spiritual gift. Why do we receive only one spiritual gift? So you can *nurture and develop* it by concentrating on it. You can become a jack of all trades and a master of none. An old hymn of the faith challenges us to "give of your best to the Master." We need to master our spiritual gifts as best as we can for the Master.

Many parents push their children to be involved year-round in a number of different sports or extracurricular activities. Those of us who have a child participating in sports would not mind having our child excel in one of those sports so that he or she would receive an athletic college scholarship. But many have a tendency today to overextend their kids in several sports in which they may do very well. The problem with participation in multiple sports is that it dilutes concentration and excellence in one sport. And that is what it takes to earn an athletic scholarship. The athlete who participates in more than one sport at the college level or professionally is an exception.

The same reasoning applies to spiritual gift development. The Lord wants us to nurture and develop our main spiritual gift so that we can *excel* in it. By receiving only one major motivational spiritual gift, you can concentrate on it, nurture, and develop it so that you can excel for the Lord in the area of service to which He has called you.

Furthermore, we receive only one main spiritual gift to make us realize our *need and dependency* for each other. I have the motivational spiritual gift of prophecy. What motivates me in my ministry role as a pastor is to preach the Word of God. If I have been true to the Word of God, then I have done what God has motivated me to do through the spiritual gift He has given me.

If the work of the church, though, was solely dependent upon the pastor, the work of the church would not be complete. The preaching of the Word is to be the focal point of the church coming together for worship, but there are other ways that a church is to minister.

We have a benevolence committee in our church. This committee must exhibit qualities of the spiritual gifts of mercy and giving. Everyone on the benevolence committee may not have the motivational gift of mercy or giving, but some do, and the characteristics of those gifts must be exemplified by the members of this committee. They help to relieve physical and material needs of residents in our community, or transients passing through our area, who have such needs. Hopefully, the needy are also ministered to spiritually in the process of receiving help from our church. If it was dependent upon me, those kinds of needs may not be met. Churches are called upon almost daily with benevolence requests. I need others in our church to take care of the area of benevolence so that I can spend the necessary time in prayer, studying, and sermon preparation.

We have others in our church who are gifted in teaching the Bible and who do so as teachers in our Sunday school. There are those in our church who have a unique ability to work with children or with some other special group in our church, and they are more gifted in those areas than I am.

Praise the Lord! I am thankful that I do not have to worry about those programs and ministries, if the ones who lead out in those areas do their job, heartily, as unto the Lord (Col. 3:23). I can concentrate on what God has called me to do. As the senior pastor of our church, I need and depend upon other church members to serve with me in making a difference for Jesus in our world, and especially, in our corner of the world. If all of us are responding appropriately to what God uses to motivate us, we, being many, will work together as one body in Christ (Rom. 12:4-5).

Discovering Spiritual Gifts

How do you discover your spiritual gift? Here are several practical helps.

First, *accept* Jesus Christ as your Lord and Savior. You need to be saved. Spiritual gifts are for Christians. The potential of your spiritual gift is within you, but it will not be developed within your life until you are born again spiritually.

After you have accepted God's free gift of eternal life through Jesus Christ (Eph. 2:8-9; Rom. 6:23; 5:1,8), *acknowledge* Him in all your ways, and God promises that He will direct your paths (Prov. 3:6). God will lead you down the pathway of discovering your spiritual gift, if you strive to obey Him in all that you do.

As you are *active* in serving the Lord where you are, you will begin to sense what motivates you to serve Him.

Admit your need of help where there is difficulty with an area of sin in your life. You need to confess your sins to God (1 John 1:9). Keep your sin list short by confessing and asking God's forgiveness as you become aware of your acts of sin.

In the first eleven chapters of Romans, Paul explains how to get saved and conquer sin. Then, in Romans 12, he addresses spiritual gifts. They are not explained and dealt with until *after* sin has been identified and defeated in the life of the believer in Christ.

One reason many Christians don't use their spiritual gift, or even know what their gift is, is because there are unconquered areas of sin in their lives.

Affections can also help you to discover your spiritual gift. As a spiritual gift is to be for the good of the body of believers, the way affections can help you determine your spiritual gift is in how you concentrate on the needs of others. What motivates you to do what you do in your church to help other people?

Affirmation from others can assist you as well. People will see qualities in you, and they will let you know it. As you learn the qualities of the different spiritual gifts, others affirm in you certain qualities dominant to a particular gift, which point you to your gift. It did not take long for me to learn the specific spiritual gift of the first two men who served as chairman of the deacons at my first pastorate. One has the gift of organizing, and the other has the gift of serving. They, and others who know them, agree. The qualities of those gifts stand out in those two men, and it is obvious to others.

Along the line of affections and affirmation, is *ambition*. Discern your real ambition in life; not so much by what satisfies or benefits you, but what motivates you to respond in helping people.

Another trait that can guide you to discover your spiritual gift is *annoyance*. I bet that you had not thought of what annoys you as being a way to determine your spiritual gift. Identify what other Christians do that irritate you. There are things that fellow Christians do not do, or ways they respond or do not respond to a situation, that make you think they are either insensitive or not very alert. Rather than frustrating or irritating you, this should be a signal that confirms your motivational spiritual gift. Their gift does not alert them to such circumstances and situations, but yours does. Most likely, your spiritual gift is to be activated in that particular situation where you become irritated with other Christians. Your spiritual gift allows you to see needs that are overlooked by the other spiritual gifts.

You need to *analyze* the diversities and divisions of spiritual gifts to understand their different categories and functions. This will help you to discover your gift and to be of assistance in helping others to discover their gift.

As you analyze, you will learn to *associate* the characteristics as well as the misuses of each gift. Most problems we face come as we try to fulfill our spiritual gift in the energy of the flesh, rather than by the energizing power of the Holy Spirit. Some people discover their spiritual gift by detecting misuses of natural abilities and characteristics common to a particular spiritual gift.

I stated previously that being active in serving the Lord is a way to determine your spiritual gift. I want to expand that suggestion even further in the idea of *assimilation*. Assimilation is the process by which nourishment is changed into living tissue. By getting involved in service in the body of Christ at a local church, you will find what nourishes you spiritually and how you spiritually nourish other Christians. That will give you a realistic picture of your spiritual gift.

Another practical step to find your spiritual gift is the most basic of those that have been mentioned thus far. Surprisingly, it is many times the last resort for some seekers instead of being the first choice.

Ask God to reveal your spiritual gift to you (Matt. 7:7-8). Most likely, He will work through the other means that have already been given, but the process of finding your spiritual gift will be more greatly advanced by beginning with the One who chooses your spiritual gift for you.

Several components make up God's design for spiritual gifts. Each person is given one major motivational spiritual gift by God to nurture and develop by concentrating on it. But you need to discover which of the seven motivational spiritual gifts is the one that God has given to you. Several practical steps have been given to assist you in discovering your spiritual gift. As you serve the Lord in your local church by exercising your spiritual gift, as others do likewise, it is for the profit of all (1 Cor. 12:7).

Diversities Of Spiritual Gifts

It is necessary to understand two more classifications of spiritual gifts before studying each of the individual motivational gifts.

Let's look at 1 Corinthians 12:4-6:

> Now there are diversities of gifts, but the same Spirit. And there are differences of administrations, but the same Lord. And there are diversities of operations, but it is the same God which worketh all in all.

The same Greek word has been translated in the King James Version Bible as *diversities*, in verses four and six, and as *differences*, in verse five. In English, we tend to avoid repeating a word too much. Maybe that is why the translators of the King James Version used *differences* in verse five.

I prefer the translation *diversities*. To be *different* can give the idea of being unlike. To be *diverse*, two things can be alike, but their function or approach to a shared goal or project may not be done the same way. The analogy given in 1 Corinthians 12 likens the function of spiritual gifts to the way the parts of the body work together. The hand and foot are alike, in that both are part of the body, but their functions in helping the body to operate properly are not the same. So it is with spiritual gifts. Paul has classified them as diversities of **gifts** (v. 4), diversities of **administrations**, and diversities of **operations** (v. 6).

In verse four, Paul states that there are diversities of gifts. The Greek word used in 1 Corinthians 12:4 and 1 Peter 4:10 for *gift* actually means *grace gift*. You have one grace gift. You are motivated to express it by God giving you the desire and power to do His will.

Paul also informs us that there are diversities of administrations through which to use your grace gift (motivational gift). The word translated *administration* in 1 Corinthians 12:5, and as *minister* in 1 Peter 4:10, is the word from which we get our English word *deacon*. The basic responsibility of deacons is to be servants of the Lord (Acts 6:2-3), who lead out in seeing that the more practical work of the church is properly administered. Likewise, your grace gift is to be a serving gift. It finds its meaningful expression and fulfillment in the ministries (*administrations*) and outreach of the local church.

There are also diversities of operations (1 Cor. 12:6). The word translated *operations* is where we get our English word *energy*. First Corinthians 12:7 declares, "But the manifestation of the Spirit is given to every man to profit withal." To manifest something is to show it and make it clear to those who see it.

As you use your grace gift through service (ministry) in a local church, the effect (operation) of it is seen (manifested) in the response of others to it.

So, there are diversities of motivational gifts—seven, to be exact. These motivational spiritual gifts are exercised through the ministries of a local church. The diverse operations of these spiritual gifts are manifested in various ways by the effect they have on others. It is our responsibility to develop our motivational gift. It is the church's responsibility to provide ministries and to confirm what this book will refer to as ministry gifts. The Holy Spirit will manifest Himself through our gift to reward the use of the gifts for the profit of all.

Division Of Spiritual Gifts

From the Bible passage describing the diversities of spiritual gifts, it also makes a distinction for **the division of spiritual gifts**. First Corinthians 12:4 refers to the *motivational gifts*, verse five makes a distinction for *ministry gifts*, and verses six and seven address the *manifestation gifts*. These three divisions of spiritual gifts are expanded upon through other verses in the Bible – the motivational gifts in Romans 12:6-15, the ministry gifts in 1 Corinthians 12:27-31, and the manifestation gifts in 1 Corinthians 12:7-11. Since the emphasis of this book is upon the motivational gifts, I will not go into much detail regarding the ministry and manifestation gifts. But I do want you to see how those two divisions of spiritual gifts are distinguished from the motivational gifts.

Motivational Gifts

Seven motivational spiritual gifts are given in Romans 12:6-8:

> *Having then gifts differing according to the grace that is given to us, whether **prophecy**, let us prophesy according to the proportion of faith; Or ministry **(serving)**, let us wait on our ministering: or he that teacheth, on **teaching**; Or he that exhorteth, on **exhortation**: he that **giveth**, let him do it with simplicity; he that ruleth **(organizing)**, with diligence; he that showeth **mercy**, with cheerfulness.*

Prophecy - A prophet is motivated to expound the Scriptures and expose sin by boldly speaking the truth. Old Testament prophets predicted judgment for the sins of God's people. Prophets use the Scriptures to reveal unrighteous motives and actions.

Serving - A server is alert to meeting practical needs in the lives of others and to freeing others to achieve what the server feels to be more important tasks.

Teaching - A teacher is motivated to confirm, clarify, and communicate truth.

Exhorting - An exhorter is motivated to stimulate the spiritual progress of others by sensing one's potential, then suggesting steps of action that are practical.

Giving - A giver is motivated to invest money in ministries as the Lord impresses to advance His work. Motivated to give gifts as God guides, the gifts of a giver have impact and significance because they are received as answers to prayer.

Organizing - An organizer is motivated to conceive, coordinate, and complete a project that involves others working together in one accord for the Lord to reach a common goal.

Mercy - A mercy giver is motivated to relate to and remove hindrances and hurts that others experience. Just as the server focuses on physical needs and assistance, and as the giver meets financial need, one with the gift of mercy concentrates on giving empathy, encouragement, comfort, and cheer, particularly during times of distress.

Ministry Gifts

Paul reveals in 1 Corinthians 12:5 that there are differences of *administrations*. Another way to say it is that there are diversities or varieties of *ministries* in the body of Christ. The ministry gifts are listed in 1 Corinthians 12:28:

> *And God hath set some in the church, first **apostles**, secondarily **prophets**, thirdly **teachers**, after that **miracles**, then gifts of **healing**, **helps**, **governments**, **diversities of tongues**.*

A similar list is found in Ephesians 4:11, in Paul's letter to Ephesus: "And he gave some, **apostles**; and some, **prophets**; and some, **evangelists**; and some, **pastors** and **teachers**." In verse twelve, Paul also explains why God gave the ministry gifts to the church: "For the perfecting of the saints, for the work of the ministry, for the edifying of the body of Christ." The context of those verses begins in verse seven where Paul states: "But unto every one of us is given grace according to the measure of the gift of Christ." The Greek word used for *gift* in that verse means a *free gift or present*.

Ministry gifts are given by God to the church to edify (build up) the body of believers. Our motivational gift becomes a gift of blessing as we express it through one of the following ministries.

Apostles - In the New Testament, the *apostles* originally referred to the twelve disciples of Christ. The word means *one sent forth*. Paul describes himself as an apostle. Today, the ministry of an apostle is fulfilled in the role of a missionary. In Ephesians 4:11, Paul adds, *evangelists* and *pastors*, not previously listed in 1 Corinthians 12:28. I believe the biblical concept of an apostle is also fulfilled today in the role of an evangelist and a pastor. An evangelist is one sent forth by God, who goes from place to place, to spread the gospel and to edify the church. A pastor may remain for several years, maybe a lifetime, in one location. But as part of his calling, he makes a commitment to go wherever and whenever God sends him. Evangelism, missions, and missions giving are to be a vital part of a local church.

Prophets - A pastor, as a faithful forthteller of God's divine truth, is an example of fulfilling the ministry of a prophet. The prophetic ministry in a local church is most effectively accomplished in its pulpit ministry, although that certainly is not the only way the ministry of a prophet is expressed.

Teachers - The teaching ministry in a local church is exemplified through such ministries as Sunday school, discipleship training, special Bible studies (for example, Kay Arthur's Precept Ministry), music education, missions education, and other similar programs. Those who are instructors in such ministries are fulfilling the role of teachers. The pulpit ministry of the pastor is also meant for teaching, as well as fulfilling the role of a prophet. There must be balance.

Miracles - Miracles are natural or supernatural events God accomplishes with precise timing in order to draw people to Him. The ultimate purpose for miracles is salvation. The works (miracles) that Jesus performed were to bear witness through Him that He had been sent by God so that people would believe in Christ unto salvation (John 5:20,24,34,36). The ministry of prayer is the most effective means by which to fulfill the ministry of miracles today.

Healings - This was part of Christ's earthly ministry, and it should continue to be a part of a local church ministry now. It refers not only to physical healing, but also to spiritual, emotional, and mental healing. Bringing healing to the spirit and soul is often a prerequisite to physical healing. The ministry of healing does include miraculous healings, which are preceded by prayer. A local church can also have a part in this ministry through supporting recreational programs of a church, as well as through medical missions. God uses doctors and medicines as a means of healing, but medicines should not be abused, and only doctors who operate their practices according to biblical principles should be entrusted with medical mission leadership.

Helps - A local church should do its part to help meet physical and financial needs of those around them. There are several ways churches can be involved in this ministry. A clothes closet, food pantry, special funds and offerings for benevolence needs, and a church benevolence committee are a few examples of the ministry of helps. Especially included under the ministry of helps is the taking care of the fatherless, the widows, and the poor.

Governments - This ministry refers to those who guide the local church. Usually, the ministerial staff are the most visible ones who fulfill this ministry, but others in elected and appointed church leadership positions are also included. It is significant that this gift was listed near the end of the list. Organization which is the most effective is that which is least visible.

Diversities of Tongues - This ministry gift in a local church concerns the use of language in introducing people to the Gospel and in maturing them in the faith. One way a local church can fulfill this ministry is by ministering to an ethnic group who do not speak English. Even the sign ministry to deaf people can be identified as a diversity of tongues.

Manifestation Gifts

There are also diversities of operations. Paul declares in 1 Corinthians 12:6-7:

> And there are diversities of operations, but it is the same God which worketh all in all. But the manifestation of the Spirit is given to every man to profit withal.

The word *manifestation* in verse seven, is the key to a third division of spiritual gifts. As mentioned previously, the Greek word which the King James Version Bible translates *operations* is where we get our English word *energy*. In its use in verse six, this word refers to the results of the energy of God. Using the word *manifestation* in verse seven, is another way of expressing the idea of verse six. There is a manifestation – a result that God has in mind – from the use of your motivational gift through a ministry gift. Manifestation gifts are the effect of expressing your motivational gift through one of the ministry gifts. A list of the manifestation gifts is found in 1 Corinthians 12:8-11:

> For to one is given by the Spirit the **word of wisdom**; to another the **word of knowledge** by the same Spirit; To another **faith** by the same Spirit; to another the gifts of **healing** by the same Spirit; To another the working of **miracles**; to another **prophecy**; to another **discerning of spirits**; to another **divers kinds of tongues**; to another the **interpretation of tongues**.

As I have done with the other two divisions of spiritual gifts, I will list each of the manifestation gifts with a brief description.

Word of Wisdom - The manifestation of the word of wisdom is being able to see life from God's perspective. Wisdom is the application of what you know. It is manifested in the way you use what you know. It begins with a fear of the Lord (Prov. 1:7). You may be the beneficiary of a word of wisdom that you receive from the comment of a Sunday school teacher about a verse of Scripture. That is just one example of how the process can work. A word of wisdom can always be confirmed by Scripture.

Word of Knowledge - Knowledge is what you already know. It comes as the Holy Spirit opens one's understanding, because the things of God are spiritually discerned (1 Cor. 2:14). The manifestation of the word of knowledge comes in using knowledge truthfully.

Faith - Faith is taking God at His Word and living according to it. It is the result of hearing the Word of God (Rom. 10:17), believing it, and acting upon it. Faith is manifested in being able to visualize what God wants to accomplish and seeing it through.

Healings - The manifestation of the gift of healing is the removing of disease(s) from the spirit, soul, or body. Some diseases of the spirit are bitterness, greed, and guilt. Examples of the diseases of the soul are discouragement, worry, jealously, and other such destructive attitudes (see Ps. 103:1-3). Many physical illnesses are not originally physical in their source. Although this is certainly not always the case, the diseases of the spirit and soul can result in physical problems.

Miracles - Miracles are natural or supernatural events that occur with precise timing to bring glory to God. As the ministry gift of miracles basically comes through the expression of prayer, it is the function of the Holy Spirit to direct our prayers in praying for God to work miracles (Rom. 8:26).

Prophecy - The manifestation of prophecy is bringing to light the secret motives of the heart. It is the ministry of the Holy Spirit to convict of sin, righteousness, and judgment to come (John 16:8-11).

Discerning of Spirits - The manifestation of this gift is being able to recognize what is of God as opposed to what is of the world, the flesh, or the devil. Discerning of spirits must be done by the power of the Holy Spirit. He bears witness with our spirit when something or someone is not right or is not of God.

Divers Kinds of Tongues - The manifestation gift of tongues is glorifying God through language and music. The Holy Spirit energizes the tongue to edify believers through language and music.

Interpretation of Tongues - The interpretation of tongues is manifested by an unfamiliar language being interpreted into the language of the recipients of a message from God. For example, I have a preacher friend who made a mission trip to the Soviet Union. Most of the preaching he did while there was not to English speaking audiences. But he had a Russian interpreter with him. As he preached in English, his interpreter spoke the message in the language the audience understood. It always resulted in people being saved as the Gospel presentation was interpreted from English into the Russian language. Interpretation of tongues is for the purpose of relaying a message from God for the salvation and edification of people.

Conclusion

God has given us different gifts, as it hath pleased Him, in order for us to serve one another. You have one major motivational spiritual gift from God, but there are many areas of ministry through which to use your gift. There are also many positive effects (manifestations) resulting from the use of your spiritual gift, especially as you serve the Lord through a local church. As you develop characteristics of all the gifts, Jesus in you always equips you for the moment with whatever gift is needed at the time. But you will tend to see things and people from a different perspective, depending on your motivational gift.

As we move on to a detailed study of the individual motivational gifts, our purpose for learning about them is not just so you will know what your motivational gift is and how to identify the other gifts in other people. You also need to do some self-evaluation once you have discovered or reconfirmed what you believe to be your motivational spiritual gift.

Are you a spectator or are you serving the Lord? Are you exercising your motivational gift? What motivates you to do what you do for the Lord? Is it love or is it for selfish reasons? Is it more for the benefit of others or more for the benefits you receive? Your motivational spiritual gift is a grace gift from God to you. It is your special gift of blessing. Although you will receive personal blessings from the proper use of your gift, as you give away your gift to others from your exercise of it, your special gift of blessing becomes a channel of blessing to others whom your life touches. May these words from *"Make Me A Channel Of Blessing,"* be lived out through each of our lives:

> *Is your life a channel of blessing?*
> *Is the love of God flowing through you?*
> *Are you telling the lost of the Savior?*
> *Are you ready His service to do?*
>
> *Make me a channel of blessing today;*
> *Make me a channel of blessing I pray;*
> *My life possessing, my service blessing;*
> *Make me a channel of blessing today.*[1]

Identifying Your Spiritual Gift

2

The Spiritual Gift of Prophecy

"A More Sure Word"

*Having then gifts differing according to the grace that is given to us, whether **prophecy**, let us prophesy according to the proportion of faith; ...Let love be without dissimulation. Abhor that which is evil; cleave to that which is good. (Rom. 12:6,9)*

Prophecy is the first gift listed in Romans 12:6-15, the pivotal Bible passage for motivational gifts.

The prophet is to *make sure the Word of God.* After you have heard a prophet, and you begin doing something sinfully wrong, the word of the prophet may come back to you and make sure the Word of God. His words remind you: "No, you are not living how you ought to live. This is not right. This is not sure according to the Word of God."

Second Peter 1:19-21 illustrates the motivation of one who has the spiritual gift of prophecy:

We have also a more sure word of prophecy; whereunto ye do well that ye take heed, as unto a light that shineth in a dark place, until the day dawn, and the day star arise in your hearts: Knowing this first, that no prophecy of the scripture is of any private interpretation. For the prophecy came not in old time by the will of man: but holy men of God spake as they were moved by the Holy Ghost.

Prophets spoke what they believed to be *"a more sure word"* as they were moved by the Holy Spirit. The person with the gift of prophecy is probably the most misunderstood because of the manner by which a prophet may express his gift.

In the New Testament, Peter exemplifies the gift of prophecy. However, in the Gospels, his gift of prophecy often manifested itself in the weakness of the flesh. But we should not be quick to criticize Peter because of that. If we are not careful, our motivational gift will come out in the weakness of the flesh, when we are not walking in the power of the Holy Spirit. Peter really did not understand his spiritual gift until the Day of Pentecost, when he was filled with the Holy Spirit. On that day and thereafter, his motivational gift of prophecy was manifested in a mighty and powerful way as he witnessed for the Lord.

When God uses a prophet in a church (particularly if people do not know the prophet very well), there can be misunderstandings because he says things very bluntly, at times. People may feel that the prophet is mean-spirited and not a loving person. But the Bible says that it takes more love to correct a problem than to ignore it (Prov. 27:5 paraphrased). Sometimes, a straightforward approach to dealing with a situation is the best way to handle it. Such circumstances call for the prophets to come to the forefront.

A prophet will be God's spokesman, telling you exactly what you are doing wrong, and you may even know what he says is the truth, but you do not necessarily like it. If you really want to understand a prophet, read through 1 and 2 Peter. You will see the heart of prophet who is under the control of the Holy Spirit. Peter strongly expresses what he says, but his love for his readers is also evident. That is very important to understand in the life of one who has the motivational gift of prophecy.

Let us see the composite the Bible gives of one with the spiritual gift of prophecy.

A Composite: The Gift of Prophecy

Explanation of the Gift of Prophecy

In the eighteenth chapter of Deuteronomy, an explanation is given about prophecy and what a prophet is to do:

> *I will raise them up a Prophet from among their brethren, like unto thee, and will put My words is his mouth; and he shall speak unto them all that I shall command him. And it shall come to pass, that whosoever will not hearken unto My words which he shall speak in My name, I will require it of him.* (Deut. 18:18-19)

This passage indicates that a prophet is to *speak God's words* and to *speak them in His name*. Peter gives an idea of another expectation of a prophet:

> *Wherefore I will not be negligent to put you always in remembrance of these things, though ye know them, and be established in the present truth. Yea, I think it meet, as long as I am in this tabernacle, to stir you up by putting you in remembrance.* (2 Peter 1:12-13)

A prophet is not only to speak God's words in the name of God, but he is to *stir us up*. He is to stir us up by calling to our minds the remembrance of those things in our lives that are not as they ought to be. He is to stir us up concerning the commandments of the Word of God. The prophet may exemplify his special gift through speaking, teaching, praying, and even when singing by reminding us of an area of our life where we are disobedient to God or not living the way we should.

We have had prophets whose messages are recorded in the Bible. They are classified as the Major Prophets and the Minor Prophets. That does not mean, though, that what the major prophets had to say was more important than what the minor prophets had to say. The major prophets just said more of it. Their writings are much longer than those of the minor prophets. But everything a minor prophet said had just as much credence and force to it as Isaiah, Jeremiah, and Ezekiel, who were among the major prophets.

Our society tends to view a prophet as one who foretells future world events, and some prophets have done that. But the explanation from the Bible, as to what a prophet was to do, is that he was not so much to be a *foreteller* of future world events as the prophet was to be a faithful *forthteller* of the Word of the Lord.

Today we have the Bible to tell us about future prophecy and about world events that we can expect. A real prophet today is not spending most of his time talking about what we call "prophecies." He is not spending all his time in the Book of Revelation. He is spending time in those other portions of Scripture that get people saved and that get people ready for Revelation. The prophets of today motivate Christians to live the kind of life that honors the Lord and that makes a difference for Christ. Prophets want to bring people to the place that they will be spiritually ready when those future world events happen.

Those who spend the most time on prophecy, trying to figure out what the prophecies mean and when they are going to occur, probably have the motivational gift of teaching. It is because their main concern is accuracy and clarification. The preacher who has the spiritual gift of prophecy does not necessarily do a lot of what we normally think of as prophetic preaching. Prophets are motivated to speak God's Word, to speak in His name, and to stir us up spiritually because they believe that they have a more sure word from God that we need to hear.

Examples of Prophets

The Bible contains examples of those who had the motivational gift of prophecy. Moses referred to himself as a prophet, prior to speaking what God had spoken to him (Deut. 18:17-20) about the Prophet whom God would raise up – a promise and prophecy of the coming Messiah – whom God said was like unto Moses. In Deuteronomy 18:15, Moses said, "The Lord thy God will raise up unto thee a Prophet from the midst of thee, of thy brethren, like unto me." Most likely, Moses had the motivational gift of prophecy. He claimed to be a prophet. He does, though, exhibit qualities of the other spiritual gifts at different times in his life. But when one is specifically referred to in the Bible as a prophet, it is safe to assume that prophecy was their main motivational gift. Israel was a very organized nation, under the leadership of Moses, but he was not the one with the gift of organizing. He had to have his father-in-law, Jethro, tell him how to get properly organized. Moses followed his father-in-law's instructions, and the Bible's record of that process will be one of our references for the gift of organizing.

Samuel was a prophet of God. The Bible says, "And all Israel from Dan even to Beer-sheba knew that Samuel was established to be a prophet of the Lord" (1 Sam. 3:20). Nathan was a prophet of God (2 Sam. 7:2) who was sent by God to King David for the purpose of telling the king that he had committed a great sin (2 Sam. 12:1,7). Elijah was so mighty and committed a prophet of God that he stood alone against 450 prophets of Baal, and the Bible records: "Then said Elijah unto the people, 'I, even I only, remain a prophet of the Lord; but Baal's prophets are four hundred and fifty men'" (1 Kings 18:22). But he knew, as our modern day saying goes, "God and me are a majority." Elisha succeeded Elijah as special prophet to Israel (1 Kings 19:16,19; 2 Kings 2). Isaiah was a prophet of God (2 Kings 20:1) and one of those classified as a major prophet.

Another of the major prophets was Jeremiah. He knew that he was called to be a prophet of God. He recorded in his writings, "Then the word of the Lord came unto me, saying, 'Before I formed thee in the belly I knew thee, and I ordained thee a prophet unto the nations'" (Jer. 1:4-5). This confirms that you do not simply choose what you want your motivational gift to be. You are born with it instilled in you. Jeremiah fulfilled what God had called him to do, and it was confirmed by another prophet. Daniel acknowledged that Jeremiah was a prophet (Dan. 9:2). What a great compliment it was to Jeremiah to be acknowledged as a prophet by another prophet.

Although it appears that those who are known as prophets had the motivational gift of prophecy, this may not have always been the case. Amos was known as a prophet, and his book of the Bible is classified under the writings of the Minor Prophets. Yet Amos said, "I was no prophet, neither was I a prophet's son; but I was an herdsman, and a gatherer of sycamore fruit: and the Lord took me as I followed the flock, and the Lord said unto me, 'Go, prophesy unto my people Israel'" (Amos 7:14). Perhaps he had another major motivational spiritual gift, but he was exhibiting the characteristics of a prophet, as commanded of God, during the time of his life we know about through the Bible. But unless one of those who is known in the Bible as a prophet says he was not a prophet, it is reasonable to assume that their motivational spiritual gift was prophecy.

Habakkuk (Hab. 1:1; 3:1), Haggai (Hag. 1:1,3,12), and Zechariah (Zech. 1:1,7) referred to themselves as prophets, and there are others in the Bible. But those who have been mentioned are ones who specifically called themselves prophets of the Lord.

In the Bible, most of the illustrations of the gift of prophecy are found in the Old Testament, but the New Testament has a couple of excellent examples. John the Baptist was a prophet. He was commissioned a prophet before he was born (Luke 1:12,17), confirmed in this purpose for his life at birth (Luke 1:76), and committed to fulfilling it in his life (Luke 3:3-4).

Jesus is the other New Testament example of a prophet. He perfectly exemplifies all of the motivational gifts. He is the Prophet Moses spoke of in Deuteronomy 18:15,18.

Jesus exemplified Moses' prophecy when He cleared out the Jerusalem Temple of all the moneychangers and merchants who were unfairly turning a profit from the worshipers. Temple worshipers needed the services of moneychangers and merchants for the offerings that were part of their worship of God. These entrepreneurs took advantage of those who came to worship. They did not have a reverence for the House of God or a respect for the Word of God. When Jesus saw what was happening, in righteous indignation, He drove those dishonest, disrespectful scoundrels out of the Temple area. He said to them: "It is written, 'My house shall be called the house of prayer; but ye have made it a den of thieves'" (Matt. 21:13).

The prophet in Jesus surfaced. He confronted unsaved sinners and those who did not believe in Him, as well as the religious leaders who opposed Him. Seeing the glaring inconsistencies in their lives, Jesus severely reprimanded those who claimed to be the religious and spiritual leaders of His people.

Exhortations To Prophets

The Bible gives special *exhortations* to those with the motivational gift of prophecy. Three exhortations to prophets are found in Romans 12:9: "Let love be without dissimulation. Abhor that which is evil; cleave to that which is good." The prophet is exhorted to love without hypocrisy. People sometimes think a prophet is hypocritical in saying that he loves someone, especially when the prophet can seem so hard on the person he says he loves. Since the prophet is to expound the Scriptures and expose sin, he is exhorted to abhor evil. To keep balance with the stand the prophet takes against evil, he is to cleave to that which is good.

What, then, needs to come out in the life of a prophet from these exhortations? First, one with the motivational gift of prophecy is to *be believable*. A prophet has to be very careful in coming up to someone and saying, "I want you to know that I really love you," because he is going to have to make a special effort to convince the person that he really loves them. It is because the prophet will rebuke that same individual if the prophet believes the person is out of line spiritually in some area of his life. There are those who do not realize that it takes more love to correct a problem than to ignore it (Prov. 27:5). A prophet is motivated in such a way. But there are those who just cannot accept a loving rebuke. So the prophet has to strive extra hard to be believable, and it has to carry over into all facets of his life. Whatever the area of truth may be that a prophet defends or expounds, he is going to have to back it up. If a prophet says that he spends 12 hours a day in prayer, then he is going to have to prove it. He has got to be believable in the eyes of people to be effective.

Second, a prophet is exhorted to "abhor that which is evil." That simply means he has got to *be bold* in exposing sin and evil. Prophets are those whom God uses to expose evil and sin, whether it is in the world or whether it is in the church. A prophet is motivated to stand up and defend the truths and principles of the Word of God, especially when public figures try to explain them away as irrelevant or illogical in applying to our world today. There is a natural reaction in the prophet to point out inconsistency and evil. As a result, people who do not understand or appreciate the prophet's gift will be critical of him and accuse him of being mean-spirited. He is exhorted to be bold, because the prophet may shy away from expressing his gift in order to avoid criticism. If those with the motivational gift of prophecy do not expose sin in the world today, nobody else is likely to do it.

Third, a prophet needs to "cleave to that which is good." Why does the prophet need such an exhortation? Because prophets have to spend so much time telling people what is wrong with them, and what is wrong with the world, that prophets can become very negative people. So the Bible exhorts the prophet to *be balanced* in his life. He should not always talk about negative things. The prophet who is a preacher especially has to strive to preach on positive and uplifting themes. He needs to balance exposing sin with sermons that are more encouraging and positive in helping people to grow and mature in their Christian faith.

If you are a prophet, be believable by living what you proclaim. Be bold in expounding the truth of God's Word and exposing sin, but do not get out of balance. Be influenced by good and also proclaim the good things about life.

Expectation Prophets Need To Exercise Most

First Peter 3:15-16 is so relevant to prophets:

> But sanctify the Lord God in your hearts: and be ready always to give an answer to every man that asketh you a reason of the hope that is in you with meekness and fear: having a good conscience; that, whereas they speak evil of you, as of evildoers, they may be ashamed that falsely accuse your good conversation in Christ.

Here, in verse 15, Peter basically says, "You be ready. Anytime someone asks you about your faith, be bold." But he also says to balance your boldness with meekness and fear. Witness boldly, but as kindly as possible.

Then he gives the expectation that prophets need to exercise the most: a *clear conscience*. Otherwise, he will not have much of an effect on others.

Why does a prophet need a clear conscience? It is so that he can speak the truth boldly in love (Eph. 4:15). That is the only way a prophet can be believable and stay believable. The fallen prophets of our day have greatly hurt the ministries of the faithful prophets of God. Whenever a well-known minister has fallen morally, it has caused people to wonder who is really a true prophet of the Lord.

A true prophet of God stays consistent. He walks his talk. He boldly proclaims the truth because he lives his message. It has been interesting in our day to see some men who exhibited the gift of prophecy and preached with the apparent blessings of God. Eventually, though, some horrible inconsistencies came out concerning their lives. If a prophet does not have a clear conscience, eventually it is going to come through loud and clear.

Characteristics of Prophets

Specifically, there are four main areas that distinguish one with the motivational gift of prophecy: *verbal expressions, valid impressions, valiant professions* and *voluntary confessions*.

Verbal Expressions

One of the first keys to identifying a prophet regards *verbal expressions*. A prophet has got to say it. That was a characteristic of the life of Peter. Peter urged the readers of his first epistle to "be ready to give an answer to every man" (1 Peter 3:15) because that was how he was motivated. A prophet is always ready to say something. As a matter of fact, you are not ready for them to say it to you, but they say it anyway. A prophet must verbally express himself, especially when matters of right and wrong are involved.

Just think through the Gospel accounts. Other than Jesus, who spoke the most in the Gospels? It was Peter—the person in the Bible who best illustrates one who has the motivational gift of prophecy. Most of the other disciples are heard, at some time, in the Gospels. But there were some of whom the Bible does not record anything. This gives evidence that different spiritual gifts were spread among the disciples.

Peter, though, was nearly always the one who had something to say. Peter, more than any other disciple, was the first one to speak up. When Jesus asked a question, the one to answer was more often Peter than any of the other disciples. The fourteenth, fifteenth, and sixteenth chapters of Matthew record three instances right together that show us how Peter was usually the first one to respond. In Matthew 14:27-28, which describes Jesus walking on the water, the Bible says, "But straightway Jesus spake unto them, saying, 'Be of good cheer; it is I; be not afraid.' And Peter answered Him and said, 'Lord, if it be Thou, bid me come unto Thee on the water.'"

In Matthew 15, Jesus ends a parable with a question. Who answered the question? "Then answered Peter and said unto Him, 'Declare unto us this parable'" (v. 15).

In chapter 16, Jesus asks His disciples what the people were saying about Him. Then He asks them, "But whom say ye that I am?" (v. 15). Peter answers with: "Thou art the Christ, the Son of the living God" (v. 16). Now that brings us to another interesting trait of Peter. He answered that question well. But a few verses later, we find him going overboard with his efforts (v. 22). As a result, the Lord had to rebuke him (v. 23). The other disciples, with their spiritual gifts, gave matters a little more thought. But Peter was always ready to reply. He usually did—but sometimes, without thinking it through.

Not only are prophets the first to speak, most of the time, but they are *foremost* in addressing a matter, especially within a group. Peter was not only the foremost in answering the questions of Jesus, sometimes too impetuously. He eventually became the foremost spokesman for the disciples and the early church. On the Day of Pentecost, Peter was the one who stood up and preached with such mighty results (Acts 2:14,41). Soon thereafter the disciples were arrested on two different occasions because of their proclamation of the risen Lord. They were questioned by the Sanhedrin and even beaten after their second arrest. Peter was the one who spoke boldly on behalf of the believers (Acts 4:8; 5:29).

Prophets also have a very *fluent and influential* way of saying what they want to say as they verbally express themselves on a matter. A prophet has a special ability to articulate, especially in defining what is right and wrong. Again, we turn to the Book of Acts for a good illustration of the fluent and influential way the prophets articulate matters. Peter is our example, once again. Let us look at a brief excerpt from his sermon, as he preached on the Day of Pentecost under the mighty power of the Holy Spirit:

> *Ye men of Israel, hear these words; Jesus of Nazareth, a man*
> *approved of God among you by miracles and wonders and signs,*
> *which God did by Him in the midst of you, as ye yourselves*
> *also know: Him, being delivered by the determinate counsel*
> *and foreknowledge of God, ye have taken, and by wicked hands*
> *have crucified and slain. (Acts 2:22-23)*

A less articulate preacher may have come out and simply said, "You people killed the Lord." And the people would have probably been ready to kill the preacher next. But in that powerfully fluent and influential manner by which Peter verbally expressed himself, the intended message got through to the listeners clearly, but convictingly. The conclusion of the sermon provides the proof. Peter closes his message with these words: "Therefore let all the house of Israel know assuredly, that God hath made that same Jesus, whom ye have crucified, both Lord and Christ" (Acts 2:36). What was the effect? The fluent way in which he preached his sermon influenced the people to the desired result: "Now when they heard this, they were pricked in their heart, and said unto Peter and to the rest of the apostles, 'Men and brethren, what shall we do?'" (v. 37). Peter told them what they should do (v. 38), and those who were sincere did it (v. 41).

Verbal expression—it is just something that the person with the gift of prophecy is going to do. For those of you who do not have the motivational gift of prophecy, turning a deaf ear to a prophet can be a great disadvantage.

Valid Impressions

Another major characteristic of prophets is their *valid impressions*. Prophets can make quick impressions of people. They have to be careful, though, that they do not make them too quickly before they get all the facts. But people with the gift of prophecy are very discerning. They can quickly size up someone, being particularly alert to dishonesty. Within a few minutes, a prophet can usually tell whether someone is real and sincere.

Prophets tend to make quick judgments on what they see and hear—at times, too prematurely. But they have an amazing ability to sense when someone or something is not what it appears to be. Prophets react harshly to any form of deception or dishonesty.

Peter reacted harshly to the dishonesty of Ananias and Sapphira (Acts 5:1-10). Peter knew when this husband and wife each came to him separately that they were lying concerning the price of property for which they had been paid. They held back some of the money for their personal use, which they had the right to do. But they made everyone think that they were giving all their money from the sale of their land. Peter immediately discerned that Ananias was lying. It resulted in the death of Ananias because the Holy Spirit wanted to keep the young church in Jerusalem from deceit. When Sapphira came in later, Peter did not say, "Let me tell you what your husband said." He did not tell her what had happened with her husband. He asked her how much they had been paid for the sale of their land. Peter wanted to see how honest Sapphira was by testing her before he confronted her with his knowledge of the real story. That incident is a classic example of how a prophet is motivated to operate.

Prophets have very valid impressions, and they are usually very *fast* to decide or comment on a matter. Why? Because prophets want to cut through details right to the real heart of a matter.

As prophets make valid impressions, they are also *firm*. In being firm, prophets are very direct and want to deal with a concern immediately. They have such a desire for justice that they will cut off those who sin so that others will be warned. Peter asks Jesus on one occasion, "Lord, how oft shall my brother sin against me, and I forgive him? till seven times?" (Matt. 18:21). Jesus answers that there is no limit to forgiveness. To Peter, there had to be a point at which you no longer forgave someone, if they kept sinning against you. In such cases, a prophet has to work at it. The prophet is motivated to make examples of people so that other people will not fall into the particular sin the prophet is exposing. Balance is the key for the prophet in such situations.

As prophets are fast and firm in their impressions, they are very *fair*. A prophet will deal with his friends just as he would with others who oppose or disobey the Word of God. That was a characteristic trait in the life of Peter. He wrote, "For the time is come that judgment must begin at the house of God: and if it first begin at us, what shall the end be of them that obey not the gospel of God?" (1 Peter 4:17). Peter was not just firm in dealing with those in the world who were enemies of the gospel. He also indicated that the church needed to be spiritually right. If sin was not exposed and dealt with among Christians, Peter knew that there would be no difference between the saved and the unsaved, and the church would not make a difference for Christ in the world.

Valiant Professions

In addition to verbal expressions and valid impressions, another major characteristic of prophets can be classified by the term, **valiant professions**. If something becomes a conviction in the life of a prophet, it sticks! When the prophet determines that under no condition will he compromise a particular belief, it is for life. Unless something drastically happens to make him believe otherwise, which he is convinced is of the Lord, the prophet does not change his mind. He adheres to a belief even when no one else will. If everybody is caving in on a matter, the prophet who is Spirit-filled will stay true—very valiantly, at times.

Prophets are sensitive to and against those who question or cut down the work of God. They have a genuine concern for the reputation and program of God, whether it is at the prophet's church or at another church. They have a strong dependence upon the Scriptures to validate their convictions and all that they have to say about a matter of right and wrong. If it is in the Bible, a prophet believes it. If it is not in the Word, and you cannot validate their opinion from the Bible, to the prophet, you are wrong.

The prophet does not base his feelings on personal opinion alone. He bases what he believes, says, and does upon the Word of God.

To have valiant professions, one must be *faithful*. Prophets are very faithful. They are openly loyal and committed. If you are their friend, they will stick with you, even when things are not spiritually right in your life. But they stick with you to try to correct you and to try to get you right where there is an area of sin in your life with which you are having problems. If it finally gets to the point that you do not want to change, the prophet is more loyal to the truth, even if it means cutting off relationships. If you are true to the faith, though, a prophet will be a faithful friend through thick and thin. When many of the followers of Jesus "went back, and walked no more with Him" (John 6:66), Jesus asked His twelve disciples if they were also going to desert Him. Peter acknowledged Jesus as the Christ, and he faithfully continued to follow the Lord, as did the other disciples. Peter said that he would not deny Jesus, even if it cost him his life (Matt. 26:35). Of course, we all know so well that Peter did deny the Lord, on the night that Christ was arrested and sentenced to die. But so did all the other disciples (Matt. 26:56). After all the disciples had fled, Peter had enough of a boldness to follow Christ to where He was first taken after being arrested. When Peter was later confronted there, concerning his being one of the followers of Jesus, he did verbally deny being a follower of the Lord. Although Peter did slip, it was temporary. That humbling incident in his life eventually resulted in Peter's becoming a more faithful follower of Jesus than he had been previously.

Along with being faithful, a prophet is *fervent*. Once a prophet becomes committed to a cause, he gets wholeheartedly involved in it. Prophets are quick to respond to situations and opportunities. When Jesus walked on the water, Peter was the first one to say something. When he knew that it was Jesus, he was the first one to get involved with the Lord. After Jesus spoke to him, just to make sure it was real, Peter said, "Lord, if it's You, tell me to come out there to You." Jesus said, "It's Me. Come on." Peter did not give it a second thought. Sometimes, that was his problem, but sometimes, it worked to his advantage. Peter got out of the boat, and as far as we know, he was the second man to walk on water. That is, until he got his eyes off Jesus, and he began thinking, "What am I doing?" Prophets get involved, and they are very fervent in the right kind of way, when they are focusing on the Lord.

Prophets are also *forbearing*, when it comes to their valiant professions. They have a willingness to suffer for what is right. The Book of Acts records that after the first time the disciples were arrested and told not to testify about the risen Lord (Acts 4:18), as soon as they were released, that is exactly what they did once again. The religious authorities had them arrested a second time (Acts 5:17-18). When they were brought before those who were responsible for their arrest, they were asked, "Did not we straitly command you that ye should not teach in this name? And, behold, ye have filled Jerusalem with your doctrine, and intend to bring this man's blood upon us" (v. 28). Peter replied, "We ought to obey God rather than men" (v. 29). The disciples were beaten, warned not to speak in the name of Jesus, and released (v. 40). The Bible says, "And they departed from the presence of the council, rejoicing that they were counted worthy to suffer shame for His name. And daily in the temple, and in every house, they ceased not to teach and preach Jesus Christ" (vs. 41-42). I believe that Peter was the chief among the disciples in rejoicing because they had been counted worthy to suffer shame for Jesus.

Voluntary Confessions

One more key characteristic of the prophet is manifested in **voluntary confessions**. When you really get to know a prophet, you find that although he can be so harsh toward those who presumptuously commit sin, he can also be such a "teddy bear" on a personal level. When prophets get under preaching that is convicting, they are likely to be seen at the altar more than anybody else.

Prophets are hard on other people, but even harder on themselves. When a prophet realizes that something is not right in his life, he is miserable until he gets it right with God. Very open about their own faults and failures, prophets are willing to be broken in order to be better.

Honesty is also a steadfast trademark of a prophet. A prophet's tax return contains information the Internal Revenue Service does not even require. When a prophet trades for a new car, he will tell the car dealer everything that he knows is wrong with the car he is trading. The prophet is painfully honest about his personal life. When Peter first confronted the Lord, he and his mates had been fishing all night without a catch. When Jesus told them to go out again and lay down their nets, Peter objected. But he and his fishing partners went out again, and did as Jesus advised them. They fetched a phenomenal catch of fish. Upon personally experiencing the power of the Lord in his life, Peter "fell down at Jesus' feet, saying, 'Depart from me; for I am a sinful man, O Lord'" (Luke 5:8).

Prophets are very humble, too. When Peter fell down before the Lord, he bowed before Christ in *humility*. Although tough and firm, prophets are normally very humble people. The humility of Peter bleeds through in the books of 1 and 2 Peter.

Holiness is another hallmark of prophets. They stress holiness in their lives and in the lives of others. Peter states that since we are going to "an inheritance incorruptible, and undefiled, and that fadeth not away, reserved in heaven for you" (1 Peter 1:4), we are to be "as obedient children, not fashioning yourselves according to the former lusts in your ignorance: But as He which hath called you is holy, so be ye holy in all manner of conversation; Because it is written, 'Be ye holy; for I am holy'" (1 Peter 1:14-16).

A prophet also voluntarily comes forward. You do not have to prod and prompt prophets to confess when things are not right in their lives.

Verbal expressions, valid impressions, valiant professions, and voluntary confessions—those are the major characteristics of one with the motivational spiritual gift of prophecy.

Cautions For The Gift Of Prophecy

There are some **cautions for the spiritual gift of prophecy**. For those who do not have this motivational gift, there are some things you need to be cautious about to keep from misunderstanding prophets.

For prophets, there are some misuses of your gift that you need to be careful to avoid.

Misunderstandings

Those with other spiritual gifts may have some *misunderstandings* about what motivates prophets. If you do not have the gift of prophecy, you really need to pay attention to what is said here.

The reason we see so much conflict in churches is because people with a particular spiritual gift do not understand another spiritual gift, and they may become critical of the way a person with another spiritual gift reacts to a situation. It is because they do not understand the motivation behind the other spiritual gifts. A clear understanding of all the spiritual gifts is needed.

Keep in mind, that <u>misunderstandings</u> regarding a motivational gift are not <u>misuses</u> of the gift. It is that spiritual gift responding to a situation the way the person with that gift is motivated by God to respond. Among those who do not have the spiritual gift of prophecy, let us look at some of the misunderstandings others have about the way prophets react to various situations.

One misunderstanding is that prophets are *imposing*. Since prophets are usually the first ones to speak out, they are often viewed as overly outspoken. The prophet always seems to want to say something. Many may feel that the prophet imposes on what others would like to say.

In one of the churches where I served on the ministerial staff, Dicky and Carol were two of our best friends. Carol is a prophet. Her husband, Dicky, has the gift of giving. My wife, Wanda, has the motivational gift of mercy. Whenever we went out together for dinner, our conversations were usually two-sided. Who did most of the talking? The two prophets. It was all in good fun, but Dicky and Wanda said that we never gave them the opportunity to speak. When they waited for a break in the conversation to say something, the other prophet spoke up as soon as the other stopped speaking. Carol and I did learn not to always give our opinions first and to allow Dicky and Wanda the opportunity to speak. But prophets have to work at it. They are naturally motivated to speak out.

Another misunderstanding about prophets is that they are *impatient*. They are looked upon by some as being too hasty in acting on some matters. Prophets want to avoid details and get right to the issue at hand. Peter knew the situation with Ananias and Sapphira (Acts 5:1-11) needed to be handled immediately. The young church needed to see deceit as a serious matter. Peter knew that "a little leaven leaveneth the whole lump" (Gal. 5:7-9). If presumptuous sins were not dealt with immediately, especially in those early days of the church, it would quickly stifle the growth of the church. To the prophet, sins need to be dealt with as quickly as possible.

Prophets are also misunderstood as *inordinate*. Some would think a prophet is too harsh in exposing sin and dealing with it. There are those who feel that the prophet goes for the overkill. The religious leaders felt Jesus dealt too harshly with the moneychangers and merchants who desecrated the Temple. They knew, though, that He had a legitimate cause in doing so. It is just that they were getting "kickbacks" from the money that the merchants were making. The religious leaders were actually part of the desecration. Jesus knew that it was a situation that needed to be firmly and openly corrected.

Some people misunderstand the prophet as being *insensitive* because the prophet's strong interest in truth is often interpreted as disinterest in other people. Prophets are sometimes misjudged as being haughty. But the motivation of the prophet is to expose sin and to punish where it is needed. A prophet can be very frank in doing so. Peter's dealing with Ananias and Sapphira resulted in a reverent awe and respect for God (Acts 5:11).

Prophets are also misunderstood as *insincere*. They are often looked upon as not being genuine. Some people forget that it also takes love to expose wrongdoing and to correct it. Especially when a prophet admits to his own shortcomings, he is susceptible to being called a hypocrite. Those with a critical eye will be quick to comment about the prophet not being what he claims to be because the prophet is so transparent. But what really makes the prophet so effective is being quick to confess when he is aware of a shortcoming in his own life.

Misuses

Let us now turn our attention to **misuses** of the motivational gift of prophecy. When prophets act in the strength of their flesh instead of in the control of the Holy Spirit, the gift can be misused.

When a prophet operates in the flesh (see Rom. 8:1-17 for a biblical explanation of being in the flesh as compared to being in the Spirit), he can be *intimidating*. He will tend to have an opinion about everything, and he will always think that he is right. To get his opinion across, the prophet will dwell on the negative, especially about someone else. He will lead others to be negative and critical of that person. In the flesh, a prophet is very unmannerly and inconsiderate.

A prophet who misuses his gift can be *impetuous*. Such prophets do not always get all the facts or think before reacting. They may take a statement out of context to prove their point. Even though they may be uninformed, prophets who misuse their motivational gift may hear information, which may be secondhand and unsubstantiated, and jump to the wrong conclusion. During election campaigns, just think of all the statements made by candidates about other candidates that have to be retracted. Very likely, a prophet, who is in the flesh, is behind a statement about another candidate that has to be retracted when all the facts are known.

In the flesh, prophets can be too *intolerant*. It is one thing to rebuke someone, but there is a tactful way to do it. A prophet may lack tact in rebuking someone when the prophet is not Spirit-controlled. It is hard for the prophet to separate the sin from the sinner. In the flesh, the prophet has a tendency to vengefully cut off sinful people. In such cases, prophets can be very unforgiving.

Another misuse is *insufficiency*; a prophet feels insufficient when he makes a spiritual mistake. Prophets can get very self-critical of their mistakes and feel worthless when they fail. If a prophet allows the feelings of the flesh to be more dominant, he becomes useless. Jesus made it a point to express His need of Peter after Peter had denied Him (John 21:15-19). This was to encourage Peter so that he would not reach a state of insufficiency, becoming useless as a witness for Christ.

Oh, that Christians would walk in the control and power of the Holy Spirit. If Christians will be mighty in Spirit, their spiritual gift will not be misused. If you are walking in the Spirit, the misunderstandings that others typically have about your gift will not be exhibited toward you very often. It is because you will have developed a sensitivity about not letting the negative characteristics of your gift come out as the most dominant. Spirit-filled and Spirit-controlled Christians also learn to balance their special gift of blessing with the needed use of the other spiritual gifts. When you are mighty in the Spirit, you will know when it is right for your motivational gift to be the one that comes to the forefront.

Conclusion

The prophets of the church keep us centered on the will of God by making us sure of and sure to the Word of God. Of all the motivational spiritual gifts, it is probably the most noticeable one when the prophet misuses it. Peter misused his gift of prophecy a few times, as we can surmise from reading through the Gospels. Because he was so vocal, and he nearly always responded when Jesus asked or allowed a response, Peter's blunders are known more than the other disciples'. But he learned from his mistakes, and after the Lord ascended into heaven, Peter became mighty in the Spirit in the use of his spiritual gift.

The Bible says to "despise not prophesyings" (1 Thess. 5:20). That verse is included in a passage that gives God's plan for a successful church (1 Thess. 5:12-22). Prophets tend to say things that hit a nerve within us. We do not necessarily like what the prophet has to say. But remember, it is dangerous to disagree with the truth that sets us free. The prophet who is mighty in the Spirit is going to be true to the Word of Truth—the Word of God, the Bible, and the Living Word, Jesus.

You may not like the prophet, but you must listen to what God says through him. Do not listen to the words of the prophet as much as you listen for the Word of God spoken through the words of the prophet. Prophets are supposed to stir us up. Listen to them. Learn from them. When they speak the Word, it is a more sure word, because they speak it as holy men and women of God, moved by the Holy Spirit.

3

The Gift of Serving

"Naturally Caring"

*Having then gifts differing according to the grace that is given
to us, whether prophecy, let us prophesy according to the
proportion of faith; Or ministry [service], let us wait on our
ministering [serving]: ...Be kindly affectioned one to another
with brotherly love; in honour preferring one another. (Rom.
12:6-7,10)*

Timothy best illustrates the gift of serving. In a passage in which Paul
talks about Timothy, from the second chapter of Philippians, the major
characteristics of the gift of serving are found. Let's see what these verses
have to say and how they are relevant to this motivational spiritual gift.

*Yea, and if I be offered upon the sacrifice and service of your
faith, I joy, and rejoice with you all. For the same cause also
do ye joy, and rejoice with me. But I trust in the Lord Jesus to
send Timotheus shortly unto you, that I also may be of good
comfort, when I know your state. For I have no man like-minded,
who will naturally care for your state. For all seek their own,
not the things which are Jesus Christ's. But ye know the proof
of him, that, as a son with the father, he hath served with me in
the gospel. Him therefore I hope to send presently, so soon as I
shall see how it will go with me. (Phil. 2:17-23)*

In this passage, Paul tells us that he just loved serving the Lord, and
what a joy it was to be a servant of the Lord. His joy was enhanced

because of the service of the church at Philippi. As the thought of serving the Lord was upon his mind, he thought of Timothy. The statements Paul made about Timothy, to the Philippians, beautifully illustrate the life of one with the gift of serving.

Timothy was both a herald and a helper in exercising his motivational gift of serving. In his epistle to the church at Corinth, Paul writes, "For this cause have I sent unto you Timotheus, who is my beloved son, and faithful in the Lord, who shall bring you into remembrance of my ways which be in Christ, as I teach every where in every church" (1 Cor. 4:17).

Timothy was sent to Corinth as a spokesman for Paul to teach them in the Lord exactly as Paul would have done it if he had personally been there. In 1 Thessalonians 3, we are given an example of Timothy as Paul's special helper: "Wherefore when we could no longer forbear, we thought it good to be left at Athens alone; And sent Timotheus, our brother, and minister of God, and our fellow labourer in the gospel of Christ, to establish you, and to comfort you concerning your faith" (vs. 1-2).

A servant not only comforts, but *naturally cares* for others (Phil. 2:20). Those two words give a simple, but accurate description of what motivates one who has the spiritual gift of serving. The server is alert to meeting practical needs in the lives of others in order to free them to achieve what the server feels to be more important tasks. If it were not for the servers, there are many practical needs that would never be met and practical things that would not get done around a church. Let us take a detailed look at these less recognized members of the body of Christ who make the more recognized members – the spiritual leaders – the effective leaders they are.

A Composite: The Gift of Serving

The word for "service" or "serving," as normally used in the Bible, literally means "through dust." It gives the picture of dust being stirred as the serving person is going to meet the need of someone. A servant is an obedient person, if he does his job well. Obedience is doing exactly what you are told to do, when you are told to do it.

But serving goes beyond simple obedience. One with the spiritual gift of serving does exactly what needs to be done, even more, before being asked to do it. That is the real joy of a person with the spiritual gift of serving. Their motivation is to do something before anybody thinks about it and before being asked to do it. Bill Gothard defines service as simply "demonstrating love by meeting practical needs."

One of the ways we misuse those with this spiritual gift is that we have a tendency to ask them to do something that is needed. They will usually do it, too. But the key to what joyfully motivates servers is to let them be led to needed tasks before someone asks them. If you have the spiritual gift of serving, that is an important consideration to keep in mind. Take it upon yourself to offer your services when you feel led to meet a need. Do it before you are asked and before a leader in the church has to beg for help where there is a need in the church that you can help to meet. That is when you receive your greatest joy. As Paul said (Phil. 2:17), it is like a sacrifice of joy. It is more joyful to offer to do something before you are asked to do it.

Explanation of the Gift of Serving

The earliest picture the Bible gives of the gift of serving is found in the fourth chapter of Exodus. Aaron performed a special service for Moses, his brother. God had told Moses that He wanted him to free the Israelites, acting on behalf of God. But Moses was unsure because he did not have speaking ability. With little confidence in himself, Moses said to God: "O my Lord, send, I pray Thee, by the hand of him whom Thou wilt send" (Ex. 4:13). Now God became angry at Moses, and basically told him, "I called you to do something, and if I have called you to do it, I am going to equip you to do it." But Moses remained reluctant. So "the anger of the LORD was kindled against Moses, and He said, 'Is not Aaron the Levite thy brother? I know that he can speak well. And also, behold, he cometh forth to meet thee: and when he seeth thee, he will be glad in his heart'" (Ex. 4:14). And so, Aaron became a helper to his brother, and gladly so.

A servant naturally becomes glad helping people. God further told Moses, "And thou shalt speak unto him, and put words in his mouth: and I will be with thy mouth, and with his mouth, and will teach you what ye shall do. And he shall be thy spokesman unto the people" (Ex. 4:15-16).

A server is often a "spokesman" on behalf of someone. The word *herald* is often used in the Bible to apply to one with the gift of serving who fulfills the role of spokesman for someone else. Aaron fulfilled his role as a server in being the spokesman for his brother Moses.

Joshua was also used to help Moses in his God-appointed leadership role as deliverer of the Israelites. Until I began to study spiritual gifts, I had not thought of Joshua as having the gift of service. Those who possess this gift are usually not in leadership positions. Although we think more of Joshua as the successor to Moses, he was groomed for the position of leadership, while fulfilling his motivational gift of serving as a special assistant to Moses. Joshua became the leader of a great nation.

In Joshua 1:1, the Bible illustrates the "helper" aspect of the gift of serving. The Bible records, "Now after the death of Moses the servant of the LORD it came to pass, that the LORD spake unto Joshua the son of Nun, Moses' minister." That word "minister" actually means *helper*.

A couple of other verses show Joshua fulfilling this serving role as a helper to Moses. Exodus 24:13 says, "And Moses rose up, and his minister Joshua: and Moses went up into the mount of God." In Exodus 33:11, the word "servant" is used in the same way as "minister." This verse says, "And the LORD spake unto Moses face to face, as a man speaketh unto his friend. And he turned again into the camp: but his servant Joshua, the son of Nun, a young man, departed not out of the tabernacle."

In the Bible, there is that aspect that one with the gift of serving may be a special helper to someone God has led him to serve.

Joshua had to be strongly encouraged by God to get out there and do what God wanted him to do. A server lacks confidence in his spiritual abilities. The confidence of a person with the gift of serving is in doing things that are more physical that in doing spiritual things.

But Joshua, as well as Timothy, acted on behalf of men who had great spiritual insight—Moses, who was a prophet of God, and Paul, who was an exhorter. Those mentors prepared two servers to move into high positions of leadership. Another prophet, Elisha, also dealt with someone who was a server.

Second Kings 4:8 says, "And it fell on a day, that Elisha passed to Shunem, where was a great woman; and she constrained him to eat bread. And so it was, that as oft as he passed by, he turned in thither to eat bread." The Hebrew, translated in the King James Version as "constrained," literally means "laid hold on him."

Have you ever noticed how one with the gift of serving will tell you, "You've got to have a second helping! You need to eat another piece of pie!" They almost constrain you to eat beyond your normal capacities. That is just natural for them to do. Servers want to make sure you have enough to eat, and that you are comfortable.

Elisha knew if he visited the Shunammite woman's town, he better plan on taking time to stop by her home. If he tried to get through town without stopping at her home, and she happened to see him walking by her home, she would not let him get by without constraining him to come inside and get something to eat or drink. God used this woman and her family in a special way to serve Elisha. Second Kings 4 shows us how God used them in the life of Elisha: "And she said unto her husband, 'Behold now, I perceive that this is an holy man of God, which passeth by us continually. Let us make a little chamber, I pray thee, on the wall; and let us set for him there a bed, and a table, and a stool, and a candlestick: and it shall be, when he cometh to us, that he shall turn in thither'" (vs. 10-11). In this way, a server may exercise service as a *hostess* or *host*. This is evident in many who have the gift of serving. If one with the gift of serving finds out that you are coming into town, their reaction will be, "You're going to stay with us. Don't you even think about staying at a hotel." A server wants you to stay in their home. It is natural and enjoyable for them, because it is how they are motivated.

The hostess aspect of serving has some excellent New Testament examples. The word "constrained" is little used in the Bible. A familiar reference where this word is used is a statement by Paul: "For the love of Christ constraineth us" (2 Cor. 5:14). This word is an excellent Bible word for one with the gift of serving. When Paul came to Philippi, Lydia was one of the first converts Paul won to Christ in that city. Her motivational gift of serving was immediately put to use. The Bibles says, "And a certain woman named Lydia, a seller of purple, of the city of Thyatira, which worshipped God, heard us: whose heart the Lord opened, that she attended unto the things which were spoken of Paul. And when she was baptized, and her household, she besought us, saying, If ye have judged me to be faithful to the Lord, come into my house, and abide there. And she constrained us" (Acts 16:14-15). That is not an offer that would be easy to turn down. Lydia was simply acting in a manner that was normal for her. You may feel like some with the gift of serving constrain you, more than you want to be constrained, sometimes, but that is how they are motivated.

Another example of a server who was gifted as a hostess was Martha. From her story in the Bible, we learn that you can work in the flesh with your spiritual gift. Many of us are familiar with the story of Mary and Martha. Let's observe Luke's record of a sisterly disagreement:

> *Now it came to pass, as they went, that He entered into a certain village: and a certain woman named Martha received Him into*

her house. And she had a sister called Mary, which also sat at Jesus' feet, and heard His word. But Martha was cumbered about much serving, and came to Him, and said, 'Lord, dost Thou not care that my sister hath left me to serve alone? bid her therefore that she help me.' And Jesus answered and said unto her, 'Martha, Martha, thou art careful and troubled about many things: But one thing is needful: and Mary hath chosen that good part, which shall not be taken away from her.' (Luke 10:38-42)

A person with the gift of serving, especially in the role of a hostess, usually gets encumbered in serving until everything falls in place. Jesus acknowledged Martha's gift of serving and her sensitivity to people's needs. But He showed her that she had missed the point for that particular occasion. At that moment, a spiritual need needed to be met more than anything else. Jesus tenderly pointed that out to Martha.

The family of Lazarus, Mary, and Martha provides another biblical explanation of the gift of serving in an incident recorded in the eleventh chapter of John. Jesus had a special relationship with this family. Upon the death of their brother, Lazarus, Jesus came to their home. The way Martha reacted to the Lord's arrival shows a typical response of one with the motivational gift of serving. The Bible says, "Then Martha, as soon as she heard that Jesus was coming, went and met Him: but Mary sat still in the house" (John 11:20). You react to certain situations according to your spiritual gift. I have noticed at social gatherings, such as family reunions, the various reactions as different ones arrive. I may be sitting down talking to somebody, when someone says, "Look who's here!" Immediately, two or three people will jump up and go to the door. They may be in the middle of a conversation with you, but they leave you sitting there, not even allowing you to complete the statement you were making. Most likely, those are the servers. They get up to meet someone and to receive them into the gathering.

In chapter twelve of John, the consistency of Martha is confirmed.

After Jesus raised Lazarus from the dead, He came back for another visit at the home of His dear friends, and they had dinner for Jesus. Verse two says, "There they made Him a supper; and Martha served." That same night, Mary also helped to meet a need in a special way she served. Actually, she gave something. She anointed Christ with some very expensive perfume. I believe that Mary probably had the spiritual gift of giving.

In the gift of serving, one can be a herald, a spokesman for another person, or a minister to someone as their special helper. A herald, a helper, and a hostess: these are some of the biblical roles explaining the gift of serving.

Examples of Servants

Several *examples of the spiritual gift of serving* have already been mentioned: Aaron, Joshua, the Shunammite woman, Timothy, Lydia, and Martha possessed the motivational gift of serving.

Mark's Gospel centers around the servanthood of Christ. In chapter after chapter in the Book of Mark, incidents are mentioned, one after another, in which Jesus met a practical need in the life of someone before He met a spiritual need. That is what a person with the gift of serving notices. When you read the Gospel of Mark, you are reading a book that was inspired by the Holy Spirit, but written from the perspective of service.

Mark 10:43-45 shows serving was exemplified in the life of Jesus: "Whosoever will be great among you, shall be your minister: And whosoever of you will be the chiefest, shall be servant of all. For even the Son of Man came not to be ministered unto, but to minister, and to give his life a ransom for many." The word "minister" can also be translated "servant" as a noun, and "serve" as a verb. As previously mentioned, all spiritual gifts culminate in Jesus Christ.

Exhortations to Servers

The special *exhortations to servers* are given in Romans 12:10:

> *Be kindly affectioned one to another with brotherly love; in honour preferring one another.*

To be "kindly affectioned one to another" means to *be responsive*. For the person with the motivational gift of serving, when you are prompted to do something, do it! It is because God gives you a special ability to be alert to the needs of people. You may not even know for certain that there is a need concerning where you are prompted to help. But if you are prompted by the Holy Spirit, then respond accordingly. If not, you may miss an opportunity where God wants to work through you. Be kindly affectioned in responding to the needs of others by being loving and caring as you do it.

Servers are also exhorted to serve with brotherly love. The emphasis behind the exhortation is to *be related*. Be responsive as if you are related to the person you are serving.

One noteworthy trait of close families is that they are supportive of one another. Such families are loyal. If you are a server, be loyal to whomever you are serving, just as if they were your mom, dad, brother, or sister. Be cooperative, too. When do families function the best? When the family members fully cooperate with one another.

Another exhortation to servers is to honor one another. Servers are to honor those they serve as we should honor those in authority over us. As a server, you need to *be respectful*. The prophet keys in on truth and speaking a message. A server keys in on meeting a need. Often, that is all the server sees. If the server is not respectful of others' authority, and working through proper channels, he will walk all over other people. When that is the case, the server wants whoever is in his way to get out of the way so that he can be about his service.

A true servant must learn to be less. A song a few years ago stressed the importance of thinking a little more of others and a little less of me.

The server must make it a priority to let Jesus increase while "I" (the server) decrease (John 3:30). Servers must make it a priority to put others first. The server must learn to be considerate and compliant. In being compliant, the server works within proper channels.

A server needs to be responsive to the needs of others. When responding to those needs, the server is to serve those whom he helps as if he is related to them. The server is to always show respect for all who are involved in a situation where the server is providing assistance and leadership.

Expectation Servers Need to Exercise Most

If servers are going to most effectively use their gift, the server needs to exercise *control* in his life. It is not that the server is to be in authority over other people, but that he is to be in control of his life. The person with the spiritual gift of serving can get so consumed in many different projects that he does not get any of them done the right way. The result will often be that the server quits before completing a project. The server has to learn when to say, "when." A server has got to say "no" at times. Being in control of his life, by being under the control of the Holy Spirit, gives the server protection for the management of his time. Paul told Timothy, "Till I come, give attendance to reading, to exhortation, to doctrine. Neglect not the gift that is in thee, which was given thee by prophecy, with the laying on of the hands of the presbytery" (1 Tim. 4:13-14). Paul was confirming Timothy's motivational gift in those verses. A server has got to carefully avoid the neglect of his spiritual life. Timothy had the motivational gift of serving. He eventually exercised his gift through the ministry of the pastorate. He had to stay in control of his life, especially giving attention to the study of the Word and to prayer. Otherwise, he may eventually have been consumed by his motivational gift, especially when trying to exercise it through his ministry gift, which required great spiritual depth.

Characteristics of Servers

More is revealed in the Bible relating to this gift than the others. Maybe it is because there are various means by which this gift can be exercised within the body of Christ. If those who have the gift of serving do not have a good understanding of their gift, and how it is to be expressed, practical areas of the Lord's work will be neglected and left undone. If those practical areas are overlooked, it will negatively affect the spiritual power and effectiveness of a church.

Let us now examine the **characteristics of the spiritual gift of serving**. They are given in the passage from the Book of Philippians (Phil. 2:17-23), which was referred to earlier in this chapter.

Find Opportunities to Assist

Paul said of Timothy, in Philippians 2:20: "I have no man like-minded, who will naturally care for your state." That is characteristic of a person with the gift of serving. When a server is in the Spirit, it is just natural for him to *find opportunities to assist*. In finding opportunities to assist others, servers are *alert to practical needs*. Some needs may seem insignificant to most people, but they catch the eye of the server. Usually, the needs are physical. The server knows that his assistance will bring encouragement and strength to those who have the particular need.

Servers are exceptionally *attentive to people*. The word "attended" was used about Lydia (Acts 16:14) in her attending unto the things said by Paul. First, she received spiritual truth. She attended to what really mattered the most. You remember that Martha failed to do that on one occasion (Luke 10:39-42). Second, Lydia began to attend to the special kinds of needs that Paul had in his life as a minister. Many servers have an amazing ability to find out and remember the likes and dislikes of people. They can remember special dates. Have you ever taken notice of the people who remember your birthday, and your mate's birthday, and your children's birthdays, and other special dates and occasions? That comes naturally for many who have the gift of serving.

Servers also like to make all occasions special. For some of you husbands, if your wife has this motivational gift, you might open your lunch box at work, and notice a little bow on it. Your fellow workers probably razzed you, and said something like, "How, sweet!" Your wife probably enclosed a nice cloth napkin, instead of a paper one, along with a couple of peppermints with your lunch. She even put in a little love note for you. By the time you read the love note, your fellow employees probably said something jokingly like, "I love you, sweetie!" Can you identify with that scenario? It may embarrass you a little, but such is life for the husband of a server. Don't let the kidding of your fellow employees bother you. They are probably just jealous!

Servers find ways to serve, adding special touches along the way.

Free Others to Achieve

Philippians 2:21 provides us with another major characteristic of the motivational gift of serving: "For all seek their own, not the things which are Jesus Christ's." A server is motivated to *free others to achieve*. The person with the gift of serving finds greater joy in doing what they believe is a menial task so that someone whom they feel has a more important responsibility can succeed. Have you ever noticed how Paul either had Mark or Timothy with him for most of his travels as a missionary. They were a part of the success of Paul's ministry. Paul did not have to worry about certain concerns because of the assistance of Timothy and Mark. Paul had a genuine concern for all the churches he had helped to start or to whom he had ministered. He wanted to *personally* care for all those churches, but it was impossible. But he had someone he could send out in his place. Several references in the Bible indicate that he sent Timothy on his behalf to minister to the churches.

Several years ago, I went to interview with a church concerning their minister of youth position. A meeting was arranged with all those who were volunteers in any aspect of that church's youth program. As everyone shared with me their involvement in the youth ministry of that church, two women made as great an impression on me as any of the rest. One of the ladies said that her involvement in their church's youth ministry was "dipping ice." I looked at her inquisitively. She explained, "I help serve food, dip ice, or do whatever else needs to be done in the way of providing refreshments for fellowships and other youth activities." The next lady said, "I take care of all the food for you. When you need refreshments or a meal for a youth ministry activity, I'll plan the menu, get whatever you want, and I'll be in charge of serving it and cleaning it up." I remember thinking to myself, "Lord, I've found youth ministry heaven on earth!" Many youth ministers will admit that counseling teenagers, or preparing a Bible study, a sermon, a youth retreat, and other special activities is not that difficult. But trying to figure out how much food and drinks are needed for a youth activity, taking time to get it, and seeing that it is served properly is more wearying than just about anything else connected with youth work. Those two ladies did not think their help in the youth ministry of their church was all that important. But it was a far greater service they were providing than they realized. Servers usually prefer to work behind the scenes and out of the limelight. But the service of those two ladies added to the success of "out front" workers in their church's youth ministry.

Servers are very important in a church. Servers are needed in Sunday schools to fulfill support responsibilities, and to meet other needs, so that the teacher can devote time to teaching. If others in church leadership positions are going to lead us effectively, they have to be freed from some of the less noticeable tasks that can take up so much of their time. We may even refer to such tasks as menial tasks, but they are not. If certain tasks are overlooked, someone may lose respect for a teacher or the pastor or some other church leader. Servers, that is why it is extremely important for you to be responsive to do what God prompts you to do in freeing up time for your spiritual leaders.

If you are a server, do not ever feel that what you do is menial, unnoticeable, or insignificant. Several years ago, at a major university, a study was conducted with the former participants in the football program of the school. The purpose of the study was to trace what had happened in their lives since graduation. Those who conducted the study wanted to see who had succeeded in their vocations and what they had accomplished. The study revealed the team position that produced the most successful graduates. What position on the football team do you think produced the most successful people?

It was not who most people would guess—the quarterback. It was not one of the other high profile positions, such as running backs, receivers, kickoff returners, or punt returners. It was not one of the positions that calls for a special aggressiveness, such as exhibited by those on the defensive unit. It was not the position of kicker or punter that calls for specializing in one aspect of the game of football. It was not the offensive guards or tackles, or the other not so recognized and appreciated positions on a football team. The answer probably will be an unexpected one for nearly everyone.

Who on a college football team had gone on to the most success in life? The managers.

You see, the managers for the football team had learned to develop a server's spirit. Didn't Jesus say that if you want to be the greatest, then you needed to be a server (Matt. 20:26-27)? Oh, the managers for a football team do not get a lot of recognition. When they run onto the field, you do not hear the public address announcer or radio announcer tell you the name of the manager on the field who served the players water, and wiped the sweat off their faces and necks. Managers are not those you know by name (unless you are their parent).

I know two football managers of my alma mater, the University of Tennessee, who validate this survey. Other than the former Tennessee Volunteer football players who have made it in pro football, the two managers I am thinking of have attained far more than most of the football players whom they served. Both of those managers are still working in capacities that provide a service for athletes and sports fans.

One is now a sports agent for some of those athletes for whom he was a manager, as well as for some of the other top names in professional sports. He is now a manager for them in a different role, but he still uses the qualities of a server. The other former manager is now one of the associate athletic directors at his alma mater.

Those with the gift of serving like to free others to accomplish important tasks. But the servers are just as much a part of the success achieved by the ones they assist. It may mold the tangible success the server may later attain in his personal life.

Fulfill Obligations to the End

A third major characteristic of the server is found in verse 22 of the passage in the second chapter of Philippians: "But ye know the proof of him, that, as a son with the father, he hath served with me in the gospel." The word "proof" is an interesting word here. Paul was living proof of what he proclaimed.

My subtitle for the Book of Philippians is "Living Joyfully Everyday." As Paul was the writer of Philippians, he was one who was living proof of living joyfully everyday, regardless of the circumstances he encountered in life.

Timothy was living proof, too. Timothy *fulfilled obligations to the end*. He faithfully served with Paul, as they served the Lord together. A person with the spiritual gift of serving fulfills obligations to the end.

When servers are Spirit-controlled, and when they are in control of their schedules, they get the job done.

There is a caution, though, to which the server must be sensitive. Servers tend to be *available and accepting to all proposals* that come their way. A server has difficulty in saying, "No." As a server meets one need, someone else may think, "He's good at that. I am going to ask him to do the same thing for me." The server will probably accept your request, although he may not be prompted to do it. We have to be careful that we do not take advantage of someone with the spiritual gift of serving.

I have been told that someone would be good at doing something for the church where there is a need. But there was a condition to it: "He's the kind of person who will do anything for you, but you've got to ask him." Well, my response to such offers is usually the same: "No, I am not going to ask him." I would rather God prompt a person to do what we have need of in our church. That is when the person with the gift of serving is in the Spirit and properly exercising their special gift for blessing. If God has prompted you to do a task, do it. It may seem insignificant, but your fulfilling it to the end may make your church more successful. It could mean the difference in your church leading twice as many people to Christ because you may free up someone who has an exceptional ability to witness to the unsaved, but they are bogged down with other responsibilities that limit their time and opportunities to do more soul winning.

In fulfilling obligations to the end, a trait of servers is that they get *absorbed in a project*. When a server gets absorbed in a project, he disregards weariness and freely uses up personal assets of time, money, and strength. The server's focus is not on himself, but on the completion of tasks.

When we moved to Milan, Tennessee, in 1982, Dixie was a great help to us getting moved in and settled. Her motivational gift is serving. She came to us and offered her help. For those first few days, Dixie was there every day. I remember a statement she made right after we first arrived in town. None of us knew much about spiritual gifts then. She told us, "You may see me everyday for three or four weeks, then you may not see me for awhile. I want you to know that it does not mean I don't like you anymore. But it's just the way I am." Sure enough, she helped us get our new home in order. As an interior decorator, she made our little apartment look like a New York City penthouse suite. After about three weeks, when things were in order, she was not around much. That's just a server. We were Dixie's special project. When the need was fulfilled (the project was finished), she was ready for another project. That's her life because that is how she is motivated as a server.

I want to add two more story lines to our relationship through the years with Dixie. When we left Milan and moved to Memphis, 95 miles away, during our first week in Memphis, Dixie came to Memphis with two other ladies to help Wanda get our new home in order. She brought two helpers because she was only able to spend one day with us. They got it done, too!

We were in Memphis for five years. Then I accepted the pastorate of Dixie Lee Baptist Church, near Knoxville, Tennessee. By the way, it is one of those unusual coincidences, but the full name of this dear server friend is Dixie Lee. Five and a half years after moving from Milan, I returned to preach the ordination service of a young man who had been in the youth group when I was minister of youth at the First Baptist Church there. He had been called to his first pastorate. The ordination was at First Baptist Church, Milan. I had driven to Milan after the morning worship service at Dixie Lee Church. The over 300 mile drive gave me just enough time to drive straight to the church for the ordination service. I had not taken care of getting a hotel room. At the end of the service, Dixie and her husband, Mickey, made their way to me as quickly as they could. She said, "Bobby, I don't know what I was thinking of. Some-how we missed that you were coming in for the ordination service. But you know that you are going to stay with us tonight." I was constrained to spend the night with them, and what wonderful hosts they were. I know that you know someone like Dixie. Aren't you thankful that God has placed such wonderful servants in the body of believers?

People with the gift of serving become absorbed in a project. One thing you can count on, too, is that they will give it a *special touch*. The server puts extra touches to jobs and tasks they perform. At times, they almost go overboard. You have to give them limits, and tell them you do not want to go beyond a certain scale. When I was in youth ministry and singles ministry, I would schedule a small, simple occasion, such as an after-church fellowship or potluck dinner. But if one with the gift of serv-ing was in charge of the occasion, my planned simple, informal gather-ing almost became a formal banquet.

Servers do things with a special touch that usually adds a lot of class to even the smallest occasion. That is the way they naturally approach what they do. You have to tell them, "I don't want it quite that big and that involved." They do more than is expected. The server not only wants to delight the one being served, but the server wants to delight the Lord. Servers go the second mile.

A key to our understanding of one with the motivational gift of serv-ing is this: do not give them long-range projects. Servers like to see vis-ible results. Otherwise, unless they are right with God and filled with the Spirit, they may not stick with it. Paul had to tell Timothy several times to stick with it and be diligent about his duties (see 1 Tim. 4:16; 2 Tim. 2:1, 3; 4:9, 21). Timothy had the spiritual gift of serving, and if the server does not see things happening, he may get discouraged and move on to something else.

I believe the need to keep it short term with visible results had something to do with John Mark deserting Paul and Barnabas on one of their mission trips. Mark had the motivational gift of serving. Maybe, the positive visible results were not as great as he expected. They were encountering opposition on their mission trip, too. So Mark quit, and went back home. It is wonderful that Mark did get back under the control of the Holy Spirit, because Paul later requested for Timothy to bring Mark (1 Tim. 4:11) to him. Paul said that Mark was profitable to his ministry. But that had not always been the case.

A characteristic of servers is that they prefer *short-term* projects. A server is motivated to see a task fulfilled. The server is attracted to immediate needs. Servers get frustrated with long range planning or a continuous project where they see little visible progress.

Follow Orders to Expectation

The next characteristic of the server is found in verses 19 and 23 of Philippians 2. Paul said, "But I trust in the Lord Jesus to send Timotheus shortly unto you, that I also may be of good comfort, when I know your state...Him therefore I hope to send presently, so soon as I shall see how it will go with me." Paul said that he was going to send Timothy, on his behalf, to the church at Philippi. From other writings of Paul, we know that when he sent Timothy on a mission, Timothy was faithful to fulfill Paul's instructions. Servers *follow orders to expectation*, if they know what is expected of them. A person with the spiritual gift of serving has got to know exactly what you want him to do. If a server is given orders, they are *acknowledged if perceived.*

Servers will faithfully follow orders, but expectations must be given to them and fully understood by them. Timothy faithfully followed what Paul asked him to do because Paul made it clear what was expected of Timothy. In the references in the Bible where Paul addressed Timothy, or referred to him, he would normally have some encouraging and complimentary things to say. But Paul was also clear in making known what was expected of Timothy. There were times when Paul was very specific with Timothy, so that Timothy would know the orders to follow. In Acts 17:15, Paul got word to Silas and Timothy "to come to him with all speed." The Bible says, "they departed." Paul purposely used language with Timothy that got the point clearly across:

> This charge I commit unto thee, son Timothy, according to the prophecies which went before on thee, that thou by them mightest war a good warfare. (1 Tim. 1:18)

> Hold fast the form of sound words, which thou hast heard of me, in faith and love which is in Christ Jesus. (2 Tim. 1:13)

> Thou therefore, my son, be strong in the grace that is in Christ Jesus. (2 Tim. 2:1)

> I charge thee therefore before God, and the Lord Jesus Christ. (2 Tim. 4:1)

Those are just a few examples, but they give a good illustration of how Paul wanted to make it clear to Timothy what was expected of him.

The reason why you need to make orders clear to servers is because they like to *accelerate the process.* Servers like to produce. They want to see results. If not given guidelines, servers will try to avoid committees and "red tape." To avoid delays, servers will use personal funds to speed up the process. Sometimes, it gets them in trouble. I have a ministry friend, who has the gift of serving. To help expedite the process of getting a celebrity speaker for a youth camp, he put up $2000 of his own money to cover the celebrity's travel expenses and performance fees. He expected to get reimbursed from the planners of the camp. But he never got reimbursed. He learned a valuable lesson. He had to take out a personal loan and pay it off over three years. Instead of waiting until the camp organizers had the money in hand to pay for the celebrity guest, he expedited the process and it got him in trouble.

A server must be careful not to avoid guidelines. Even when you think that it is okay to move ahead with a project, remember, some will take advantage of a server, especially when offered use of personal funds.

Feel Appreciated for their Efforts

In Philippians 3, there is one more major characteristic given for those who have the motivational gift of serving. There is one preposition that is a key to keeping the server in the Spirit. See if you can spot it in verse 22: "But ye know the proof of him, that, as a son with the father, he hath served with me in the gospel." The last phrase gives the key preposition and the basis for the next characteristic of a server. "He hath served **with** me in the gospel." Paul does not say of Timothy that he served *for* me, but *with* me.

Servers need to *feel appreciated for their efforts*. Servers love to be with people. The person with the gift of serving nearly always wants to be around people. It is because servers prefer working <u>with</u> people rather than <u>for</u> people. The server is one who just seems to *always be with people*, and who prefers it that way. If you do not have the motivational gift of serving, be careful in referring to any servers who assist you as ones who work for you. In reality, they may work for you, but be sensitive in not drawing attention to it, especially if it is in a voluntary capacity. Keep servers happy by making them feel that they serve and work with you in your mutual involvement.

Paul was careful to refer to Timothy as one who served with him in the ministry in Philippians 2:22. It is also how he mentioned his relationship with Timothy in his other writings. In his first letter to the church at Corinth, Paul referred to Timothy as "my beloved son" (1 Cor. 4:17). In his first letter to the church at Thessalonica, Paul mentioned Timothy as "our brother, and minister of God, and our fellow labourer in the gospel of Christ" (1 Thess. 3:2). Timothy followed orders to expectation, as Paul gave them to him, but Paul used every opportunity he could to make Timothy feel appreciated for his efforts. Servers need *affirmation from their peers*. It confirms to the server that the work he is doing is necessary. Paul praised Timothy more than any of the others who assisted and served with him in the ministry. With Timothy's motivational gift of serving, Paul motivated and encouraged Timothy to keep on keeping on.

This characteristic of the server is an important fact to keep in mind for those who have another motivational gift. Be an encourager to a server. Just a small thank-you note is a big confirmation to a server that he is following the Lord's promptings. Servers like to feel appreciated for their efforts. It is not because servers like the pat on the back. It shows servers that what they are doing is necessary. It is like saying to a server, "Hey, you are doing exactly what God wants you to do." If you know of a server who has been of help to you, why not send a thank-you card or make a phone call to let that server know how appreciative you are of the service he performed.

Cautions For The Gift of Serving

Let us now direct our attention to the **cautions for the spiritual gift of serving**.

Misunderstandings

One of the first misunderstandings that others may have about servers is that they are *nosy*. Because servers often give help or offer help without being asked, some people think that servers are just naturally nosy people. Servers do have a tendency to stick their nose into where they see a need. The server does not necessarily consider that someone may already be involved in the process of meeting what is an evident need to the server. All the pieces may not yet fit together in an apparent need being met. To a server, he still sees a need that has not been dealt with. The motivation of the server is to meet the need. Sometimes, the server's unrequested help is greatly appreciated. At other times, a server's unrequested involvement may cause a problem.

The word *notoriety* summarizes another misunderstanding that others have about servers. Have you ever heard someone make a comment about someone else, who is always leading out in a church project, that "someone else" is trying to impress the preacher? It is because "someone" has misunderstood the motivation of the "someone else" who is a server. Servers are not so helpful in order to gain recognition for their own personal advancement. Servers are not serving to impress anybody. It is what a server is naturally motivated to do. There is no motive for self-advancement, although that may possibly be a result of serving.

Sometimes, servers are misunderstood as being *neglectful*. It may appear that a server is neglectful personally. Because a server is so involved in various projects, others may feel that the server is neglecting his own home and personal responsibilities. Some may feel that a server is neglectful physically. As servers often work beyond physical limits, they may look run down if that is the case. How do you know when you are taking on too much as a server? Your family will let you know and your body will let you know. Those without the gift of serving also may misjudge a server as being neglectful spiritually. I must admit that, until I studied spiritual gifts, there were active church members who did many good things, but they did not seem very spiritual to me. I tended to have a critical attitude toward those individuals. They were busy doing things for the church, but they seldom, if ever, participated in outreach or soul winning visitation. They were the kind of people who would travel half-way around the world to build a church, or they would travel great distances to serve food to victims of disasters. Yet, they would not make the same sacrifices to go verbally witness to a neighbor across the street. As we will learn in the final chapter of this book, some of the motivational gifts are more speaking gifts and some are more serving gifts. We ought to believe in personal soul winning, and we ought to share our faith with others. But let us not limit witnessing to our favorite method. God can use a hammer and a hot meal as a tool in witnessing as effectively as he can use our tongue or a gospel tract. Remember, servers free up those who are gifted with their tongues to use their tongues for the Lord.

Another misunderstanding that others have about servers is that they are *negative*. It is because a server may react critically or negatively to people whom the server thinks are overlooking obvious needs. Servers just assume that others see what they see. Servers do have to be careful not to judge or jump too quickly on someone who does not respond to a need as the server feels someone should.

One other misunderstanding about servers is that they are *nervous*. So is everybody else, at times. When a server is working under a close deadline, and everything is not ready, he can get extremely nervous. Servers do get frustrated with time limits, so they can get in a rush and appear to be nervous until a project is ready and rolling.

Now it's one thing to be nervous because of time considerations, but when a server gets out from under the control of the Holy Spirit, he may fall apart from worry. Paul exhorted Timothy to not worry about what God had called him to do (2 Tim. 1:7). Paul informed the church at Corinth that he was sending Timothy to them, and he said: "Now if Timotheus come, see that he may be with you without fear: for he worketh the work of the Lord, as I also do. Let no man therefore despise him: but conduct him forth in peace, that he may come unto me: for I look for him with the brethren" (1 Cor. 16:10-11). The fear of Timothy that Paul referred to was not due to physical danger, but because of many who did not accept Timothy's authority. That was probably a worry to Timothy prior to his going to Corinth.

Servers worry about fulfilling obligations, because they wonder if they are qualified. Several times, the Bible records that Paul exhorted Timothy to "neglect not" a duty, or to "be diligent" to do something. Paul knew that Timothy might become so frustrated and nervous that he would feel like he was on the verge of falling apart emotionally and be tempted to quit.

Misuses

Since there are so many servers in the church, who are needed in the body of Christ, more misuses seem prevalent with this gift than with the others. Obviously, the more you have of something, the more you notice it, especially when it is not functioning properly.

Even though a server is motivated to assist others, without Spirit control, the server can be *intrusive*. In the flesh, servers tend to force their ideas on others. It may come to the point that a server puts force or pressure on others, verbally and emotionally, to get them to cooperate.

Another misuse of the gift of serving is *interference*. All of us have to be particularly sensitive in this area, but the server especially has to be careful not to get in God's way. One of the greatest misuses of the gift of serving is when a server interferes with the will of God in God's discipline upon a person's life. God may have put someone in a state of need as punishment. His purposes may be frustrated where the server seeks to meet a need that God meant to bring about repentance.

What would have happened to the prodigal son if the needs of that young man had been met in the "far country"? (See Luke 15:11-32) Because of his rebellious and wasteful lifestyle, the "husks that the swine did eat" began to look good to him. He had to get to that position in his life or he probably would have never returned home and been restored with his father and family. What if somebody along the way, who had the gift of serving, had seen his need in the "far country" and met it? They would have interfered with God's will.

Irresponsibility is another misuse of the gift of serving. For example, if a server is not careful, he may neglect his own family in serving others. I heard a story about a man who was a Mr. Fix-It. He could fix just about anything. His friends and neighbors were always asking him to fix something at their homes. Yet the kitchen sink in his own home had been leaking for months. Because he was so busy serving others, his own home was neglected. His wife finally had enough, and laid down the law to her husband: No more service elsewhere until you take care of servicing needed at your own home.

Illness can come upon servers as a result of misusing their motivational gift. Servers can work beyond physical limitations and become ill. When servers get overinvolved and pressure builds up, they are especially susceptible to stomach problems. Paul had to tell Timothy to take some medicine for his "stomach's sake and thine often infirmities" (1 Tim. 5:23). Due to overworking his body and his nerves in his role as a server, Timothy developed stomach problems, as well as other illnesses. Some individuals with the gift of serving seem to get sick more than normal. It is because they are busy doing something nearly all the time.

When a server ignores the Holy Spirit's control, he often becomes *imbalanced*. Servers can get so involved in non-spiritual duties, that they neglect their spiritual life. Their life becomes out of balance spiritually.

The server needs to make daily quiet time in prayer and Bible study a priority (see 1 Tim. 2:1; 2 Tim. 3:14-17). This needs to be a priority for all of us, but because of the nature of his motivational gift, the server may neglect the spiritual needs in his own life.

A server can also become *insistent*. The insistent server says: "I want something done, and I want it done my way, no matter what." When that is the case, the server may use his own resources, and it can hurt him. It can be financially or physically straining, but the server's attitude is that I am going to go on and do it. Such thinking and action may lead to conflict. If you feel what you want is God's will, but others do not yet feel that way, you need to wait. Give God time to change the minds of others. You may push your way through to get something when you want it. But you may cause some hard and hurt feelings among those with whom you once walked in sweet fellowship.

A server must also guard against becoming *inconsistent*. Servers can take on too many projects at one time, to the extent that some of the projects drag on long-term. Since servers want to see visible results, they move on to other projects without completing existing ones. Paul regularly reminded Timothy to "continue in them" (1 Tim. 4:16) and "to endure hardness" (2 Tim. 2:3). It was because Timothy needed to be encouraged to stay at it even when he was not always seeing positive results.

A server misuses his gift when he becomes too *independent*. Servers do not always observe the rules. Since they have a tendency to bypass "red tape," servers can become too independent. A server will just do it himself if he does not feel a need is being met. That is not always bad, but there are some servers who get used to operating by themselves all the time. Not allowing others to help deprives those who have the gift of serving from using their gift.

Servers can also misuse their gift by being *inconsiderate*. Why? If they do not have a schedule, or they try to have a schedule, they want you to adjust your schedule in order to meet theirs. Without the control of the Holy Spirit, servers rush people around their schedules, or actually, their lack of one. A server can get so involved that it is useless for him to try to abide by a schedule. Twenty-four hours in a day are not enough hours to fulfill all the commitments of such a server.

In the flesh, servers can also be very *irritable*. Servers can react critically to others who do not see what the server feels are obvious needs. The server will disrespect such people. Servers also become irritable and resentful if they do not feel their efforts are appreciated. They have ways of letting it be known. They may even drop out of church because they did not get patted on the back enough and became bitter because of it. As servers can get frustrated with time limits, they can fall apart with worry. With so many factors involved, servers can become so irritable that people do not even want to be around them, and might even seek to keep irritable servers from leading projects in a church.

If servers do not deal with the misuses of their gift spiritually, the ultimate, final misuse is that they become *inactive*.

Servers who operate in the strength of the flesh tend to become quitters. They may not be seeing things happen as quickly as they want to see them happen, and they tend to dwell on what is not being accomplished. Or they feel unappreciated, and they get bitter, dwelling on the lack of appreciation shown to them. They may believe that people do not like them. With all those factors, their serving is no longer a joy, so they quit. Most once active church members who have become inactive are probably servers who were misunderstood or felt unappreciated.

Oswald Chambers wrote about Christian workers that: "A worker has to disentangle himself from many things that would advantage and develop him but which would turn him aside from being broken bread and poured out wine in his Lord's hands."[2]

One with the gift of serving can be involved in many good things, but not in the best things, through which he can most effectively serve the Lord and grow in his faith. That is when he can easily become a quitter. Chambers also said: "Whenever a worker breaks down it is because he has taken responsibility upon himself which was never God's will for him to take."[3] This is where servers must be so very careful. Responsibilities taken beyond the will of God make quitters out of servers.

Conclusion

A server mighty in Spirit responds to the needs of others and seeks to meet needs with a respectful attitude. Servers need to keep their lives in control, by wisely handling their schedules, and by being obedient to the promptings and restraints of the Holy Spirit.

Such servers will find the right opportunities to assist others and will effectively free others to achieve. They will also fulfill obligations to the end by following orders to expectations. The natural response of others will be appreciation for the efforts of a helpful, cooperative Spirit-filled server.

Those with the motivational spiritual gift of serving just love to meet needs. That is how God has gifted them. They just love to be involved in the work of the Lord because they love to serve other people in the name of the Lord.

4

The Gift of Teaching

"Knowing with Certainty"

*Having then gifts differing according to the grace that is given to us, whether prophecy, let us prophesy according to the proportion of faith; Or ministry, let us wait on our ministering: or he that teacheth, on **teaching**;...Not slothful in business; fervent in spirit; serving the Lord. (Rom. 12:6-7,11)*

There are those of you who are about to read this chapter who do not believe that you are motivated as a teacher. You would not consider the gift of teaching as your motivational spiritual gift. But after reading the characteristics of a teacher in this chapter, you may discover that this motivational gift, indeed, is yours.

There are ministries in the church where teaching is used, but teaching is not the motivational gift of the ones who are teaching. More than anything else, a teacher wants to confirm that something is true, to clarify it so that other people can understand it, and then, most of the time, to communicate it.

You see, the person with the motivational gift of teaching is really not concerned with being the one who communicates the truth. The teacher strives to equip someone to effectively communicate truth.

The first chapter of Luke outlines the major characteristics of a teacher:

Forasmuch as many have taken in hand to set forth in order a declaration of those things which are most surely believed among us, Even as they delivered them unto us, which from the beginning were eyewitnesses, and ministers of the word; It seemed good to me also, having had perfect understanding of all things from the very first, to write unto thee in order, most excellent Theophilus, That thou mightest know the certainty of those things, wherein thou hast been instructed.

In the New American Standard Version of Luke 1:1-4, characteristics of the teacher are defined more clearly.

*Inasmuch as many have undertaken to **compile** an account of the things accomplished among us. (v. 1)*

Teachers **compile information**.

*Just as those who from the beginning were eyewitnesses and servants of the word have handed them down to us, it seemed fitting for me as well, having **investigated** everything carefully from the beginning. (vs. 2-3a)*

Teachers **carefully investigate** all the material they compile.

*To write it out for you in **consecutive order**, most excellent Theophilus. (v. 3b)*

Teachers like to **consecutively organize** everything and build toward a theme. To a teacher, one word should be placed before another word in a listing because it comes before the other in alphabetical order. That is how a teacher considers how to clarify and make information memorable.

*So that you might know the **exact truth** about the things you have been taught. (v. 4)*

Teachers **communicate exactly** that which is discovered. He begins from the motivation to **confirm accuracy**. A teacher hears something, but must confirm it if he does not already know it to be factual. He has to know with certainty that it is true.

I have titled this chapter, "Knowing with Certainty" (Luke 1:4). The prophet wants to give you "a more sure word." Prophets believe that they have a more sure word to give you on a matter than you have ever heard before. The server is "naturally caring," motivated to serve and assist others. Teachers want others to "know with certainty" absolutely reliable and truthful information.

Luke is our main biblical example of one with the gift of teaching. He wrote the two longest books in the New Testament: the Gospel of Luke and the Book of Acts.

Why were Luke's books so long in content? As a teacher, he really gets down to proving the facts in detail.

A Composite: The Gift of Teaching
Explanation of the Gift of Teaching

Some books of the Bible can be associated with the individual motivational gifts. One section of the Bible is known as the "Major Prophets," while another section is known as the "Minor Prophets."

Apparently, most authors of biblical books were motivated by the gift of prophecy. In the Book of Judges, an ***explanation of the spiritual gift of teaching*** is illustrated through the lives of some of the judges, as well as some other biblical examples.

The sixth chapter of Judges records the account of Gideon's "throwing out a fleece." As a teacher, Gideon wanted to verify God's voice. Judges 6:12 describes how Gideon responded when the angel of the Lord first came to him: "And the angel of the LORD appeared unto him, and said unto him, 'The LORD is with thee, thou mighty man of valour.'" Instead of saying, "Thank you," he responded as a teacher, by asking questions.

> *And Gideon said unto him, 'Oh my Lord, if the LORD be with us, why then is all this befallen us? and where be all His miracles which our fathers told us of, saying, Did not the LORD bring us up from Egypt? but now the LORD hath forsaken us, and delivered us into the hands of the Midianites.' (Judges 6:13)*

Gideon's response was basically, "Where's the proof? Show me the accuracy of what you are telling me. I'm not with you at this point." The dialogue continues in a similar vein for a few more verses.

> And the LORD looked upon him, and said, 'Go in this thy might, and thou shalt save Israel from the hand of the Midianites: have not I sent thee?' And he said unto Him, 'Oh my Lord, wherewith shall I save Israel? behold, my family is poor in Manasseh, and I am the least in my father's house.' And the LORD said unto him, 'Surely I will be with thee, and thou shalt smite the Midianites as one man.' (vs. 14-16)

The angel of the Lord responded to Gideon's question. Then Gideon questioned again the logic of the angel's response. The angel of the Lord reconfirmed that He would be with Gideon to give him victory. But Gideon was still not convinced. So he said to the angel, "If now I have found grace in thy sight, then shew me a sign that Thou talkest with me" (v. 17).

In verses 19-21, God gave Gideon a sign. Verse twenty-two reveals Gideon's response: "And when Gideon perceived that He was an angel of the LORD, Gideon said, 'Alas, O Lord GOD! for because I have seen an angel of the LORD face to face.'" Gideon's response confirmed the accuracy and the truth of what he had been told because he had seen the proof to back it up. But later, he still asked for further confirmation in his "throwing out the fleece" experience (vs. 36-40).

From Gideon's story, several traits are revealed that are common to teachers.

Teachers *inquire* (Judg. 6:13). They want to know the why and the where of something. A few chapters later in the Book of Judges, chapter 13 tells about an incident that happened to Manoah, the father of Samson. An angel of the Lord came to Manoah's wife and told her that she and her husband were going to have a son. Well, Manoah did not tell his wife that he did not believe her, but he wanted some proof. The angel of the Lord appeared personally to Manoah. Just like Gideon, Manoah started asking him questions. He wanted to know the why, where, and when of it.

Teachers like to inquire because they want *evidence*. They ask questions like "Shew me a sign" (Judg. 6:17)? The teacher prefers to know from *experience* that something is true or factual. Therefore, they often say: "Because I have seen" (Judg. 6:22).

In Judges 8:16, Gideon *instructed* the people. The Bible says that he "taught the men of Succoth." That particular occasion was not a pleasant experience for the learners. Gideon beat them because he did not trust them. He used force to enlighten them.

Solomon, another teacher, and the author of Ecclesiastes, was known for his wisdom. How do you get wisdom? By searching and investigating. That was Solomon's purpose for writing Ecclesiastes. In the first chapter he states: "And I gave my heart to seek and search out by wisdom concerning all things that are done under heaven" (v. 13). In Ecclesiastes 2:1, Solomon declares, "I will prove." Similar statements are found throughout Ecclesiastes. Solomon had to have proof. However, when one must have proof, it often weakens the element of faith.

Solomon strove to discover by experience. And he did. He learned by experience that some things were not good. Most of the time, it is better to learn from the mistakes of others than to make the same mistakes yourself. By the time we get to the last chapter of Ecclesiastes, we learn what Solomon found: "And moreover, because the preacher was wise, he still taught the people knowledge; yea, he gave good heed, and sought out, and set in order many proverbs. The preacher sought to find out acceptable words: and that which was written was upright, even words of truth" (Eccl. 12:9-10).

In Ecclesiastes 13:12, Solomon shares his ultimate discovery: "Let us hear the conclusion of the whole matter: Fear God, and keep His commandments: for this is the whole duty of man."

In verse 10, Solomon promises his readers that they could trust his conclusion: "The preacher sought to find out acceptable words: and that which was written was upright, even words of truth." Paraphrased, Solomon's statement means: "Everything that I have written in this book is the truth, folks, because I have personally checked it out." He communicated it exactly the way he had found it to be. He did it the way he had said that he was going to do it. Solomon said that he was going to seek and search (Eccl. 1:13). He said that he would inquire and get the evidence. He revealed from the start, before he disclosed his findings, that he had done just that: "I have seen" (Eccl. 1:14). He got his evidence from first hand experience because he felt that was what he had to do to prove his findings (Eccl. 2:1). He proved it by wisdom (Eccl. 7:23). When Solomon found the proof of what he was searching for, he instructed others about what he felt was the truth. The Bible says that he taught the people (Eccl. 12:9). His record of what he discovered—the Book of Ecclesiastes—is still teaching the truth of his findings to people today.

The Old Testament reveals that teachers inquire about everything, gather evidence gained from personal experience, and instruct others concerning their discoveries. The New Testament supports the Old. In his Gospel account, Luke sets forth a declaration (Luke 1:1). To do that, he inquired. He got his evidence from eyewitnesses, as it was delivered to him (Luke 1:2). He wanted us to understand and believe it because he had perfect understanding of it (Luke 1:3). Luke had experienced it personally. Therefore, he stated that he was writing with certainty and that we could know with certainty that what he wrote was true (Luke 1:3-4).

Examples of Teachers
Biblical examples of teachers include Gideon, Manoah, Solomon, and Luke.

Two of the twelve disciples, Bartholomew and Thomas, were also teachers. When Philip found Bartholomew (Nathaniel) and told him, "We

have found the Messiah" (John 1:45), Bartholomew responded skepti-
cally, saying: "'Can there any good thing come out of Nazareth?' Philip
saith unto him, 'Come and see'" (John 1:46). When Bartholomew met
Jesus, who revealed some perceptive insights about him, Bartholomew
responded with questions (John 1:48-49).

After the crucifixion and resurrection of Christ, Thomas was not
present when Jesus first appeared to all His disciples. When the other
disciples revealed to Thomas their visit with the resurrected Lord, he
responded, "Except I shall see in His hands the print of the nails, and put
my finger into the print of the nails, and thrust my hand into His side, I
will not believe" (John 20:25).

Both Bartholomew and Thomas responded as typical teachers. They
asked questions and wanted firsthand evidence. But when they got it
firsthand, each man was quick to instruct those around them of what
they had learned (John 1:49; 20:28).

These biblical examples, by no means exhaustive, are exemplary with
regard to teaching.

Without question, our perfect example of a teacher is Jesus, often
referred to as Master or Teacher by those who followed Him or who
asked questions of Him.

Exhortations to Teachers

Romans 12:11 gives some special *exhortations to teachers:* be "not slothful in business; fervent in spirit; serving the Lord." Teachers are given
these three exhortations to especially heed.

First, the Bible exhorts the teacher to be "not slothful in business."
Teachers tend to be perfectionists and strive to *be flawless.* When a teacher
sets out to research something, he seeks to ascertain facts accurately,
which takes endurance to accomplish. A person with this motivational
gift spends much time alone searching for correct answers. Even though
it is tempting to allow one's mind to wander without accountability, Scrip-

ture exhorts teachers to flee slothfulness to be as flawless as possible in work.

Teachers are also exhorted to *be fervent* in spirit. In order to be fervent, one needs to enthusiastically endure, striving for excellence.

Through the years, you may have known some teachers who were less than enthusiastic. You probably did not enjoy their instruction. It may have had a negative learning effect on you. However, if a teacher is enthusiastic about his subject, chances are greater that his pupils will catch some of that enthusiasm. As a result, learning will be enhanced. Thus, teachers are exhorted to be fervent.

A third exhortation to teachers is that they are to serve the Lord. Sometimes, teachers become so engrossed with education that they lose the element of faith.

Seminary professors who deviate from the literal truth of the Scriptures are proof of this. They think that they have found truth above biblical teachings. In their minds, they cannot absolutely prove the truth of a Scripture, so they make a judgment that leaves out the element of faith.

But Matthew 10:24 tells us that a servant cannot be above his master. Such a teacher is not serving the Lord. Even if a teacher does not fully understand a portion of the Scriptures, or cannot totally prove it, the teacher has to believe it and back it with faith.

Teachers, be earnest in serving the Lord first. *Be faithful* to the Lord above all else and all others. Always keep in mind whose you are and what you are all about as you flawlessly, fervently, and faithfully serve the Lord.

Expectation Teachers Need to Exercise Most

Just as a prophet needs to have a clear conscience so he can speak the truth in love, and a server needs to have control over his life, the teacher needs to learn to *concentrate on the Word of God above all else.*

Teachers must make an effort to give quality time to meditation upon the Scriptures so that they can be mighty in the Spirit.

Philippians 4:7-8 brings out something we all need to do, but it is something a teacher should give extra effort to: "And the peace of God, which passeth all understanding, shall keep your hearts and minds through Christ Jesus. Finally, brethren, whatsoever things are true, whatsoever things are honest, whatsoever things are just, whatsoever things are pure, whatsoever things are lovely, whatsoever things are of good report; if there be any virtue, and if there be any praise, think on these things." Where can all these elements be found? The Word of God. Therefore, a teacher should concentrate on the Word of God and center that concentration on Christ. Our belief is based on faith. As Christians, we do not always have tangible proof before us. The expectation that teachers need to exercise the most is concentration on Christ through meditation upon the Word of God, making the words of Christ central above all other sources of knowledge.

Characteristics of Teachers
Confirm Accuracy

Teachers *confirm accuracy*. Luke acknowledged that one of his purposes for writing his Gospel was that his readers might know with certainty that his account of the life of Christ was accurate. Not only does a teacher desire to be accurate, but he wants others to be accurate.

Teachers keep the church *doctrinally pure*. They help to keep our theology in line with the Word of God. The conflict in the Southern Baptist Convention was born out of a concern that the denomination's seminaries had professors who did not adhere to the inerrancy of the Bible. Those whom God has raised up in this denomination to call the seminaries to doctrinal accountability have not been the most educated individuals in their denomination. But some of them have the motivational gift of teaching. They know what the Bible says as the standard for our beliefs.

God often uses less educated teachers to keep well-educated professors true to the Word of God and doctrinally pure.

In their desire to confirm accuracy, teachers want others to *define precisely* whatever they are explaining, teaching, or talking about. The teacher puts an emphasis on the importance of words and their shades of meaning. A teacher will often ask, "Just what do you mean?" If one with the gift of teaching has doubts about someone who says that he believes the Bible, the teacher will want to know what the person means when he says that he believes the Bible.

For instance, the teacher will want to know if the person believes the Genesis account of creation. The teacher wants to get specific. He will ask the person if he believes in the virgin birth of Christ and in the other miracles in the Bible. To the teacher, if someone does not believe all of the Bible is the inspired, inerrant, infallible (completely reliable) Word of God, then the person does not believe the Bible. That is why the teacher gets very specific and wants others to define their beliefs precisely.

Teachers also want others to *declare properly* what they believe because teachers are alert to false instructors. A teacher wants to know the background of guest speakers. When someone is scheduled as a revival preacher at a teacher's church, the teacher will have a natural interest in the background of the evangelist and why he was asked to preach the revival. The teacher investigates the education, pastorates, and other pertinent information pertaining to that speaker. In this way, the teacher confirms that his church is getting the right person to preach or speak to their congregation.

When a teacher speaks before a group for the first time, he will usually give his own qualifications and tell his audience why he has selected his chosen lecture topic. If he had planned to speak on another topic but changed his mind, the teacher will tell you why. To most of us, that does not matter. But teachers want to see truth presented in balance. They desire to take their own and others' experiences and see how they relate to the Scriptures.

A teacher who is properly motivated interprets experiences in light of the Scriptures, not vice versa. An improperly motivated teacher seeks to interpret the Scriptures in light of experiences. That leads to doctrinal error.

In making sure that information is declared properly, a teacher remains quiet until he has heard all the information, observes what is visibly presented, and verifies it. The Gospel of Luke does not contain personal statements by Luke about what he believed. At the start of his Gospel, he proclaims that what he relates is the truth because he has searched it out. Throughout the Book of Luke, he quotes Jesus, or someone else, but he does not impart his personal feelings. His beliefs are expressed through the ones he used as resources for his information.

In confirming accuracy and making sure that information is declared properly, teachers seek to clarify misunderstandings. If a teacher's facts appear to be wrong, the teacher cannot rest until he goes back and sees where he made the mistake.

A seminary professor of mine did this. If someone questioned something he had said in class, and it appeared he had made a mistake, the next day in class he would tell you where he was wrong and how he had made his mistake. Most of the time, though, this seminary professor was not the one who was in error. It was the student. A person with the gift of teaching can keep you humble. This professor did it in a way, not to put a student down, but to get the student to search it out for himself. In correcting misunderstandings and correcting mistakes, the teacher's motivation is to help the student discover where he got off track and why. But even when the teacher makes a mistake, he will find out why and where he got off course so that he can help others from making the same mistake.

If a teacher is in charge of a publication, it will be a *dependable publication*. The teacher will make sure that everything in the publication is true and has the facts to support it. Teachers have a knack for spotting mistakes and misinformation in any publication they read. My seminary professor's wife told me that her husband cannot help but correct mistakes when he reads a book or article. He will make notations where he believes a sentence is improperly punctuated, a word is misspelled or missing, or there is some other typographical error. But do not misjudge such a teacher. He is motivated to make sure that what we hear, read, and see is accurate.

Compile Information

Teachers also like to **compile information**. Luke stated that he "set forth in order a declaration of those things which are most surely believed among us" (Luke 1:1). He compiled the information, then he wrote it out in a clear manner. To do that, a teacher must *gather facts*. A teacher has a greater delight in doing research than in the actual act of teaching.

When a teacher does report his findings, it is usually not done within a few minutes. Teachers are often too detailed for most people. But you have to gather facts to get it exactly right, and it takes time to present the facts.

Luke is the most prolific biblical writer with just two New Testament books. In his Gospel account, he thoroughly defines details not found in Matthew, Mark, and John. Luke's Gospel contains unique information and incidents.

Teachers gather facts, and they prefer for those facts to be *gained firsthand*. Gideon said, "I have seen" (Judg. 6:22). Solomon said, "I have seen" (Eccl. 1:14). If unseen, teachers seek information from an eyewitness (Luke 1:2).

In compiling information, teachers prefer to *go with familiarity*, relying on primary resources that they can trust. Teachers tend to use the accepted works of recognized authorities to confirm statements on a particular matter. They will also tend to remain loyal to those sources. When others deserted Paul, Luke remained with him (2 Tim. 4:11). Much of Acts centers on Luke's writings about the life of Paul. Luke remained with Paul because he recognized Paul as the authoritative chief spokesman and missionary of the Christian faith. Like prophets, teachers are very loyal to remain with those whom they trust.

In sharing what they have found, teachers *give fairness*. They want to know all the views on a subject. They will hear you out, if they are convinced you have something credible to say. They want to be fair, but when they compile all their information and gather all the facts, they will confirm what they believe is accurate and truthful.

Carefully Investigate

Furthermore, teachers *carefully investigate* a matter. Luke wrote his Gospel account after "having investigated everything carefully from the beginning" (Luke 1:3 NAS). While carefully investigating a matter to know with certainty, a teacher will *filter the facts*. Teachers have a desire to verify what they have heard, so they will digest the data they compile in detail. A teacher will spend hours and hours by himself. Without discretion, the teacher can lose track of time trying to filter through information he accesses.

Luke gives precise descriptions of events, conversations, and physical conditions in his Gospel and in Acts. He includes more names, titles, dates, events, and sidelights than any other Gospel writer.

When Jesus responded to Jairus' urgent request to come and heal his daughter, Luke weaves a story within a story. He relates the account of a woman with a blood disease, who was healed when she touched Jesus' garment (Luke 8:41-48). That secondary incident happened while Jesus was on the way to the home of Jairus. This is typical of Luke's writing style.

As those with the gift of teaching carefully investigate a matter by filtering through the facts, it is so they can *find the factual.* It is wonderful when one with the gift of teaching manifests the gift in the profession of teaching. But there are other professions where those with the gift of teaching can use their gift effectively.

After a teacher has filtered through the facts, found the factual, and deliberated to the point of confirmation, he will *fix it firmly* in his mind. When one with the motivational gift of teaching has confirmed what is accurate, he stays by his decision and determines that he will not change his mind. In his mind, he has found the truth on a matter. The teacher then may defend his findings with confidence.

Consecutive Order

Luke wrote: "Just as those who from the beginning were eyewitnesses and servants of the word have handed them down to us, it seemed fitting for me as well, having investigated everything carefully from the beginning to write it out for you in consecutive order" (Luke 1:3 NAS). As part of that process, teachers will use a kind of *systematic sequence* because they like to develop and build their findings around a theme.

Most of the time, teachers organize information *chronologically.* They like to put events, circumstances, and facts in the order in which they occurred. Why do teachers like to put things in a chronological order? So that they can more *efficiently explain* what they want to communicate.

Sometimes, a teacher will deviate from chronological order. If the teacher feels that a concept can be taught and more efficiently explained, he deals with it thoroughly and exclusively, even if it is out of chronological order. Mainly, a teacher keeps everything in chronological order.

Some Gospel writers occasionally wrote about a happening in Christ's life ahead of its chronological order since it was a proper place to insert it to expound upon and enhance a fact about Jesus or a truth being presented by the Lord.

Teachers will use whatever they feel will make it easier for them and others to remember what they are trying to communicate.

A popular preaching method for outlining a sermon is called alliteration. This method calls for all the major points of a sermon to begin with the same letter of the alphabet. Alliteration may even be used for the sub-points of the sermon, although it does allow for use of other letters of the alphabet than the one used for the main sermon points. This technique helps the preacher to remember his outline, but it also helps the listeners to pick up on the key thoughts of a sermon. Teachers use similar methods to efficiently explain what they want to communicate.

Why do teachers go to such great measures? So we might have *clear comprehension*. Teachers want to clearly present their information to bring understanding to others. Students may think teachers purposely try to make learning difficult, but most teachers purposely try to make it as easy as possible to explain and understand for clear comprehension.

Communicate Exactly

Prior to Luke 1:4, Luke informs his readers that he had compiled information about the life of Christ, carefully investigating it to confirm its accuracy. He arranged his findings in consecutive order. He told his readers it was "so that you might know the exact truth about the things you have been taught" (v. 4 NAS). Luke wanted to ***communicate exactly*** to his readers what he had discovered. He wanted them to know how he had come to his conclusions so that they might know with certainty that he was imparting truth. When a teacher says, "Here is the report. This is what I have come up with," you can be assured that *thorough research* has gone into the report. You can be confident that the teacher has sat down and *thoughtfully recorded* what he has found through his research. If the teacher is the one to report his findings, rest assured that it will be *truthfully reported* because a teacher is motivated to be *totally reliable* in finding and supporting the truth on a given matter.

Luke assured the readers of his Gospel that it was thoughtfully recorded ("compile an account" - v. 1) because he had put thorough research into it ("investigated everything carefully" - v. 3). He also assured that it was truthfully reported ("from the beginning...in consecutive order" - v. 3) so that his readers could be confident that it was totally reliable ("that you might know the exact truth" - v. 4).

Cautions for The Gift of Teaching
Misunderstandings

Teachers are often misjudged as being *too skeptical*. Because teachers ask many questions, people think they are doubting and skeptical. Perhaps, you have thought that someone who often asks questions must not believe what they are hearing when they seem to question everything they hear. But that certainly is not necessarily the case. The questioner may actually believe what he is hearing, but he wants to know the why, when, and where. The teacher wants to know all the facts that he is learning so that he can accurately share those facts with others. The teacher desires to know with certainty so that he can help others to also know with certainty.

Teachers are often misunderstood as being *too specific*. They do tend to be detailed. Because they are very specific, the misunderstanding comes in others thinking that teachers are rigid, boring, and complex. To get all the facts, though, one often has to be very specific and detailed.

A teacher is sometimes looked upon as being *too selective* because he tends to stick to reliable sources. When people think a teacher is too selective, they may also misjudge the teacher as being prejudiced. If a teacher knows that there is a certain book that he can trust as a resource, or a person whose opinion he values greatly, the teacher will quote that book or person often. The teacher will usually go to that source first, even to the exclusion of other sources.

We may think that teachers are *too schematic*. To us, things do not have to be put together in a certain order, if it is not really necessary. But a teacher does things in an orderly fashion. They have schemes for how they judge something to be true and for the way by which they put their information in order. Teachers are not very flexible to new procedures, unless they are convinced that the new procedure is a better, more efficient way to do it.

A teacher may be misjudged as being *too secular*, especially those not known for their Christian faith. It is because such teachers do not appear to depend upon the teachings of the Bible enough as much as they depend upon the skills they have learned in finding facts and putting their findings together. Teachers do stress human reasoning in determining how to communicate truth. That is why they may be misjudged as de-emphasizing the factor of faith.

Some misjudge teachers as being *too structured* because they are adamant about putting everything in proper order. Teachers have a certain way or procedure by which they want to do things, and it is also how they want others to respond. I have had teachers who would give a student a lower grade if the student wrote his name on a paper or test somewhere other than the upper right hand corner. In the teacher's mind, such structure makes it easier to grade papers, record the scores, and return them to the students.

Too strict is another misunderstanding toward those with the motivational gift of teaching. Teachers tend to observe rules with no exceptions. If the rules and regulations say it is to be done a certain way, a teacher goes right by the book. I have previously referred to one of my seminary professors whom I believe has the spiritual gift of teaching. I know that there were students who thought he was too strict in his demands that a paper be graded as much for form as for content. Since graduating from seminary, as with some of my other professors, I am thankful for their strictness. It has helped me to develop a discipline to do things correctly and in proper order that has carried over into all facets of life. I believe that I am a better minister and person because of it.

At times, teachers can come off as *too showy*. People who have researched and are knowledgeable about a subject can appear as show-offs, especially with those who do not know much about the same subject. But all teachers are not trying to be showy when they tend to do what is natural for those who are motivated as teachers. They are insistent on making sure that what is presented is the truth. If it causes them to correct the mistakes of others, and they're publicly giving the correct facts when something has been incorrectly given, such actions might look showy. But that is not the intention of the teacher. The teacher is simply motivated to see the truth correctly communicated.

Teachers are also misjudged as being *too square*. Because teachers are conservative in expression until they get all the facts, and they are slow to change to new ways, they are often judged as boring and behind the times. As you think of someone who has appeared to be square to you, one or more of your former schoolteachers may come to mind. But you might find it surprising how much you favor that person now in some of your attitudes and actions.

Misuses

A teacher can become very *contrary*, focusing too much on the negative and pointing out flaws. Ninety-nine percent of what someone does can be right, but the teacher emphasizes and dwells on the negative instead of reinforcing the positive.

Teachers can misuse their gift by being overly *critical*. When a teacher misuses his gift, he may despise a lack of credentials in someone whose teaching he may be sitting under. In the teacher's mind, the person teaching him is not as educated, so he disavows that person as a qualified teacher because of it. A teacher who is not Spirit-controlled will be critical of anyone who does it differently from how he does it.

One who is motivated as a teacher may misuse his gift by becoming *confined*. A teacher can get to the point of spending too much time isolated in research. You may have heard some professor referred to as being eccentric. Why is he considered eccentric? It is because the professor may spend so much time in research that he has lost touch with reality. He may have gained much knowledge in research, but by staying alone and isolated so much, he has lost the ability to express himself in a way that people are open and understanding to what he has to say. Teachers need interaction regularly with other people in order to stay balanced.

There is a danger that comes when one gets out of balance and involved in a new truth or trying to find a new discovery. That person can become *consumed*. In the spiritual realm, this is where we see most cults originate. Someone gets so involved in a discovery or acceptance of what is a new truth or fact to them, and they take it to extremes. It results in truth out of balance.

Teachers can misuse their gift by becoming too *complex*. Teachers can become so dependent on structured systems of determining truth that they become too thorough, intense, and unrealistic. One person said of a preacher with the motivational gift of teaching, who had become too complex, that "he can go down deeper, stay down longer, and come up drier than anyone I have ever heard before."

Another misuse of the gift of teaching is becoming *cocky*. A teacher becomes cocky when he becomes too proud of his learning and knowledge so that he feels above others. If such a teacher does not learn to deal with his cockiness concerning his credentials and intellectualism, he will become a *conceited* person. That kind of reputation will be difficult to dispel. Conceited teachers do get very showy by showcasing research skills and showing disdain for those who do not have equal credentials or who have been in error.

A teacher who is not Spirit-controlled can become *callous*. Because teachers are so intent on things being done by the rules, correctly, and without exception, they can become hardened to the fact that learning still happens, even when errors are made. When a teacher becomes callous, he becomes neglectful of practical values of learning, even when something is not 100% correct.

A callous person who does not deal with his callousness will become *cold* in his relationships with other people. Teachers can become cold in their demeanor and personality because they are more concerned with presenting the facts than they are with a response. A teacher's motivation is not necessarily based upon what others think. A person with the gift of teaching is more motivated to do research, stick it under the door of the one the results go to, with a note attached that says, "Here are the facts." They make good writers of Bible study materials, such as those used by classroom teachers and students in Sunday schools and Bible study groups. The teacher who writes the material is completely content with someone else teaching the material that the teacher has researched and put together in lesson form.

He says: "Hey, folks, I have told you the truth. It is up to you whether or not you believe it. I have done the studying and research. I have found the facts, and this is the truth right here as I have presented it to you. Now you have to deal personally with what you have heard."

Conclusion

"Knowing with certainty"—that is what a person with the motivational spiritual gift of teaching wants to do in his life and make possible for others. Some of you who have read this chapter may have learned a lot about yourself. You may have thought that you had some other spiritual gift because you are not the kind of person who could ever teach a class or subject of any kind. You may never teach a Sunday school class or

Bible study group at your church or anywhere else. You may never teach as a ministry gift, but you may have discovered that you have the motivational gift of teaching. You may be the person in a Sunday school class whom God uses to keep the teacher sharp. As you may be used to keep the teacher on his toes, though, do not misuse your gift. Do not become contrary, critical, or callous and let things get out of hand.

I do believe that there are more teachers now after this chapter has been read than there were before it was read. Having the motivational gift of teaching does not mean that it has to be fulfilled in a teaching role. For some, though, this is not only your motivational gift, but it is what you will also do as a profession.

We need to be thankful for the teachers in our churches who keep us right theologically and doctrinally. They keep us true to the Word of God and in the things that please Him. If this is your major motivational spiritual gift, remember to endure. Be as flawless as possible in what you do. Keep fervent in spirit by being enthusiastic. And above all, be faithful to the Lord by earnestly serving Him in all the things you do. We need you to point the way in leading us to follow faithfully the teachings of Jesus, the Master Teacher.

5

The Gift of Exhorting

"As a Father Does His Children"

Having then gifts differing according to the grace that is given to us, whether prophecy, let us prophesy according to the proportion of faith; Or ministry, let us wait on our ministering: or he that teacheth, on teaching; Or he that exhorteth, on **exhortation**:...Rejoicing in hope; patient in tribulation; *continuing instant in prayer. (Rom. 12:6-8,12)*

A confessed exhorter, Dr. James H. Smith, describes himself here:

The man I have in mind has been a preacher of the gospel for more than 45 years. More than half of these years he spent as pastor of five different churches. He took each one of these churches when they were torn apart by internal strife and were on the verge of complete splits. One was in dire financial stress and another was in desperate need of a new building which seemed to be absolutely impossible. By the end of his pastoral experience, each of these churches had become a growing, mature, giving, ministering, loving fellowship. His enthusiasm and ability to encourage had caused the members of these churches to realize that they were the people of God, the body of Christ. For more than 20 years, he has been the chief executive officer of two church denominational agencies. Each of these was in a condition of distress at the time he was called. His ministry of reconciliation has built a spirit of trust, confidence, hope, and steadfastness. Employees have often said that he has the unique ability of being able to encourage and motivate. He is always willing to give the person in doubt another chance. His children, who are all grown now, often quote him as saying, 'Problems are for the solving.' I am that man. I have the gift of exhortation.[4]

Upon retirement from the presidency of the Brotherhood Commission of the Southern Baptist Convention, Dr. Smith pastored an inner city, multi-ethnic church and helped them deal with some key concerns.

Another exhorter, the apostle Paul, wrote to the church at Thessalonica:

For yourselves, brethren, know our entrance in unto you, that it was not in vain: But even after that we had suffered before, and were shamefully entreated, as ye know, at Philippi, we were bold in our God to speak unto you the gospel of God with much contention. For our exhortation was not of deceit, nor of uncleanness, nor in guile: But as we were allowed of God to be put in trust with the gospel, even so we speak; not as pleasing men, but God, which trieth our hearts. For neither at any time used we flattering words, as ye know, nor a cloak of covetousness; God is witness: nor of men sought we glory, neither of you, nor yet of others, when we might have been burdensome, as the apostles of Christ.

But we were gentle among you, even as a nurse cherisheth her children: so being affectionately desirous of you, we were willing to have imparted unto you, not the gospel of God only, but also our own souls, because ye were dear unto us. For ye remember, brethren, our labour and travail: for labouring night and day, because we would not be chargeable unto any of you, we preached unto you the gospel of God. Ye are witnesses, and God also, how holy and justly and unblameably we behaved ourselves among you that believe: as ye know how we exhorted and comforted and charged every one of you, as a father doth his children, that ye would walk worthy of God, who hath called you unto His kingdom and glory. (1 Thess. 2:1-12)

As a whole, 1 Thessalonians beautifully illustrates the person with the gift of exhorting expressing his gift.

A Composite: The Gift of Exhorting

An exhorter stimulates the spiritual progress of others by sensing their potential, then suggesting practical steps of action for growth. The exhorter wants to see other Christians mature in their faith.

Explanation of the Gift of Exhortation

Several Bible verses, other than the passage in 1 Thessalonians 2:1-12, provide an *explanation of the spiritual gift of exhortation*. An exhorter challenges believers. From the examples of Paul, Barnabas and Jude, we see an emphasis upon contending for the faith by cleaving unto the Lord so that one will continue in the faith.

Jude exhibits some of the characteristics of an exhorter in his short biblical book. In verse three of his epistle, he says: "Beloved, when I gave all diligence to write unto you of the common salvation, it was needful for me to write unto you, and exhort you that ye should earnestly contend for the faith which was once delivered unto the saints." That verse reveals one explanation of what motivates one who has the gift of exhorting. Exhorters like to *challenge* people.

Jude challenged those to whom he wrote to contend for the faith. He challenged them to combat heresies plaguing the early church. His words are a relevant and applicable challenge to the church today.

In Acts 11, Barnabas further explains how an exhorter puts his motivational gift into practice. Barnabas certainly exhibited characteristics of this gift. His name literally means "Son of Encouragement" (Acts 4:36).

You may recall that he and Paul eventually parted ways as a missionary team. When people are similar, eventually, their view on an issue or the handling of a circumstance will differ. The problem escalates when neither one will give in.

For example, an unresolvable conflict arose between Paul and Barnabas. They disagreed over Mark's accompanying them on their next missionary tour because he had deserted them on the previous tour (Acts 13:13; 15:36-40). The rift ripped their missionary team apart. Paul took Silas, and later Timothy, to serve with them. Paul's ministry came to the forefront. But Barnabas helped Mark, whose motivational gift was serving. He had given up, in Paul's eyes, on the previous tour. If Mark had not had an exhorter like Barnabas, who wanted to help him become strong in his faith again, as a father to a son, we may very well have never had the Gospel of Mark. Barnabas took Mark from the point where he had failed, and he helped him to get his spiritual life back in order again and on the right track.

Acts 11:23 gives a profile in just a few words of what made Barnabas such a great man of God: "Who, when he came, and had seen the grace of God, was glad, and exhorted them all, that with purpose of heart they would cleave unto the Lord." Barnabas had been "sent forth" by the church in Jerusalem to minister, encourage, and exhort the Grecians in Antioch who had become new believers in Christ. He challenged them to cleave unto God. To contend for the faith, one needs to cleave unto the Lord.

In Acts 14:21-22, Paul challenged the believers of Lystra, Iconium, and Antioch to continue in their faith:

> And when they had preached the gospel to that city, and had taught many, they returned again to Lystra, and to Iconium, and Antioch, confirming the souls of the disciples, and **exhorting them to continue in the faith**, and that we must through much tribulation enter into the kingdom of God.

Paul also said: "And now I exhort you to be of good cheer: for there shall be no loss of any man's life among you, but of the ship" (Acts 27:22). Paul's exhortation to "be of good cheer" was an unusual one. Those to whom he was speaking thought they were losing their lives. As Paul was on his way to Rome to stand trial before Caesar, their ship was tossed and driven by a severe storm. They had reached a point where they had no control over its course. Those on board had gone days without eating. Sheer panic and fear robbed them of appetite.

But an exhorter has a great faith in God and knows the Lord will always come through. Even in the worst circumstances, the exhorter wants to *cheer* up others. Paul told his fellow passengers and the crew members to be of good cheer, in what to them was a hopeless situation in which they feared for their lives. He was there to encourage them. He confidently did so because God had promised Paul that He would come through on their behalf: "For there stood by me this night the angel of God, whose I am, and whom I serve, saying, 'Fear not, Paul; thou must be brought before Caesar: and, lo, God hath given thee all them that sail with thee.' Wherefore, sirs, be of good cheer: for I believe God, that it shall be even as it was told me" (Acts 27:23-25).

Exhorters also like to *comfort* people. From the passage in 1 Thessalonians 2, a third aspect of the motivational gift of exhorting is given: "Ye know how we exhorted and comforted and charged every one of you, as a father doth his children" (v. 11).

Other verses in 1 Thessalonians bring out this quality of those with the gift of exhorting. In the beautiful passage from the fourth chapter, which describes the Rapture of the church, Paul concludes his exhortation by stating, "Wherefore comfort one another with these words" (v. 18). In chapter five, verse eleven, Paul proclaims, "Wherefore comfort yourselves together, and edify one another, even as also ye do." The word "comfort" could have been translated as "exhort" in those two verses.

In his letter to the church at Corinth, as Paul was following up his teaching about spiritual gifts, and the greatest gift of all, love, he said, "But he that prophesieth speaketh unto men to edification, and exhortation, and comfort" (1 Cor. 14:3). Even prophets are to learn to use their gift in an exhorting way so that they will encourage, build up, and comfort others. As has already been mentioned in the first chapter, we are to learn to develop characteristics of all the spiritual gifts. The prophet, Peter, even provided a fourth aspect of exhorting. As he neared the end of his sermon on the Day of Pentecost, the Bible records:

Now when they heard this, they were pricked in their heart, and said unto Peter and to the rest of the apostles, 'Men and brethren, what shall we do?' Then Peter said unto them, 'Repent, and be baptized every one of you in the name of Jesus Christ for the remission of sins, and ye shall receive the gift of the Holy Ghost. For the promise is unto you, and to your children, and to all that are afar off, even as many as the Lord our God shall call.' And with many other words did he testify and exhort, saying, 'Save yourselves from this untoward generation.' (Acts 2:37-40)

Exhorters also *convince* people. Peter used many words to convince his hearers that they needed to be saved from the penalty of their sins by repenting of their sins and believing that Jesus died for the pardon of their sins. Paul also exemplified this aspect of exhorting, as illustrated in the Book of Titus, when he spoke of the role of the bishop (pastor). He said that a bishop was to hold "fast the faithful word as he hath been taught, that he may be able by sound doctrine both to exhort and to convince the gainsayers" (Titus 1:9).

What motivates an exhorter is to stimulate the faith of others, whether it is to challenge them in their faith, to encourage others by cheering them up, to comfort others in a particular area, or to convince others of something that they need to do.

Examples of Exhorters

Barnabas, Jude, and Paul were exhorters. I cannot definitively name an Old Testament personality whom I believe had the gift of exhorting. Ezra may have been an exhorter, although he also had several characteristics of the gift of teaching, too. In Luke 4:16-22, Jesus, the perfect exhorter, read from the Scriptures and gave a word of exhortation during the segment of the Jewish worship service that was designated for that purpose. (See Acts 13:15 where Paul was given a similar opportunity).

Exhortations to Exhorters

The special *exhortations to exhorters* are given in Romans 12:12: "Rejoicing in hope; patient in tribulation; continuing instant in prayer." A
person with the gift of exhorting is first exhorted to *be positive*, then also
to encourage and comfort people.

To do this effectively, an exhorter is exhorted to rejoice in hope. He is
to be positive about the prospect of what the future holds. When an exhorter resists control of the Holy Spirit, we do not have the encouragement in the church we need. Exhorters are placed in the church to encourage us.

A second exhortation to exhorters is to *be patient* in tribulation. An
exhorter knows that difficulties are eventually going to work out for good
(Romans 8:28), so sometimes an exhorter may get impatient. The exhorter may discern that God is trying to teach someone through a difficult circumstance. The exhorter wants to see the result come about concerning what God is trying to teach a person, so the exhorter may not
want to wait for God to do what He is going to do. Because the exhorter
has such great faith that eventually everything is going to work out right,
he feels like saying, "God, why are You dragging out the process for
three more months? Let's go on and get the lesson finished right now."
The Bible says to be patient and wait on God. His timing is always right.
Three more months may be needed to fully develop a person's faith regarding what God intends to teach that individual. The exhorter must be
persevering toward pressure and in times of persecution, whether he is
experiencing tribulation or it is someone the exhorter is trying to stimulate to greater maturity in the Christian faith.

A third exhortation to exhorters is to continue constantly in prayer.
Do you know who has the hardest time praying? In some cases, it is
those who have great faith. It is sometimes those who believe the Bible
without compromise. It is often those who have a faithful walk with the

Lord, who are right in their lives, and are doing what God has called them to do. Why? Because they know that God is going to be faithful to fulfill His Word. They know that He is going to take care of His people.

Exhorters have great faith, often to the extent that they try to stimulate the faith of others. Because the exhorter has such great faith in believing that God will always come through, the exhorter has to guard against not being persistent in prayer. Exhorters must strive to pray about everything. God will work out all things for good, but how does God work? What is the key that so often unlocks the door to things working out? It is prayer. There are miracles that God wants to bring about in our churches and in the lives of people. The reason that they are not happening is because we may have the faith that God will do it, but we are not using the means by which God said He will accomplish it—through prayer. Exhorters need to *be prayerful*.

Expectation Exhorters Need to Exercise Most
The **expectation exhorters need to exercise the most** is *consistency*. Why? Because exhorters make good counselors. Many of those with the gift of exhorting become counselors. They sit down with someone they are counseling and tell them that you need to do this, this, and this to overcome the problem in your life.

The counseled will not follow a counselor's advice when they do not see the counselor living it in his own life.

Consistency is the key to being an effective exhorter. In order to stimulate the faith of others, it needs to be evident that it is working in the life of the exhorter.

Characteristics of Exhorters
Stimulate Spiritual Progress
Probably the main motivation of an exhorter is to **stimulate spiritual progress**. Paul told the Christians at Thessalonica, "Ye know how we

exhorted and comforted and charged every one of you, as a father doth his children, that ye would walk worthy of God, who hath called you unto His kingdom and glory" (1 Thess. 2:11-12). Paul's exhortations were often accompanied with the word "perfect." An exhorter wants to see others become complete in their faith. He is motivated to see others reach maturity and perfection in their Christian life.

Exhorters like to see *achievement*. In 1 Thessalonians 3:9-10, Paul said, "For what thanks can we render to God again for you, for all the joy wherewith we joy for your sakes before our God; night and day praying exceedingly that we might see your face, and might perfect that which is lacking in your faith?" Paul wanted to see the Christians at Thessalonica achieve that which was lacking in their faith. As an exhorter desires to see others walk worthy of their Christian calling, it brings the exhorter joy to see others grow spiritually.

Exhorters are also motivated to help other Christians *accomplish* what God desires for their lives. In 1 Thessalonians 4:1-3, Paul spoke further exhortations to the church at Thessalonica:

> *Furthermore then we beseech you, brethren, and exhort you by the Lord Jesus, that as ye have received of us how ye ought to walk and to please God, so ye would abound more and more. For ye know what commandments we gave you by the Lord Jesus. For this is the will of God, even your sanctification, that ye should abstain from fornication.*

We have been saved, and we are to be sanctified, growing and maturing in our faith. Exhorters want to see other Christians achieve and accomplish sanctification and perfection in their lives – that process whereby the Christian is moving toward maturity and completeness in faith. Exhorters give others something to accomplish. Once one goal is accomplished, the exhorter gives you other spiritual goals to fulfill. The process helps people to abound more and more spiritually. Paul told the Thessalonians to follow his example (1 Thess. 4:1) in how they should walk in their lives.

Exhorters also desire to see levels of *attainment* reached in the spiritual lives of others. Paul wrote to the Christians in Galatia, whom he called "my little children," that "I travail in birth again until Christ be formed in you" (Gal. 4:19). He wrote to the Colossians, "Christ in you, the hope of glory: whom we preach, warning every man, and teaching every man in all wisdom; that we may present every man perfect in Christ Jesus" (Col. 1:28).

Paul wanted those whom he won to Christ to be so filled with Christ and alive to the Lord that they became Christ-like. As he was concluding his first letter to the church at Thessalonica, Paul finished an exhortation by telling them the result of obedience to his exhortation, "The very God of peace sanctify you wholly; and I pray God your whole spirit and soul and body be preserved blameless unto the coming of our Lord Jesus Christ. Faithful is He that calleth you, who also will do it" (1 Thess. 5:23-24). Paul tried to cover everything – "your whole spirit and soul and body" – in helping those whom he exhorted to be spiritually complete. He wanted them to be blameless and ready to meet the Lord. Strong faith in God was evident in Paul's life. He stated to his readers in his first Thessalonian letter that God would be faithful to do for those he called what He said He would do (1 Thess. 5:24).

Sense Your Potential

Exhorters also can *sense your potential*. He senses your potential in your Christian walk. In the first chapter of his first letter to the church at Thessalonica, Paul talked to those Christians about their potential. He said:

> And ye became followers of us, and of the Lord, having received the word in much affliction, with joy of the Holy Ghost: so that ye were ensamples to all that believe in Macedonia and Achaia. For from you sounded out the word of the Lord not only in Macedonia and Achaia, but also in every place your faith to God-ward is spread abroad; so that we need not to speak any thing. (1 Thess. 1:6-8)

Paul encouraged the Thessalonians first by complimenting their courage in the Lord (v. 6). It is evident that Paul sensed their potential. He saw what the church at Thessalonica had already accomplished and what they could attain, if they would really focus on letting God work in their lives, helping them to reach maturity.

Exhorters *discern ability*; they can determine where you are spiritually, and then strive to help you attain it. Paul told the church at Corinth, "I, brethren, could not speak unto you as unto spiritual, but as unto carnal, even as unto babes in Christ" (1 Cor. 3:1). He discerned what their ability was at that point in their spiritual lives. That is what an exhorter is motivated to do. When you are not at a certain level spiritually, the exhorter starts right where you are, stimulating your spiritual needs at that maturity level.

In sensing your potential and what you can become, exhorters also *detect obstacles*. They will find hindrances in the lives of those who are not growing spiritually. Paul pointed out to the Thessalonians: "For this cause, when I could no longer forbear, I sent to know your faith, lest by some means the tempter have tempted you, and our labour be in vain" (1 Thess. 3:5). Paul saw something that he felt was an obstacle in the lives of those Christians. From the text, we cannot readily discern the definite obstacle, but Paul knew it was there.

Then, an exhorter *deals appropriately* to help overcome an obstacle in one's spiritual life. In the situation with the Thessalonian believers, Paul sent Timothy to discover the level of their faith (1 Thess. 3:5). Timothy was able to deal appropriately with the situation. When he returned, Paul was able to write, "But now when Timotheus came from you unto us, and brought us good tidings of your faith and charity, and that ye have good remembrance of us always, desiring greatly to see us, as we also to see you" (1 Thess. 3:6). Paul sent someone he felt would take care of the situation and who would help them deal with whatever obstacle was in their lives at that point.

Suggest Steps that are Practical

The exhorter gives practical steps to other Christians to help them over-come hindrances in their Christian lives so that they can grow to spiritual maturity. The fourth and fifth chapters of 1 Thessalonians provide an excellent example of an exhorter giving steps that are practical. Here, Paul basically says, "All right, here are the practical steps I want you to follow so that you can grow and mature in your faith." In verse three of chapter four, he begins by saying, "For this is the will of God, even your sanctification, that ye should abstain from fornication." He tells them why in verse four: "That every one of you should know how to possess his vessel in sanctification and honour."

In verses eleven and twelve, Paul lists more practical steps: "And that ye study to be quiet, and to do your own business, and to work with your own hands, as we commanded you; that ye may walk honestly toward them that are without, and that ye may have lack of nothing." Chapters four and five are full of such practical steps that deal with various ele-ments of the Christian faith. Paul's exhorting style was to give those whom he exhorted some practical steps, then he told them why they should follow them and the result that would be produced.

In 1 Thessalonians 5:12-22, Paul outlines God's plan for a successful church. In those eleven verses, Paul gives about twenty practical steps to follow for making a church successful in the eyes of God. They are *steps of action*. Exhorters suggest clear, logical steps of action so progress can be visualized, hindrances can be removed, and discipline can be devel-oped.

When Timothy was a young man in the ministry, one of Paul's exhor-tations to him was to "flee also youthful lusts: but follow righteousness, faith, charity, peace, with them that call on the Lord out of a pure heart" (2 Tim. 2:22). Paul told Timothy what and who to avoid, but he also told him what was right to do and who could help him to live a life of righ-teousness, faith, love, and peace.

Exhorters like for their suggested steps of action to have *scriptural application*, centering around principles and truths of the Bible. They want you to discover insights amplified in Scripture. In reading through the books of the Bible written by Paul, you will find passages in one book that parallel passages in another book. Paul would draw from other letters that he had written to prove a point in the letter he was presently writing. Much of what Paul said was traced back to the Old Testament, too. He applied the steps of action he gave to the Scriptures.

In giving steps that are practical, the exhorter wants to *see advancement*. In most of Paul's letters to the different churches, he expressed joy over hearing about their great faith or because of some other Christ-like action of the believers whom he was addressing (see Col. 1:3-4 as an example). Paul was able to see advancement in the spiritual lives of those believers in hearing about the fruit of his labors in their lives. Exhorters give steps so that as you reach them, it is for your comfort (1 Thess. 4:18; 5:11), encouragement, and joy. As you advance, your profiting is not only for yourself, but for others, too. After exhorting Timothy about several matters (1 Tim. 4:11-15), Paul told Timothy to "continue in them: for in doing this thou shalt both save thyself, and them that hear thee" (1 Tim. 4:16).

Solve Problems

After describing his ministry among the Thessalonians as being as gentle as a mother nursing her children (1 Thess. 2:7), Paul said, "So being affectionately desirous of you, we were willing to have imparted unto you, not the gospel of God only, but also our own souls, because ye were dear unto us. For ye remember, brethren, our labour and travail: for labouring night and day, because we would not be chargeable unto any of you, we preached unto you the gospel of God" (1 Thess. 2:8-9).

Evidently, Paul sensed an obstacle that the Thessalonians had regarding paying their preachers and evangelists or taking up an offering. So

Paul and his ministry team determined that they were going to be bi-vocational for the church at Thessalonica. Paul decided that his ministry team would do whatever they had to do so that they would not be a hindrance to the Thessalonian believers and their advancing on in the faith. Paul saw a potential problem and he solved it.

Exhorters, like servers, want to step into your life and walk with you. That is how Paul approached his ministry at Thessalonica. It is evident that he accomplished that goal. He was able to tell them, "So being affectionately desirous of you, we were willing to have imparted unto you, not the gospel of God only, but also our own souls, because ye were dear unto us" (1 Thess. 2:8). Part of that stepping into your life is that an exhorter is motivated to help you solve your problems. That is why exhorters make good counselors. Exhorters like to hear someone say, "I've got a problem." That makes the eyes of an exhorter light up. They love to deal with and solve problems.

To an exhorter, a problem is an opportunity for a solution. They identify with your problems because they have probably experienced the same thing or have had a similar experience. The exhorter asks, "What's the problem?" Then, after identifying it, they inquire, "What does God want to teach you through this?" Now that is not what most of us want to hear. Most of us want someone to come in and tell us that everything is going to be all right. We hope that there is not much that we will have to do about it.

The exhorter is good at identifying what the problem is, determining what God wants to teach through the problem, and then giving steps of action to follow. They will let you know that if you follow these steps, you will be able to overcome a bothersome area of your life. The exhorter leads you to identify what a problem is that keeps you from going on in your spiritual maturity, what God wants you to do about it, and what He wants to teach you through it.

After an exhorter helps you to identify what a problem is so that it can be solved, the exhorter will next find a way to *illustrate* it for you. Exhorters will find examples from the lives of others, including their own, to motivate you in order to remove spiritual hindrances in your life. In writing to the Christians at Thessalonica, Paul informed them how they were an example to the believers in Macedonia, Achaia, and even beyond. Paul said that the faith of the Thessalonians was so well known that he did not even have to mention it (1 Thess. 1:7-8). He used the church at Philippi as an example to other churches when it came to giving (Phil. 4:15-16; 2 Cor. 11:9). The church at Philippi sent money on two occasions to support Paul's ministry when he was in Thessalonica. He surely made that fact known to the Thessalonians, who appeared to have a problem with giving to the financial support of Paul. What an illustration that was to the Thessalonians concerning their lack of giving to support the work of the Lord in their own city. The work of the Lord through Paul was made possible for them by the gifts of the believers in Philippi. Paul found personal illustrations to help teach those whom he exhorted to solve their problems.

After a problem has been identified and illustrated, the exhorter then wants to *illuminate* it. As the exhorter identifies the problem and illustrates it, they are trying to illuminate it in your mind so that you will see what the problem is and the steps that will help that problem to be solved. The Thessalonians suffered persecution for their faith in Jesus Christ (1 Thess. 2:14-16). What a wonderful example they had in Paul on how to deal with persecution. One reason that Paul wrote this letter to the Thessalonians was to help them deal with the problem of suffering for their faith. He identified and illustrated this problem in chapters one and two. In chapter three, Paul illuminated how to deal with it. He sent Timothy to encourage them by telling them how he was suffering, too, (v. 7) and how their standing fast in the Lord brought him joy (vs. 8-9). In chapters four and five, Paul illuminated how to deal with persecution, as well as other tempting areas of life that could cause one to falter in his faith. He not only illuminated how to deal with such areas of difficulty, but also how to overcome them and remain strong in the Lord.

One of the things that exhorters effectively do in solving problems is to provide peaceful solutions. When counseling a family in conflict with one another, the exhorter will give steps of action for each family member to follow that will bring peace.

Exhorters have to be especially careful in dealing with steps of action needed to bring peace when there is conflict within a church. They must take into account the whole counsel of the Word of God. If there is a doctrinal problem at the root of the church conflict, exhorters prefer to avoid the theological concerns in order to bring peace within the church, even at the expense of the truth. However, that is not dealing with the conflict biblically. The steps to solve a problem must always be in accord with the Word of God.

Share Personally

Exhorters tend to be transparent, and *share personally*. They live open lives, sharing personal *examples* and *experiences* from their own lives to encourage and stimulate growth in the spiritual lives of others.

Paul told the church at Corinth that "to the weak became I as weak, that I might gain the weak: I am made all things to all men, that I might by all means save some. And this I do for the gospel's sake, that I might be partaker thereof with you" (1 Cor. 9:22-23). What an example of transparency! Paul says: "I'll be a weakling in the eyes of others, if I need to, for the cause of Christ." That goes against the grain of what society teaches—if you want to be successful, you have got to be mentally, intellectually, socially, and physically tough. But Paul was very transparent when he told Timothy, "This is a faithful saying, and worthy of all acceptation, that Christ Jesus came into the world to save sinners; of whom I am chief" (1 Tim. 1:15). He mentioned in some of his other writings how he persecuted Christians, prior to his conversion, having them imprisoned. If a mistake in an exhorter's life can help you, an exhorter will tell you all the details, no matter how painful it is to recall.

Exhorters not only share personally, using their experiences and themselves as examples, but they will use their experiences with others, positively and negatively, as examples to caution or encourage you. When Paul was encouraging Timothy to "war a good warfare; holding faith, and a good conscience" (1 Tim. 1:18-19), he used two poor examples of faith in ones with whom he was acquainted: "Some having put away concerning faith have made shipwreck: of whom is Hymenaeus and Alexander; whom I have delivered unto Satan, that they may learn not to blaspheme" (1 Tim. 1:19-20). Whew! Remember, an exhorter wants to illustrate what he is trying to get you to see in a way that gets the point across.

As the exhorter shares personally, they enjoy face to face *encounters*. This is well-illustrated in Paul's first letter to the Thessalonian believers. In 1 Thessalonians 2:17, Paul wrote, "But we, brethren, being taken from you for a short time in presence, not in heart, endeavored the more abundantly to see your face with great desire." In chapter three he wrote, "For what thanks can we render to God again for you, for all the joy wherewith we joy for your sakes before our God; night and day praying exceedingly that we might see your face, and might perfect that which is lacking in your faith?" (1 Thess. 3:9-10). An exhorter likes it one-on-one. The person with the gift of serving likes to be with a group of people. They love a crowd. But what really motivates the exhorter is to sit down, one-on-one with somebody, because an exhorter wants to see your expressions and reactions to what he says. That is why an exhorter wants to see your face. It communicates to the exhorter if he is getting through to you.

Cautions for the Gift of Exhorting
Misunderstandings

We may see exhorters as *too pushy*. For years, I used to think that Paul was pushy. As I read about him in the Book of Acts, or in one of the books he authored in the Bible, I would think, "He's got a lot of nerve." He was not quite as overbearing as a prophet, but Paul seemed to be in face to face encounter with someone nearly all the time. He would usually begin his encounters, whether it was by a letter or in person, by complimenting those whom he was encountering. Then, he would put them in their place. It was as if he was scolding them. He even offered his opinion on some matters when he had not been asked for it. We have a tendency to think that exhorters are pushy, but an exhorter is motivated to stimulate spiritual progress and to mature others in their faith. As exhorters are motivated to stimulate growth, they look for people to get involved with as projects, some of whom do not want their help.

Often others think exhorters are *too probing*. As a teacher likes to find out all the facts, an exhorter tries to sense one's spiritual potential in the same manner. In the process, an exhorter can become very probing. To sense where someone is spiritually, an exhorter will ask a lot of questions. An exhorter may ask things of someone that are offensive. But it is not because the exhorter is nosy or means to be offensive. Probing is part of the exhorter's gift. It is a means by which the exhorter determines where one is spiritually in order that he may provide the proper steps to help that individual to further mature in his faith.

Exhorters may also be misunderstood as *too pragmatic* or *too practical*. Exhorters are always on the lookout for newer and better steps that will bring lasting results for those whom they counsel. The exhorter may get so involved with the causes and effects that it looks like he is neglecting the purpose and theory behind it. Some people think exhorters are too practical in applying steps of action in solving problems. An exhorter must be cautious in becoming too dependent upon the same steps of action, believing that those steps will bring about whatever change and growth needs to occur in the life of Christians to whom the steps are meant to apply. The preset steps of action an exhorter may have developed for various situations may not always work with every individual. Besides, if in his heart, a person is not right with God or open to doing what needs to be done to get right with God, steps of action do not mean too much.

Sometimes, an exhorter is regarded as *too personal*. The exhorter's use of personal illustrations can be embarrassing to family members. The exhorter's using other people's problems as examples can also be embarrassing to those particular individuals. Bill Gothard uses many personal illustrations in his seminars, not only about his life but about other people whom he has dealt with in his ministry experiences. Some of those real life illustrations really get to the point in telling it all about the spiritual conflicts some people have had to encounter. Gothard always gets their permission ahead of time before he will use an illustration about someone.

One other misunderstanding that others have about those with the gift of exhorting is somewhat unusual. An exhorter can come off to some people as being *too positive*. Do you know someone whom you feel is too positive about everything? I am talking about the kind of person who comes into a room, just smiling from ear to ear. Although your life and theirs may not be going very well, to them everything is just great. The weather outside is terrible, but to them it is a gorgeous day. They are so positive all the time that it almost makes you sick. The people you and I are thinking about right now may very well have the motivational gift of exhorting. Now it is okay to be that positive when it is genuine. There are some people like that. They have never had a bad day in their life. If I have just described you, make sure that it is genuine. If it is not, people will see through you, and you may become known to them as "the great pretender." Even when it is real, an exhorter may be so positive to some people that he comes off as phony and not genuine. If you know someone who is that positive, and he is not a pretender, then learn to accept their super positiveness because the Lord has a reason for it.

Misuses

Without the control of the Holy Spirit, in the flesh, an exhorter may become *unrelenting*, forcing himself upon people. The exhorter involves himself in the personal concerns and problems of individuals who are not yet ready to deal with those situations. Because that person is not ready to deal with his spiritual problems, to the exhorter that individual is not growing spiritually. Since the exhorter wants to stimulate the person's progress, he may not get down on the level where that person is at that time, and the exhorter begins to push the person beyond where he is ready to go.

Exhorters may misuse their spiritual gift by *disregarding* people, forcing issues people are not ready to deal with. For example, an exhorter may sense that a young man has great church leadership potential. If the exhorter is in a current leadership position, he will think, "He's a young man. It is time he had some responsibility. I am going to give him an area of responsibility." How many churches, especially in the "good old days," felt that when a young man got to a certain age he ought to be elected as a deacon? The young man may not have been doing much within the church, but some of the members justified electing him as a deacon because it might motivate him to be more involved.

According to the Bible, that is not how deacons are to be chosen. But some churches still choose spiritually inactive and uninvolved men to be deacons, hoping that it will motivate them to greater maturity in their Christian faith. Exhorters, who operate in the flesh, tend to have such misdirected thinking.

Another way exhorters may misuse their spiritual gift is by being *unreasonable*. They become adamant that their steps of action work for all situations. If those steps do not work, it is another's fault when they do not. The exhorter will say, "Here are the steps you need to follow to overcome this lack of growth in your spiritual life." However it does not always work that way. An exhorter must realize that every person is different. Although the exhorter's steps of action may apply to ninety percent of people, that means that those steps do not apply to ten percent of the people. If you are an exhorter, be sensitive to the fact that you cannot always come in and say, "All right, we have got a problem here, but if you do this, this, and this, everything is going to be okay."

An exhorter must also guard against becoming *unreliable*. Exhorters have to be careful not to use a Scripture verse out of context. It is important to remember that one verse should not be used to build steps upon until you know how that verse is used in its context or how it relates to other relevant Scriptures. I have heard this verse used more regarding finances than any other Scripture reference: "Owe no man any thing, but to love one another" (Rom. 12:8). In the context in which this verse is found, the Bible is not exclusively addressing financial concerns. The verse can be applied to finances, but it is really speaking more to our relationship with God and others. Exhorters, especially, must guard against using a verse unreliably.

In the flesh, an exhorter can also misuse his gift by being *unrestrictive* in going too far in the use of private illustrations. Several years ago, I heard the testimony of an adult, who had only been saved for a short time. He was a former Hell's Angel. As he gave his testimony one night before 1200 people, he got too graphic and too specific in sharing some things that he had done before he was converted to Christ. It was obviously embarrassing and offensive to many people who heard his testimony that night. Whether he was an exhorter or not, his way of testifying exemplifies why you have to be restrictive, at times, especially in how far you go in sharing personal and private illustrations.

When an exhorter uses real life examples from the experiences of others, he may also misuse his gift by being *disrespectful*. In using private illustrations, an exhorter, without the Holy Spirit's guidance, can disregard the reputation of others. If the exhorter has too much pride, he is disrespectful in how he views fellow exhorters who offer him advice on how to deal with someone he is counseling. He may feel that his plan is always right and that anybody is wrong who proposes alternative steps of action to his steps.

It has been mentioned that an exhorter's suggested steps do not work for every situation, but he may *unrealistically believe* they will. When an exhorter cannot accept that there are other remedies to problems besides his, he can become very stubborn and unrealistic in his expectations.

An exhorter must also guard against being *too unreproving*. Since exhorters usually strive for peace at any cost, there are times when one side or both sides of a conflict need reproof and correction. An exhorter misuses his gift if he avoids the needed reproof, opting for peace at the expense of divine discipline. Does a father always let his child get by with doing something wrong without helping to correct the child? Does the father always give his child a second chance? Many times, he does. But there are times when correction comes first before another chance is given.

I have noticed how some exhorters talk about the churches they have built and levels of accomplishments attained through their leadership. They never mention anything, though, about correction.

An exhorter must remember that the best way to exhort someone in some situations is to tell them, "You are out of line." Paul, the Spirit-controlled exhorter, told the Thessalonians to warn those who are unruly and to comfort the feebleminded (1 Thess. 5:14). Paul set an example for us that there are times when you need to tell someone that they are out of line. It is like a marching soldier who gets out of step with the rest of his fellow marchers. His getting out of step makes the whole squadron look bad. An exhorter must be cautious not to avoid the reproving side of his gift. The exhorter should solve problems with solutions that bring peace, but it is never at the expense of God's truth.

When an exhorter is *unremissive*, he is unforgiving. An exhorter can become impatient with those who do not quickly and consistently respond to his proposed steps of action. Sometimes the exhorter gives up on the individual he is trying to help. If someone does not respond immediately to his suggested steps, he does not give them a second chance. What happens, in such cases, is that the exhorter hasn't given a person enough time to respond.

Do you think that may have happened with Paul on one occasion? After Mark deserted Paul and Barnabas (see Acts 13:13; 15:36-41), a major disagreement arose between the two exhorters, Paul and Barnabas, over Mark accompanying them on their next mission trip. To Barnabas, Mark deserved another chance. To Paul, Mark deserted them. The missionary duo broke up over it. Paul teamed up with Silas, and eventually Timothy joined them. Barnabas, who evidently saw Mark's potential, took him as a partner in ministry. Peter had previously had a positive influence on Mark, and surely it continued. As a result, Mark's life got back on track, in time. Later, there came a time when Paul and Mark had patched things up. Mark was a partner again with him in ministry, and Paul acknowledged his need of Mark (2 Tim. 4:11).

I do not know if anyone was completely right or wrong in what happened between Paul and Barnabas over Mark. We can learn some valuable lessons from the mistakes and shortcomings from those we read about in the Bible. God took the situation and made it work for good to all concerned.

Conclusion

How wonderful it is to have exhorters in our churches! At times, we all need someone who is gifted to encourage us when we are discouraged in our spiritual lives. We need those who have a knack of stimulating us when we have become spiritually complacent.

Paul told us that the good work that God began in us through Christ will continue to the end of our earthly lives (Phil. 1:6). God uses exhorters in a special way to keep us growing and going in our walk with and witness for the Lord. Exhorters motivate churches to reach levels and goals that would not otherwise be attained. Exhorters minister to us individually in seeing the potential in us. All of us like to have someone who believes in us and who feels that we are of worth to the Lord. Let us thank the Lord regularly for the exhorters around us. We need them in our churches today more than ever before.

6

The Gift of Giving

"Living to Give"

> *Having then gifts differing according to the grace that is given to us, whether prophecy, let us prophesy according to the proportion of faith; or ministry, let us wait on our ministering: or he that teacheth, on teaching; or he that exhorteth, on exhortation: he that **giveth**, let him do it with simplicity; ...Distributing to the necessity of saints; given to hospitality. (Rom. 12:6-8,13)*

Some say that the spiritual gift of giving not only refers to the giving of monetary gifts, but also the giving of one's time. The giving of one's time to help meet a need really applies to the gift of serving. Someone who does not have much to give in the way of money can give of themselves for the work of the Lord through their service of time and effort.

Those individuals who have the gift of giving, according to what the Bible shows us, are people who give monetarily, or who give tangible gifts, to carry on the work of the Lord.

In 2 Corinthians 9, we find our source passage for the gift of giving. Although this passage is written to all Christians, characteristics are seen in these verses that are especially strong in givers. Let us see what the Bible says:

> *But this I say, he which soweth sparingly shall reap also*

sparingly; and he which soweth bountifully shall reap also bountifully. Every man according as he purposeth in his heart, so let him give; not grudgingly, or of necessity: for God loveth a cheerful giver. And God is able to make all grace abound toward you; that ye, always having all sufficiency in all things, may abound to every good work: (as it is written, He hath dispersed abroad; He hath given to the poor: His righteousness remaineth for ever. Now He that ministereth seed to the sower both minister bread for your food, and multiply your seed sown, and increase the fruits of your righteousness;) being enriched in every thing to all bountifulness, which causeth through us thanksgiving to God. For the administration of this service not only supplieth the want of the saints, but is abundant also by many thanksgivings unto God; Whiles by the experiment of this ministration they glorify God for your professed subjection unto the gospel of Christ, and for your liberal distribution unto them, and unto all men; and by their prayer for you, which long after you for the exceeding grace of God in you. Thanks be unto God for His unspeakable gift. (vs. 6-15)

A Composite: The Gift of Giving

In Romans 12:8, the Bible says that one with the gift of giving is to do it with "simplicity." Giving with simplicity means to give liberally with singleness of heart in a reserved manner. In Matthew 6:4, Jesus implied that one ought to give secretly, when that is possible, so that the giver gives in a simple, understated manner.

A giver is motivated to invest money to increase the means by which to give to ministries, as the Lord impresses, so that the work of the Lord is advanced. The Bible says that we are all to be givers. We are to give a tithe, which the Bible commands us to do. The tithe is the minimum standard at which a Christian is to base his giving. The key emphasis of the Bible, though, calls for us to give more than the tithe. We are to also give additional offerings. As a Christian, Paul said that you ought to be a cheerful giver (2 Cor. 9:7). If you are not a cheerful giver, you have a spiritual problem. It means that you are not right with God. It means that you need to get your heart and attitude straightened out.

Being a cheerful giver is not just a reference that only applies to giving a tithe. In 1 Corinthians, Paul said that one ought to give on the first day of the week (1 Cor. 16:2). We worship on the Lord's Day, Sunday, and that is when we set aside our tithes and offerings. An offering for special needs, such as missions emphases or benevolence assistance, ought to be in addition to one's tithe that supports the weekly ongoing budget requirements of a church. Those who have the motivational gift of giving go beyond the tithe in their giving, regularly. Sometimes, the amount of their extra giving is extremely generous, even staggering. The full joy of cheerful giving begins beyond the tithe. Those who are exercising their motivational gift of giving are cheerful givers who are full of the joy of Jesus.

Explanation of the Gift of Giving

Many of the Bible verses explaining the gift of giving are applicable for all Christians. Some verses, though, are more closely adhered to and carried out by those who are specifically givers.

In the Old Testament, Leviticus 23:38 and Exodus 36:3 emphasize how one should give a freewill offering, at times, above the tithe. Exodus 36:3 says, "And they received of Moses all the offering, which the children of Israel had brought for the work of the service of the sanctuary, to make it withal. And they brought yet unto him free offerings every morning." Leviticus 23:38, which says, "Beside the sabbaths of the LORD, and beside your gifts, and beside all your vows, and beside all your freewill offerings, which ye give unto the LORD," was preceded by a verse describing some other special offerings that the Lord required of His people. The giving of God's chosen people far exceeded the tithe, which is one-tenth. The percentage of income that one with the motivational gift of giving gives to advance the Lord's work is far greater than ten percent. A giver is motivated to give *additionally* beyond what the Bible requires one to give.

In Exodus 16:16, the Bible says, "This is the thing which the LORD hath commanded, Gather of it every man according to his eating, an omer for every man, according to the number of your persons; take ye every man for them which are in his tents." That verse makes reference to God's provision of "bread from heaven" (Ex. 16:4) for the Israelites when they were on their exodus from Egypt to the Promised Land. When the manna was dispersed upon the ground each day, the Lord told them to gather *accordingly*. The Israelites were to gather according to the number of family members living in each of their homes. If you look throughout the Bible, that is how God asks us to give. When we give above our tithe for a special offering or some other special need in the Lord's work, the Bible says to give accordingly (2 Cor. 8:12; 9:7), as the Lord has prospered you and as He has prompted you to give. God has prospered some people more than others. Therefore, they can give accordingly a greater gift than other people.

What matters the most to the Lord is how you give according to what you have. Jesus said of the poor widow, who was only able to give a small, two-coin offering (about a dollar) at the Temple, that her gift was greater in God's eyes than those who gave much larger gifts out of their abundance (Mark 12:41-44; Luke 21:1-4).

In giving, the Bible says to give additionally and accordingly, as well as *appreciatively*. When the Israelites gave to provide for the cost of the tabernacle and its furnishings, the Bible says that "the children of Israel brought a willing offering unto the LORD, every man and woman, whose heart made them willing to bring for all manner of work, which the LORD had commanded to be made by the hand of Moses" (Ex. 35:29).

To give willingly is to give appreciatively. Second Chronicles 29:31 describes the people's response to King Hezekiah's order to cleanse the

Temple of God and put it back into its proper state:

> Then Hezekiah answered and said, Now ye have consecrated
> yourselves unto the LORD, come near and bring sacrifices and
> thank offerings into the house of the LORD. And the congregation
> brought in sacrifices and thank offerings; and as many as were
> of a free heart burnt offerings.

Thank offerings and free heart offerings were an expression of appreciation. To provide for a tabernacle where the Ark of the Covenant could be placed, the Israelites gave as their hearts were stirred (Ex. 35:21). Whenever your church receives an offering, you ought to give as God stirs your heart and makes you willing to give. How you give above the tithe is between you and the Lord. Whatever amount God impresses you to give, give it appreciatively.

When you give toward the work of the Lord, the Lord will usually lead you to give *abundantly*. This is particularly characteristic of the person with the spiritual gift of giving. The spirit in which the Israelites gave free will offerings toward the building of the tabernacle, its furnishings, and its upkeep was phenomenal. The Bible says:

> And they received of Moses all the offering, which the children
> of Israel had brought for the work of the service of the sanctuary,
> to make it withal. And they brought yet unto him free offerings
> every morning. And all the wise men, that wrought all the work
> of the sanctuary, came every man from his work which they
> made; and they spake unto Moses, saying, 'The people bring
> much more than enough for the service of the work, which the
> LORD commanded to make.' And Moses gave commandment,
> and they caused it to be proclaimed throughout the camp,
> saying, 'Let neither man nor woman make any more work for
> the offering of the sanctuary.' So the people were restrained
> from bringing. For the stuff they had was sufficient for all the
> work to make it, and too much. (Ex. 36:3-7)

That is abundant giving! The people gave so much that they had to be asked to quit giving. Well, glory! Would not that be wonderful to see happen in our churches today? It would, if we would begin to give the way God has prompted us to give.

A giver can also give *expectantly*, knowing that his giving is going to be to the increase of others as well as to his own increase. The Bible says in Proverbs 11:24-25: "There is that scattereth, and yet increaseth; and there is that withholdeth more than is meet, but it tendeth to poverty. The liberal soul shall be made fat: and he that watereth shall be watered also himself." The one that nourishes – who gives to others – shall be made "fat" or prosperous.

Our Lord Jesus stressed how we can give *expectantly*, as Luke recorded for us: "Give, and it shall be given unto you; good measure, pressed down, and shaken together, and running over, shall men give into your bosom. For with the same measure that ye mete withal it shall be measured to you again" (Luke 6:38). What you give for the Lord will eventually come back into your own life in some way. Jesus said that you can expect it.

The New Testament echoes the Old Testament in explaining the qualities of the spiritual gift of giving. In 2 Corinthians 9:6, the Bible says, "He which soweth sparingly shall reap also sparingly; and he which soweth bountifully shall reap also bountifully." Givers also look for ways to give *additionally*, realizing that giving allows sowing financially in ways that will reap benefits for the cause of Christ.

The New Testament teaches that giving ought to be *accordingly*. Second Corinthians 8:12 says, "For if there be first a willing mind, it is accepted according to that a man hath, and not according to that he hath not." A chapter later, the Bible says that, "every man according as he purposeth in his heart, so let him give; not grudgingly, or of necessity: for God loveth a cheerful giver" (2 Cor. 9:7). Your giving above the tithe ought to be a free will offering. Those with the motivational gift of giving give accordingly and of their own free will in obedience to the promptings of the Lord. As they give of their own free will, not grudgingly, but cheerfully, they are giving *appreciatively*. God loves it when we give cheerfully and appreciatively. When our giving is done in such a manner, the Bible says that many people will abound in many thanksgivings to God (2 Cor. 9:2).

Examples of Givers

Prior to his conversion, Matthew was a tax collector. When the Lord called Matthew to become one of His disciples, he immediately followed the Lord. He went from being a "getter" to being a giver!

Soon after his conversion, he spared no expense in inviting his former co-workers and his friends to a dinner where Jesus was the guest of honor. An expensive banquet, which the giver hosts and funds, is a means a giver can use to get people to hear the Gospel who may never come to a church. To the giver, it is a wise use of his money for the cause of Christ. In his Gospel, Matthew speaks about gifts that the other Gospel writers do not. For example, Matthew described the gifts that the wise men gave to the infant Jesus (Matt. 2:11).

Zaccheus also had the spiritual gift of giving. When we are first introduced to Zaccheus, he exhibited his gift in the flesh. He cheated people. Givers, who work in the flesh, are so concerned with making a buck that they will cheat people out of their money just to make a dollar more.

But once Zaccheus was right with God, and operated in the Spirit, he provided an excellent example of how the giver responds. He gave half of his wealth to the poor, and to those he had cheated, he gave back four times the amount he had cheated them (Luke 19:8). When a giver gets right with God, the Lord begins to work through that person's life in what to us are almost miraculous ways.

Abigail also gave abundantly to David. When David and his men were in need of something to eat, Abigail's husband refused to help them. So they decided to take what was needed by force.

However, knowing the good they had done for her husband's sheep tenders (1 Sam. 25:14-17), the Bible says Abigail "made haste, and took two hundred loaves, and two bottles of wine, and five sheep ready dressed, and five measures of parched corn, and an hundred clusters of raisins, and two hundred cakes of figs, and laid them on asses" (1 Sam. 25:18). The list of food Abigail provided for David, his men, and their families was the equivalent of the amount and quality of food for a banquet.

Her great generosity appeased David and his men (1 Sam. 25:32-35). Abigail not only gave them what they needed, but more than they needed. She also offered to provide above what she had already given them.

When Mary, Martha, and Lazarus entertained Jesus at the home of Simon the leper, after Jesus had raised Lazarus from the dead, Mary gave lavishly: she anointed the feet of Jesus with ointment, described by John as costly (John 12:3). Matthew, as characteristic of one with the gift of giving, described Mary's ointment as very precious (Matt. 26:7). There is a difference between something that is costly and something that is very precious. The one who is motivated to give likes to give quality gifts. Matthew brought out more than just the fact that it was an expensive and quality ointment. One can sense in Matthew's account an appreciation for the way in which the gift was given. The one with the spiritual gift of giving wants to give a gift that has meaning for the one who receives it. The giver gives as prompted by God. The "very precious ointment," given by Mary, had monetary value that was equivalent to one year's wages. Jesus acknowledged the importance of what she had done and why she had done it: "For in that she hath poured this ointment on my body, she did it for my burial. Verily I say unto you, Wheresoever this gospel shall be preached in the whole world, there shall also this, that this woman hath done, be told for a memorial of her" (Matt. 26:12-13).

Our perfect example of a giver is Jesus. As recorded in the Bible, whenever Jesus gave something, it was either the best or it provided more than enough. When Jesus turned the water into wine, the emcee of the wedding reception acknowledged that it was the very best (John 2:9-10), given at a time when the best quality was normally not made available. When Jesus provided a meal for several thousand people, on two different occasions, not only did everyone get something to eat, but they were fed as much as they wanted, and there were leftovers (see Matt. 14:20 and Matt. 15:37). Characteristic of a giver, Jesus had the leftovers taken up and properly stored, so that they could be used for another meal.

Exhortations to Givers

The Bible makes two special *exhortations to givers* in Romans 12:13. The person with the spiritual gift of giving is exhorted to be "distributing to the necessity of saints; given to hospitality." The giver is to *be open-handed to saints* through *personal investments*. But it is to be with guidelines. When people learn the identity of a person who gives to various Christian causes, just about every para-church ministry in the country will put that person on their mailing list. The various para-church organizations will make appeals for the giver to donate money to their ministry. Such a giver might think, "Well, I need to give to all of these ministries." He may do that, but some of those ministries may not be ones the Lord wants him to support. To the Lord, all those ministries may not be viable and necessary. If givers will support God-ordained ministries as the Lord prompts them, then every legitimate ministry will have enough financial backers.

Givers are to help meet needs in the lives of Christians. So the Bible cautions givers to make personal investments, usually to someone he knows or to an organization he knows something about. Sometimes, though, givers are prompted to give to a cause without knowing someone who is personally involved or knowledgeable with the ministry, but that is not the norm. God usually directs givers to be knowledgeable of whom they support financially so that their giving is most effectively used for the cause of Christ.

People who are givers are usually prompted by God to give a certain amount of money. If it is someone whom a giver knows, the giver may not even know that the person has a financial need, but God prompts the giver to give and he does so obediently. Also, the Lord does not want the giver to give impersonally, but to give from the heart. If a giver is blessed by the Lord with wealth, the giver can become very impersonal by giving thousands of dollars for Christian causes. It may seem like a good thing, but the giver has little interaction or personal contacts with those he is financially supporting. Impersonal giving is giving without heart. God wants gifts from the heart. The Lord not only wants a giver's gift to have meaning for those who receive it, but He wants it to have meaning for the giver, too. The giver is to be openhanded to the saints, but only as the Lord prompts. God's way is for the giver to be openhanded to the saints; however, with strangers, God says for the giver to *be openhearted*.

The giver should not necessarily give money to strangers to meet financial or material needs. But just as a giver is to make personal investments in the lives of saints, he may also be called to *personal involvement* in the lives of strangers whom God prompts the giver to help. God may even ask the giver to do more than just meet a financial or material need in a stranger's life.

He may call the giver to help through hospitality. Mainly, hospitality is being nice to people one does not even know. Being given to hospitality might be to provide a job where the stranger can earn money, enjoy a meal or a place to stay for a night, a few days, or on a permanent basis. These acts may well lead them to salvation through Christ. That is the greatest and most beneficial help a giver can offer.

Expectation Givers Need to Exercise Most

Bill Gothard believes that the giver must have an idea of ownership. The idea of ownership is to realize that God owns everything the giver possesses. When the giver has the proper knowledge of divine ownership, he is not hesitant in his response to the promptings of God. The giver knows that if God leads him to give a phenomenal amount of money, it will not deprive the giver of his personal financial needs. God has given the giver what he has accumulated, and if God wants the giver to have more, the giver knows that the Lord will provide the funds.

I want to suggest an expectation that is very practical, but it ties in with the exhortations to givers. It also builds upon a giver's proper view of ownership. Those who have the spiritual gift of giving have to be in *contact* with other people. It puts the giver in contact with where needs are so that the giver has a sense of where God will direct him to give.

God has blessed many Christians with monetary wealth. A few years ago, I attended a small potluck dinner with about fifteen to twenty others who met a great man of God from India. A group of four men from that church had gone to India on a mission trip at the invitation of this brother from India. Thousands were saved in the brush arbors and other settings in which the men testified and proclaimed Christ. Through the ministry of Dr. P.N. Kurian, over two million of his fellow countrymen have been saved. Dr. Kurian comes to the United States every couple of years for fellowship and contact with the churches that financially and prayerfully support his ministry. After Dr. Kurian delivered a very moving message to the small gathering, testifying about the work of God through his ministry, he offered to answer any questions about the ministry. A question was asked about what differing amounts of financial gifts could support in Dr. Kurian's ministry. The amount needed to build a church was a figure between one and two thousand dollars. I remember tears welling up in the eyes of a giver who was in attendance. He got out his checkbook, and he said, "I have never heard anything like what this man has described." He wrote a check to cover the cost of building a church in India.

Usually the big citywide evangelistic crusades have built-in support through churches that will give toward the financial costs. Lesser-known ministries do not have such a support base. But God has those with the gift of giving whom He wants to be at a dinner where there may be only twenty people so that He can use a giver to support a lesser known ministry. At that small gathering in Milan, Tennessee, the Lord wanted a giver to be there whose two thousand dollars could be used to touch the lives of a hundred, maybe even thousands of people in another part of the world. Givers need to put themselves in positions where they have contact with men such as P.N. Kurian and lesser known ministers whom God is using in a mighty way.

Characteristics of Givers

The giver gives: *obediently, wisely, quietly, voluntarily,* and *excellently*.

Giving Submissively (Obediently)

Givers want to give obediently in responding to the promptings of the Lord. As a giver gives submissively, he is actually giving *for the Lord*. The purpose of a giver in giving is that he wants to give as if he is giving for the Lord. God's way of meeting a financial need in our lives is not winning the "Ten Million Dollar Sweepstakes." He may allow that to happen for one of us, but God has greater and more meaningful ways by which He meets financial needs in our lives. How does God meet special needs in the lives of the saints, especially those financial needs that job salaries are not adequate to cover? Usually, it is through another Christian with the gift of giving whom God prompts to help the one with the financial need. When the giver responds to such promptings, he is giving for the Lord.

To give for the Lord, it is very important for one to give himself *first to the Lord*. Paul brought this out when he talked about the churches in Macedonia who had given financially to support Paul's ministry and the financial needs of other Christians. Paul pointed out that the Macedonian Christians "first gave their own selves to the Lord" (2 Cor. 8:5). That is the key for a person with the gift of giving. The giver's priority is to first give himself to the Lord so that he can give according to God's will.

In giving submissively, wholly committed to the Lord, the giver desires for the receiver of his gift to know that it is *from the Lord*. Givers want their gift of provision to be for the recipient as if it came directly from the Lord. When I pray for special needs for myself, for others in my family, for my church, or others on whose behalf I am intervening, I ask God to work divinely and providentially through the ordinary, supernaturally through the natural, or miraculously.

When God prompts someone to send a special amount of money that is just the amount needed for a project, a personal need, or other similar needs, that is an example of God working divinely and providentially through the ordinary. In those situations, the one who sends the gift is aware of a financial need.

When a person has a financial need, and the amount comes in at just the time it is needed, with the receiver having no idea where the needed money was going to come from, that is an example of God working supernaturally through the natural. Such a gift is usually provided by one who has the motivational gift of giving. When I have been the recipient of such a gift, the giver normally had no idea that there was a need. But they felt prompted by God to give, even an odd amount of money, that was just what was needed.

I previously mentioned a man from Milan, Tennessee who has the gift of giving. God used him in a special way to meet a financial need in my life. Two years after our family moved from Milan, I felt led by the Lord to resign the church where I was serving on the ministerial staff and enter seminary. I took a part-time position directing the adult singles ministry at my home church for one hundred dollars a week. My income had been reduced about eighty-five percent. With some available money from an annuity account, the salary from my part-time position, along with some other income my wife received from keeping a friend's baby during the day, I knew that we could get by financially from October to about the second week in February. When we got to February, and we were out of the money that was necessary to cover the basic costs of maintaining a rental home and the every day needs of a family of four, we considered several alternatives. We had not made the extent of our financial needs or situation known to anyone. I remember telling my wife one day that if something did not happen that very day, then I was going to have to find a full-time job, and I was going to have to drop out of seminary.

But as a saying goes, "Where God guides, God provides." That very day, we received mail from our giver friend in Milan with a $500 check enclosed. That confirmed to us that we were where God wanted us to be, and we were doing exactly what God wanted us to do at that point in our lives. When someone gives an unsolicited gift, you ought to acknowledge it, if you know who gave it to you. We called the day we received the generous gift. He was not at home when we called, but his wife told us that he had come in from work the day before wanting to know our address. He had been prompted to send a check to us. His wife told us that he had promptings like that all the time. God would lay somebody upon his heart, and he would give a financial gift to that person. That is how the motivational gift of giving often works.

Givers live to give submissively as God prompts them to give. Much of the time a giver has no idea a person to whom he feels led to give even has a financial need. When God prompts one with the motivational gift of giving to give, a giver who is exercising his gift as God desires gives obediently.

Giving Surely (Wisely)

Can you think of some people who just seem to be able to accumulate funds? They may have the gift of giving. The person with the motivational gift of giving wants to make wise *investments*. Why? So he can accumulate the means, not to be wealthy, but to be able to give more money to the Lord's work and as God prompts him to give. Givers have the ability to discern wise investments for the purpose of making money in order to have the means to give for the work of the Lord. They are particularly sensitive to the counsel of their mate in how to invest and give money. Whether the giver is a man or a woman, if the giver is married this gift cannot be fulfilled unless the mate of the giver is supportive of it. One way givers know if they are giving wisely and surely is in waiting for God to give confirmation through their mate on how much they ought to give in a particular situation. People with this motivational gift have told me that, when God is prompting them to give to someone or some organization, the Lord will impress an amount upon their heart. Their mate will often be impressed by God that a certain amount ought to be given to the very person or organization whom God has already placed upon the heart of the giver mate. It is usually the exact amount that God placed upon the heart of the giver to give. This is how God confirms to one with the motivational gift of giving that he is giving for the Lord.

Givers also want their gifts to have *impact*. They want a gift to be meaningful to the receiver, as an obvious answer to prayer, especially when the need is not obvious. When this is the case, it gives the giver joy and confirms to him that he is in touch with God.

Perhaps, you have been the recipient of such a gift. The first time it happened, you were probably hesitant, maybe even embarrassed, to accept the help.

As my family has been the recipient on several occasions, I have learned that when God prompts someone to give, if I am not a willing receiver, I mess up the process. In my receiving the gift, it is the fulfillment of a special need in my life. When I share that with the giver, it lets him know that he is in tune with God and giving according to how God wants him to give. We need to be willing to accept the gifts that givers feel compelled to give to us.

The giver also knows that he is giving surely when his gift is an *inspiration* to the receiver as well as to other potential givers. The giver wants his giving to inspire and motivate others to give because of the blessing one receives when he gives. The giver already knows what that blessing is, and he wants others to also experience such a blessing in their lives. If God has met a special financial need in your life, testify about it when you have an opportunity. If it was given anonymously, it could be a way of getting feedback to the giver that he has done what God asked him to do.

As the giver desires to inspire and motivate others to give, one way they seek to do it is by giving matching gifts. When you receive an appeal to give a monetary gift that says an individual is going to match whatever amount is raised, the individual who is going to give the matching amount probably has the gift of giving.

Giving Secretly (Quietly)

One who is motivated to give not only has a tendency to give submissively and surely, but they often *give secretly*. The giver prefers to give quietly without recognition. Jesus told us how we ought to give. Matthew, who had the motivational gift of giving, recorded the words the Lord made about giving:

> *Take heed that ye do not your alms before men, to be seen of*

them: otherwise ye have no reward of your Father which is in heaven. Therefore when thou doest thine alms, do not sound a trumpet before thee, as the hypocrites do in the synagogues and in the streets, that they may have glory of men. Verily I say unto you, They have their reward. But when thou doest alms, let not thy left hand know what thy right hand doeth: that thine alms may be in secret: and thy Father which seeth in secret himself shall reward thee openly. (Matt. 6:1-4)

Giving alms means giving a gift or an offering to someone. We are to give with simplicity (Rom. 12:8) and without accolade. As we see above, Jesus confirmed that when a person gives quietly, even secretly, God will reward the person openly.

If there is someone whom God will tend to bless financially, it is those who have the motivational gift of giving. Why? Because they know how to handle their money and use it for the glory of God.

Those with the gift of giving like to *give simply*. In the churches where I have either pastored or served on the ministerial staff, there have been those who gave anonymous financial gifts to the church of several thousand dollars. Some of the gifts were designated in how they were to be used, but most of the gifts were given with no restrictions for their use.

Often the giver also likes to *give anonymously*, without the receiver knowing who gave the gift, so that the receiver will look to the Lord for provision, not to a person. If it was always known who the people were who have given several thousand dollars to provide for a ministry's need, whenever there was another financial need there may be others who are part of that ministry who would hound the benefactor to give another big gift. A ministry can get too financially dependent upon an individual. Financial problems may be God's way of getting the attention of a ministry that is out of His will. Such a ministry sometimes does not need a bailing out; they sometimes need a cleaning out spiritually. One reason why givers do not always let it be known to whom they give and how much they give is to avoid criticism. Others in a church or other ministries who were not recipients of a giver's financial support might accuse the giver of being prejudiced or showing favoritism. When such judgment occurs, it is a very unfair and unfounded judgment of the giver who is simply, significantly, and selectively giving to whom God prompts them to give.

If someone feels led to give a substantial gift to a church, it is because God has prompted that individual to meet a particular need in the church at that time. God may raise up someone else to meet another need later on. The latter giver will not get the blessing of giving to meet a special need if a ministry always goes to the same person when money is needed. Anyway, God does not want a ministry, especially a church, to become too dependent upon a few who have the gift of giving. When that happens, those with other motivational gifts, who have the potential and means to give more, may not give sacrificially, as God calls all of us to do, at times.

When the giver is able to give secretly and quietly, he is able to *give selectively*. The person with the gift of giving prefers to give to special needs where God has led them to give. They like to give quietly so that they are not appealed to over and over again. This allows the giver to support effective ministries—ministries that are glorifying the Lord and producing results.

We all need to experience the joy of giving. Even if we do not have the motivational gift of giving, we need to know what it is to give sacrificially. We all need to learn when God wants us to give sacrificially, without people knowing who or how much was given, where it meets a special need in someone's life. But we also need to learn when not to give or to expect one with the gift of giving to come through. Those with the motivational gift of giving give so that the receiver will not always depend upon the giver every time he has a need.

Givers like to *give significantly*. By meeting a need in a ministry to which God has led them to give, it signifies to the participants in the ministry, to the giver, and to others who are not even part of that ministry, that it really matters and has the blessing of God on it.

Giving Sincerely (Voluntarily)

A giver prefers to *give sincerely (voluntarily)*, as the Lord purposes in his heart (2 Cor. 9:7), because that is how he finds joy in giving, and it is when he can do it sincerely. When the giver gives sincerely, that is when he can do it *joyfully and heartily*. He is able to give cheerfully out of a joyful heart.

A giver is motivated to give *justly and honestly* to a God-given cause. The giver wants to give where there is a legitimate need because he wants his giving to be done in a just and honest manner. In order to give justly and honestly, givers like to receive counsel from their mate regarding how much to give. Givers also want to see if their mate has any cautions about a particular prompting the giver has received. A giver does not want his gift to corrupt or to be misused by the one who receives it.

A giver also likes to give *generously and helpfully*. When a giver is allowed the freedom to give voluntarily, he can give generously, as the Lord guides him to give. He can give without concern that he will be accused of prejudice or favoritism by groups to which the giver does not feel led to give or to give to as generously as to others. A giver's gift is not always in the form of a tangible gift, such as monetary donations. A giver will often give of his time to a particular cause or project, without pay, where it would cost to pay someone to do the job. I heard about a man who had accumulated a large amount of wealth through his business ventures, who was elected mayor of one of the major cities in the United States. He is accepting a dollar a year in income as mayor of the city. His motivational gift is evidently the gift of giving. He has made a fortune, he has given financially to various causes, and he is now giving of his time without accepting the salary that goes with his elected office. However a giver provides for a cause, it will be a wise investment that will increase in value as to its benefit to whomever it helps.

Giving Sufficiently (Excellently)

The Bible gives emphasis to gifts of excellence. Matthew mentions the quality of the gifts given to the baby Jesus by the wise men (Matt. 2:11). He also describes the quality of the precious ointment that Mary used to anoint Christ (Matt. 26:7). His emphasis on quality was also evident in his pointing out that the tomb of Jesus, provided by Joseph of Arimathaea, was a new tomb (Matt. 26:57-60). All of those gifts were quality gifts, the best that could be given. The Bible does not indicate in any way that such Spirit-led giving was overdoing it. When the disciples were critical of Mary's use of the very expensive ointment (Matt. 26:8-9), Jesus complimented Mary for her act of giving and said that she would be honored for it (Matt. 26:10-13).

And so, the giver gives gifts of *excellence*, of the highest quality, because he wants to give sufficiently. A giver desires to give what is needed to get the job done. I do not know if this particular giver testifies as being born again spiritually, but his secular life manifests the characteristics of a giver. Although enduring some financial trouble in recent years, Donald Trump's expertise in the area of investments and borrowing appear to have gotten him back on top of his vast wealth. Before he was a nationally known name, I heard him make a statement on a television show several years ago. His statement is characteristic of what motivates one with the gift of giving. I had not heard of him until I saw this program that centered on four of the most financially successful individuals in the United States. He had recently bought a piece of property in Manhattan that he said anybody in real estate would know is the most valuable piece of property in the world.

A few years later, after he had become well known, I saw another television interview of which he was the subject. The conversation centered on his purchase of an enormous, beautiful mansion and compound in Palm Beach. Eventually, the talk turned to his other properties and holdings. Mr. Trump summed up why he had made his well-known investments and real estate purchases. He said, "I buy treasures."

That is characteristic of the person with the motivational gift of giving. When a giver purchases something, it is of the highest quality. Givers do not give imitations. When they give something, they give the very best. They want the best, but for the Christian givers, it is not so they can keep it for themselves. The ultimate goal of the Christian giver in obtaining the best is in its lasting value. Something that will increase in value in time will provide more funds to be available to support the work of the Lord.

To give sufficiently, givers give gifts of *endurance*. As the giver wants to provide a gift that will be completely sufficient, he gives a gift of high quality because such gifts will endure. Unless something is mistreated, or there is some kind of accident, the better the quality, the longer an object will last and continue to be of use.

The giver also wants to give gifts of *edification*. He desires for his gifts to build up others in their spiritual life. As the giver abounds, he tends to be one who always has all sufficiency in all things (2 Cor. 9:8). He is able to edify other believers through his gifts. When the one with the gift of giving exercises his gift submissively, surely, secretly (as much as possible), sincerely, and sufficiently, his giving will be to the edification of other believers.

Cautions for the Gift of Giving
Misunderstandings

One of the basic misunderstandings about givers is that they *mishandle money*. When my home church built and moved into a new sanctuary in

1980, a member donated $50,000 for the development of a rose garden next to the sanctuary. A nice courtyard area was constructed, gardens were landscaped, and the rose garden became known as the Meditation Garden. Another pastor in the city misjudged my home church when he stated from his pulpit that churches are not to go around building $50,000 rose gardens. In his mind, that did not honor God, and he said that a church ought to use that amount of money for missions and evangelism. The one who donated the money for the prayer garden wanted a place where people could come and fellowship with one another, meditate, and pray. Characteristic of a giver, the donor wanted to provide a place that was beautiful and that provided a proper atmosphere. The donor gave as prompted by God to give for such a purpose.

I must admit, that my first reaction when I learned how much was spent on a rose garden was, "fifty thousand dollars on a garden!" At the time, I could think of a hundred ways that money could have been better used. When I learned the facts concerning why the person gave that monetary gift, I had to say, "Forgive me, Lord. You prompted that person to give because You wanted our church to have that prayer garden."

By the way, if you are a pastor, be careful about comments regarding how a sister church spends its money. We may feel that givers mishandle their money because they give for unusual, unnoticed needs that are overlooked or felt unnecessary by others. If a giver is listening to the Spirit, he gives his money as prompted by the Lord, and as he does, it will meet the right need at just the right time.

Givers may be misunderstood by some as using their giving for the purpose of *manipulation*. Some people may feel that a big gift is an attempt to influence and control a ministry or a church. When a giver is working in the flesh, that may be a motivation for giving. A giver who is in right relationship with the Lord and obedient to His promptings never gives and then says, "Here is what I want."

A giver may be accused of being *materialistic*. God gives wisdom to a person with the gift of giving on how to invest money. Because givers desire to make large sums of money, and because they give "treasures," givers are falsely accused by some as being materialistic. Givers can get extensively involved in collectibles. My father-in-law, who has the gift of giving, has amazed me at how he can buy a piece of antique cranberry glassware and in a couple of years the piece has doubled in value. He has invested in many collectible type items through the years that are far greater in monetary value than what he paid for them.

A giver wants to invest and accumulate items that increase in value. Some may wonder, "Why are they getting all this stuff?" We invest most of our money in items that are more immediate, as far as our use and enjoyment of them, but they depreciate in value the moment we buy them. But when some see a giver investing in collectible items, that sit on a shelf, and do not provide pleasure and enjoyment as something usable on a daily basis, they may misjudge the giver as collecting something that is useless clutter. But to the giver, it is a wise investment. Their collectibles not only gather a little dust, but they gain more value in time just sitting there. I know that some individuals have donated their collectibles to a church building program. When the collection was sold at its present market value, and the proceeds were donated to the church, the giver had been able to give twice as much. The collection had doubled in value from what the giver had originally paid for the various pieces. Givers strive to make more money and to wisely invest in things that increase in value in order to have more funds available to give away.

Some givers whom God has blessed financially live in nice, big homes and buy the best possessions money can buy. But givers do not always obtain much for themselves in the way of material possessions. There are some with this gift who would be considered *miserly* according to the standards by which they live.

Several years ago, I knew a lady who was a member of a church where I served on the ministerial staff. She lived in a nursing home. Prior to her death, I visited with her a few times in her room she shared with another lady. I did not think that she had much materially. The church where we were members was rapidly growing and needed to expand the parking lot, at a cost of thousands of dollars. Many members wondered how the church could raise that amount of money without borrowing money at a high interest rate. Once or twice a year, our church had some substantial funds available beyond the weekly tithes and offerings. Our pastor said, "I believe I know where we can get the money." The lady in the nursing home had a farm in another county. It had a lot of valuable timber on it, from which she received payments when it was lumbered each year. She also contracted with a farmer for the farmable part of her property, receiving a percentage of the profits on the crops. Each year, she divided the profits from her farm with her home church and a local church near her farm. Her offerings from the farm accounted for the extra funds at our church at least twice a year. Some years her farm was very profitable. One of the farm profit donations was sufficient to fund the needed parking lot.

The lifestyle of the woman in the nursing home was such that she did not need much and did not want much for herself while she was alive. Her motivational gift was giving. One would never have thought that she was one who was able to give large sums of money for the work of the Lord.

A giver may also be misunderstood as being *merciless*, at times. Because givers do not give to every appeal made directly or indirectly to them, they are misjudged by some as being uncaring and without mercy. A giver only gives as prompted by the Lord, and only to legitimate ministries. A giver may sense a cautionary revelation about a particular organization or program that God has revealed to the giver. As a result, the giver does not feel led to support that cause. To the giver, it would be like throwing his money away. Others, who do not know what the giver knows, may support what to them is a legitimate cause. For instance, a Christian organization may be raising funds to feed hungry children in a foreign land or to provide for Bibles to be sent to a formerly Communist country. There are now hundreds of groups who claim such a purpose as their ministry. Most of them are legitimate and being used by the Lord. But, some have been exposed as shams. The monies they received were not used for the purposes advertised. Chances are, if a giver is cautious about giving to a Christian cause, there may be corruption within the organization promoting the cause. When a giver, who is a faithful follower of the Lord, does not feel impressed to support a cause, it does not always mean that the organization promoting the cause is not on the level. God may have another ministry that needs financial help, where He wants the giver to send a gift.

Misuses

When the gift of giving is not exhibited in the power of the Holy Spirit, there may be *wavering* on the part of the giver. He may not give as God compels him to give. God may prompt the giver to give, but he says, "Well, God, I don't know about that." Sometimes the giver then questions God, not only on matters of giving, but on other issues, too. When a giver is not in tune with the Lord, he will not know specifically where God wants him to give. He may become hesitant and wavering in letting go of his money to ministries that need his help.

The giver can misuse his gift by becoming *worldly*. In the flesh, the giver is more concerned with accumulating money and satisfying worldly desires than he is in giving to the work of the Lord. I know a man whose family had very little materially for many years. For the first few years that I knew him, he just barely made enough to support his family. He was a very committed Christian and active church member. Eventually, his modest business began to grow. God blessed it greatly, and he became a wealthy man. Although he did give to several Christian organizations and causes, most of his giving, above his tithe to his church, was to organizations of people who were nationally renowned. He got on the inside with some of the well-known Christian personalities who headed the organizations. He then seemed to have been more motivated by the prominence and recognition he gained from being a generous giver. He has had to declare bankruptcy more than once in the past few years. Each time, he has come through it and become financially successful again. But his motivation now appears to be more material than spiritual. Making more money is a greater motivation now than letting God give it away through him.

One who misuses his gift of giving can become like a *warlord*. Such a giver intends to use his wealth to gain control and influence. His attitude is something like this: "I have given more money to our church than anybody else. I ought to have more say so than anyone else on how our church spends its money." For example, a warlord giver wants to exert influence over such decisions as who the church hires to build an addition to the present facilities, who gets to go as chaperones on a youth trip, or who gets money from the church to assist in going on a mission trip. It is an ongoing cycle. The nation of Somalia has suffered greatly because of the warlords who control that country. The warlords and their followers have what they need, but thousands of others in Somalia, especially children, have starved to death. Warlord givers are just as dangerous within a church, and the church is better off without their money.

Givers can misuse their gift by *withholding*. They misuse their gift by holding back on giving money and other kinds of gifts. Usually, when the withholding giver is a church member, it is to protest something the giver does not like that has been approved by the majority of church members. I know of churches where some of the members withheld their money because they did not get their way on some church matter. They hoped that their withholding would cause financial pressure on the church, causing other members to take their side and reverse a decision. God does not honor that kind of a protest. In most cases, when some individual or group tries to withhold money to get their way in a church matter, it just causes God to open up new avenues to bless the church financially. God will always open up other avenues of giving when givers fail to give responsibly. Most likely, a backslidden giver is the ringleader of such a protest, and other backslidden givers become part of the withholding group. A giver in a right relationship with Christ will never use his giving (or lack of it) as a means of protest. In every church where I have known of such a protest, I am thankful to testify that each of those churches is still alive and well.

Givers must especially guard against becoming *withdrawn*. When a giver remains to himself, and he is not where needs are, he is unaware of where God is working. The financially blessed giver can become comfortable, getting into a castle of wealth, isolated from those in need. Givers may be gone from their church for extended periods because of frequent pleasure trips. They become unaware of where the Lord is working and where He would like them to center their giving. When they do give, it may be in a *wasteful* manner. They still have the spirit of giving, but they give to a cause without thought for the effectiveness of the ministry, or that their gift may provide too much ease and comfort for someone. Such a gift then corrupts. It is not a spiritual blessing in the life of the receiver.

If you are a giver, I pray that you will not misuse your wonderful gift from God. What a channel of blessing you are to the cause of Christ when you manifest your gift in the power and control of the Holy Spirit.

Conclusion

Givers are not the ones who are always in the limelight in a church. In the churches in which I have been a member, I can only think of a few other members in each of those churches who had the motivational gift of giving. There were more givers in those churches, but many who have this motivational gift exercise it in a very simple, reserved manner. Attention is not drawn to them. Therefore, others are not able to easily identify the ones who have the motivational gift of giving. There is no way for a giver to avoid being acknowledged publicly for some of the gifts he bestows upon others. But most givers prefer to avoid recognition for their acts of giving.

Those with the spiritual gift of giving live to give. For those of you who have the motivational gift of giving, may God bless you. From my personal experiences as the receiver of a giver's gift, I know what your special gift of blessing has meant to me and my family. Thank you for giving so that the work of the Lord not only continues, but it is expanded. If this is not your spiritual gift, learn to develop characteristics of the gift of giving. We all need to learn the joy that comes in giving cheerfully and the strengthening of our faith that comes in giving sacrificially, knowing that God will supply all of our needs out of His abundant riches.

7

The Gift of Organizing

"Able to Endure"

> *Having then gifts differing according to the grace that is given to us, whether prophecy, let us prophesy according to the proportion of faith; or ministry, let us wait on our ministering: or he that teacheth, on teaching; or he that exhorteth, on exhortation: he that giveth, let him do it with simplicity; he that ruleth [organizing], with diligence;...Bless them which persecute you: bless, and curse not. (Rom. 12:6-8,14)*

Many of us have an admiring envy of those who have the motivational spiritual gift of organizing. How grateful we should be for the organizers in our churches, as well as in all other areas of concern, because they keep life from being utterly chaotic. The Bible has four excellent examples of organizers.

Jethro, the father-in-law of Moses, became a believer in Jehovah God, the God of Israel, although he was not a Jew. On one occasion, when he came to visit Moses, he sat down and observed his son-in-law trying to conduct the affairs of the nation of Israel as its leader. Like any good organizer, Jethro noticed where there were breakdowns in the way Moses handled his responsibilities as the leader of the Israelites.

Most of the time, organizers will sit back, observe, and usually not get involved until asked. A father-in-law who has a good relationship with his son-in-law can counsel him. Jethro advised Moses on better organization of Israel's national affairs. Jethro's counsel to Moses is recorded in Exodus 18. This passage provides insight into the gift of organizing, especially from a spiritual standpoint, as to how organizers approach a problem.

And it came to pass on the morrow, that Moses sat to judge the people: and the people stood by Moses from the morning unto the evening. And when Moses' father-in-law saw all that he did to the people, he said, 'What is this thing that thou doest to the people? Why sittest thou thyself alone, and all the people stand by thee from morning unto even?' And Moses said unto his father-in-law, 'Because the people come unto me to inquire of God: when they have a matter, they come unto me; and I judge between one and another, and I do make them know the statutes of God, and his laws.' And Moses' father-in-law said unto him, 'The thing that thou doest is not good. Thou wilt surely wear away, both thou, and this people that is with thee: for this thing is too heavy for thee; thou art not able to perform it thyself alone. Hearken now unto my voice, I will give thee counsel, and God shall be with thee: be thou for the people to God-ward, that thou mayest bring the causes unto God: and thou shalt teach them ordinances and laws, and shalt shew them the way wherein they must walk, and the work that they must do. Moreover thou shalt provide out of all the people able men, such as fear God, men of truth, hating covetousness; and place such over them, to be rulers of thousands, and rulers of hundreds, rulers of fifties, and rulers of tens: and let them judge the people at all seasons: and it shall be, that every great matter they shall bring unto thee, but every small matter they shall judge: so shall it be easier for thyself, and they shall bear the burden with thee. If thou shalt do this thing, and God command thee so, then thou shalt be able to endure, and all this people shall also go to their place in peace.' So Moses hearkened to the voice of his father-in-law, and did all that he had said. And Moses chose able men out of all Israel, and made them heads over the people, rulers of thousands, rulers of hundreds, rulers of fifties, and rulers of tens. And they judged the people at all seasons: the hard causes they brought unto Moses, but every small matter they judged themselves. And Moses let his father-in-law depart; and he went his way into his own land. (Ex. 18:13-27)

A couple of verses in this passage speak loudly regarding the purpose and benefits of organizing. Jethro told Moses that one of the reasons he needed to be better organized was so that it would be easier for Moses, and that the people would bear the burden with him (v. 22).

What beautiful advice for the way a church should be organized! Here was Moses, the spiritual leader of the nation of Israel, as well as the equivalent of being the president of Israel. He had to deal with all the small matters that came up among the people, most of which did not make a great deal of difference for eternity. Yet, they were matters that were important in the lives of those people. Moses, their leader, needed to have time alone with God. He needed time each day just to think. He needed more time for rest. He needed to be available to the people, but he needed to be more accessible than hearing one case at a time. But he was trying to do it all by himself. Moses was sitting for hours at a time, all day long, while the people came before him with their problems.

From the advice that Jethro gave to Moses, we learn that there is nothing wrong with making something easier. The counsel from Jethro did not suggest a leadership style and lifestyle in which Moses would sit back and do nothing. Jethro was basically saying to Moses, "If you will do your job right so that we all work together, we will all be amazed at how smoothly things will go, and we will not get stressed out and worn out in the process." Jethro developed an organizational plan for the nation of Israel in which the people would bear the burden (v. 23) with Moses. The plan was designed so that if everyone would do his part, then not only the leader, but everyone would be able to endure. Able to endure—that is the key phrase of the passage. There are some individuals who love to organize, and others might even think that organizers organize just to have something to do. But the ultimate purpose of organizing is to keep the process going smoothly, even when the person in charge is away for a few days and even when a change of leadership occurs.

In addition to Jethro, Joseph and Nehemiah were examples of organizers.

After Joseph's brothers sold him to Midianite merchants, he was later sold to Potiphar, an officer of Pharaoh of Egypt. Throughout Joseph's ordeal, from Potiphar's house to prison, and from prison to second in command to Pharaoh, it did not take long before those for whom Joseph worked placed him in the role of organizer and administrator over the affairs of their lives and other areas of responsibility (Gen. 39:5-6; 22-23; 41:40-41).

The book of Nehemiah provides a blueprint for organizing and the effectiveness of it. When the Israelites were in exile, Nehemiah was the king's cupbearer. He became aware that the walls of Jerusalem were in ruins and needed rebuilding. So he came in with this burden before the king. The king allowed Nehemiah to go back to his homeland to supervise the rebuilding of the walls of Jerusalem. In 52 days, Nehemiah organized his people to do what many thought was impossible and could never be done. There were those who thought the wall of Jerusalem would never be reconstructed after the exile. The enemies of the Jews did not want the wall to be rebuilt. But Nehemiah came in and organized his people to do the job. Throughout the book of Nehemiah, the Bible gives a picture of how the characteristics of organizing all come together.

A Composite: The Gift of Organizing

Proper organization, which always includes the right leadership, is the key to an orderly society.

Explanation of the Gift of Organizing

In the Old Testament, the words, *picture, plan, pray, prepare,* and *pro-*

duce help to explain an organizer, as exhibited in the lives of Joseph, Jethro, and Nehemiah.

In the Bible, we are first introduced to Joseph. In Genesis 37, the Bible says that "Joseph dreamed a dream" (v. 5), and that "he dreamed yet another dream" (v. 9). His dreams placed him in a position of authority over his parents and siblings. His brothers even referred to him as the "dreamer" (v. 19). In the next several chapters, the Bible reveals that Joseph not only dreamed dreams that eventually became reality, but he was able to interpret the dreams of others. An organizer can *picture* in his mind a potential project, or how something should be organized, and the organizer can see the whole picture through to completion.

Jethro saw the picture up close, then he gave Moses a *plan* to follow. He was so confident that his organizational plan would work that he told his son-in-law to "hearken now unto my counsel, and God shall be with thee" (Ex. 18:19). In verses 19-23 of Exodus 18, Jethro gave the plan and told Moses that if he followed it, he would be able to endure.

When a picture of the decayed wall around Jerusalem became alive in the mind of Nehemiah, he developed a plan on how to correct the situation. His plan was initiated with *prayer*. Prayer was part of his *preparation* for effectively implementing his plan (Neh. 1:4,6), as well as getting the guidance from God as to what was to be his plan of action. Before Nehemiah was able to implement and organize a plan to rebuild the wall around Jerusalem, he had to get the permission of the king to go to Jerusalem before he could *produce* results. Nehemiah preceded his request to the king with prayer (Neh. 1:11), and he was in a spirit of prayer (Neh. 2:4) while in the process of making his request. Prayer produced the answer Nehemiah desired from the king. Preparation was necessary before one stone was laid at Jerusalem.

As the perfect organizer, Jesus operated *authoritatively, efficiently,* and *orderly*. Verses one and five of Matthew 10 give an example of how

Jesus *authoritatively* summoned and directed His disciples in an organized mission endeavor: "And when He had called unto Him His twelve
disciples, He gave them power against unclean spirits, to cast them out,
and to heal all manner of sickness and all manner of disease...These
twelve Jesus sent forth, and commanded, saying, Go..."

Jesus then told His disciples where they were not to go, where they
were to go, and what they were to do.

On another occasion, Jesus *efficiently* sent and delegated seventy of
His followers in an evangelistic mission: "After these things the Lord
appointed other seventy also, and sent them two and two before His face
into every city and place, whither He Himself would come" (Luke 10:1).

In His miraculous feeding of the five thousand, Jesus accomplished
that feat in an *orderly* fashion as He first settled and divided the people.
Mark records that Jesus "commanded them to make all sit down by companies upon the green grass. And they sat down in ranks, by hundreds,
and by fifties" (Mark 6:39-40). Our Lord was gifted as an organizer.

Our working definition of the gift of organizing is to conceive, coordinate, and complete a project that involves others working together to
reach a common goal. As applied to the church, the process involves
everyone serving together in "bearing the burden" (Ex. 18:22), so that it
is easier for the church leaders. The result is that the church is "able to
endure" (Ex. 18:23), year after year, in an authoritative, orderly, and efficient manner.

Examples of Organizers

Jethro, Joseph, Nehemiah and Jesus are examples of gifted organizers.
There are others in Scripture who organized, but not necessarily from a
primary motivation of organization.

Exhortations to Organizers

Special *exhortations to organizers* are found in verses 8 and 14 of Romans 12. Verse eight exhorts organizers ("he that ruleth") to exercise their gift with diligence. Verse fourteen exhorts the organizer to "Bless them which persecute you: bless, and curse not."

If your job is in an area of organizing, you may realize that you cannot make everybody happy. In the process, people can get awfully upset with you. When anyone is in the top leadership position of a business or organization, there are those who do not have anything better to do than to blame the leader for whatever is wrong in their lives. The Lord especially had to encourage Joshua when he succeeded Moses as the leader of the nation of Israel. He stepped from his role of service, his major motivational gift, into the leader of the overall organizational structure of the nation of Israel. Three times in the first chapter of Joshua, the Bible records that the Lord exhorted Joshua to be strong and courageous. As the leader of Israel, Joshua needed the encouragement and exhorting because there are always those with the critical eye and a tongue ready to flame with criticism who try to offset the failures in their lives by placing the blame on someone other than themselves.

First, the organizer is exhorted to be diligent – to perform one's work with intense eagerness and effort. The key to being diligent is to *be conscientious*. To be conscientious is to be dutiful, meticulous, and observant. An organizer does not focus on one thing all the time, but reviews everything that is part of the process. The organizer has to be conscientious to know if someone is having a problem so that he can provide assistance until the problem is corrected. When an organizer is conscientious, he has delegated properly enough so that work continues even when the organizer is not in a hands-on position.

An organizer is also to "bless them which persecute you." The organizer is to find ways to *be complimentary* to those who are not nice to him. A popular cliché says, "If you cannot find something nice to say about someone, then do not say anything at all." Now the personality and actions of some individuals sure do make that hard to do. But the Bible exhorts an organizer to work at finding something complimentary he can sincerely say about those who cause him problems. When he is able to do that, the organizer will find that the attitude of his persecutors will change toward him. People like to have nice things said about them, even by those with whom they disagree. When an organizer can get in the habit of complimenting his critics, it usually will win them over as supporters.

The third exhortation to organizers is "Bless, and curse not." An organizer should not react the way everyone else reacts. There is a tendency in our society that when someone says something cutting about you, then you should come back with a stronger cutting comment about that person. The organizer is not to react in such a manner. An organizer is to *be courteous*. When an organizer listens to something a criticizing person says, the organizer might even be able to get a good idea from their statement. The organizer can then build on the positive.

Expectation Organizers Need to Exercise Most

An organizer needs to exercise *constraint* in order to stay centered on the project with which he is concerned and to keep from being distracted by complaints and criticism, which confuse and complicate a project. When someone is critical of how he organizes and progresses with a project, the organizer cannot allow that criticism to personally affect him to the point of discouragement.

Whatever project an organizer is overseeing, he needs to exercise constraint so that he stays centered on the project and is not distracted from the task at hand.

Characteristics of Organizers

Something unique is added to this motivational gift that does not apply to the others: **planning** and **personality**.

Planning

Jethro, Joseph, and Nehemiah all shared certain similarities in their approach, application, action and organization for projects. In the overall planning process, each practiced the following: *observation, intercession, evaluation, administration, implementation,* and *expectation.*

The Bible informs us that Jethro sat down and *observed* his son-in-law, Moses, perform his duties for one day (Ex. 18:14). Fortunately, he and Moses enjoyed a close relationship. Therefore, after a very long day on the job, Jethro was able to say, "Son, what are you doing?" He was not demeaning or demanding. Jethro inquired in a way that Moses responded to well. It was done in a way that helped Moses. Jethro observed how Moses was going about his job, and he had a better plan for Moses that would allow him to go about his work more efficiently and more effectively.

Intercession can actually begin before the observation occurs. Before Jethro actually interceded *verbally* with Moses as to how he should better organize his life, Moses and Jethro were involved in worship together. Along with some of the other spiritual leaders of Israel (Ex. 18:11-12), they had a time of prayer and worship to the Lord. It resulted from the rejoicing of Jethro that came over him after his son-in-law reported to him what God had done for Israel. After a time of *spiritual intercession* for one another, Jethro then followed with more practical intercession in his verbal suggestions of a better way for Moses to conduct his affairs. An organizer intercedes for people in two ways. He either goes to God on behalf of other people or he goes to people personally and relates to them how to do something better than they are presently doing it. A true organizer, who exercises his gift under the control of the Holy Spirit, intercedes on behalf of the people of God. A Spirit-controlled organizer has a wonderful prayer life and relationship with the Lord.

After the organizer has observed, and then gone through the process of intercession, he exercises *evaluation.* Verses 17-19 give Jethro's evaluation. In verse 17, Jethro began his evaluation by telling Moses that the way Moses was organized in fulfilling his leadership was inefficient. Jethro then told Moses why his organizational style was lacking. When an organizer gives constructive criticism, he always has a better plan for how to make things work out for the best.

The *administration* of the better plan that Jethro outlined for Moses is given in verse nineteen of Exodus 18. Organizers are sometimes the ones who are the administrators of what they have organized. They get into the process and practice hands-on administration. But there are also times when the organizer is not the hands-on person who sees that a plan is carried out.

For example, there are consultants who specialize in helping churches to raise funds for building programs. A consultant will work with a church over several months, assisting the church in organizing itself to motivate its members to financially give above what they are presently giving to the church on a regular basis. The consultant is seldom on the scene for more than a couple of days at a time. He is usually working with several other churches simultaneously. Eventually, the consultant's work is done, and he moves on. The pastor, along with a specially formed committee, will lead the church in carrying out the fund-raising program. But it is the plan that the consultant helped the church to set up. It is also the same plan that is used with all the other churches that have contracted with that particular fund-raising company. I have been a member of churches that used such services on three occasions. On each occasion, the churches raised the desired amount of money, using the program and plan that was organized for them.

Some organizers may also be the administrators of their plans. But some may operate like Jethro and the church fund-raising companies. They tell what needs to be done and how to do it. The administering of it is left to someone else.

Following the initial set up and organizing of how a plan is to be administered, there comes the actual *implementation* process. Exodus 18:20-22 records what Jethro counseled Moses that he needed to do to implement Jethro's plan for better organization. Moses was to find able, truthful men, who feared God and hated covetousness. Moses was to place them over varying numbers of people. These able men were to depend on their character, qualifications, and ability to work with the people for whom they were responsible.

When the planning has been carried out to completion, the *expectation* has been reached. One expectation in our churches is to be able to endure (Ex. 18:23). That was the ultimate purpose of the organizational plan that Jethro proposed for Moses.

Our churches ought to be organized so that they are able to keep growing and going year after year. There are churches today that are not organized to endure. For example, some churches are top heavy with older members because the organization broke down somewhere through the years in reaching new and younger members. If the organizational plan of the church in outreach does not get corrected, the church may die out in a few years. Is your church organized to reach new members? Does your church follow sound, biblical financial practices so that if there are some lean years, when membership may decline, the church can continue to operate and minister? There are many factors that can cause the numerical growth of a church to stabilize and the membership numbers to decrease, even when a church is active in outreach visitation. A church needs to be organized in such a way that it can handle such lean times. The ultimate expectation of a church's organizational structure is for the church to be able to endure.

Another example of this pattern is Joseph. His dreams had prophetic significance. God gave Joseph an ability to learn the meaning of his own dreams and the dreams of others. In his day, he was the only one who was capable of this. As a young boy, the dreams of Joseph angered his brothers (Gen. 37:19-20). His brothers sarcastically gave him the nickname, "Dreamer." But, oh, what a dreamer he was!

As the life of Joseph progressed, he was eventually sold into slavery by his jealous brothers. He was bought by some Midianite merchants who later sold him to an Egyptian. He ended up as a servant to Potiphar, who was a high ranking Egyptian officer in Pharaoh's army. Even in slavery, the Bible says that "the Lord was with Joseph, and he was a prosperous man; and he was in the house of his master the Egyptian" (Gen. 39:2). This was not unnoticed by Potiphar. The Bible says, "And his master saw that the LORD was with him, and that the LORD made all that he did to prosper in his hand. And Joseph found grace in his sight, and he served him: and he made him overseer over his house, and all that he had he put into his hand" (Gen. 39:3-4).

In the twelfth chapter of Romans, the word "ruleth" is the translation given in the King James Version that designates the motivational gift of organizing. The Greek word, translated as "ruleth" in the King James Version, is the equivalent to the Hebrew word "overseer." Both words have the same picture in their use as that of the term "bishop." The terms refer to someone who can oversee the process of getting a job done.

The Bible reveals that "the LORD blessed the Egyptian's house for Joseph's sake; and the blessing of the LORD was upon all that he had in the house, and in the field. And he left all that he had in Joseph's hand; and he knew not ought he had, save the bread which he did eat. And Joseph was a goodly person, and well favoured" (Gen. 39:5-6). Potiphar placed a great amount of trust in Joseph as an outstanding overseer.

But Potiphar's wife desired Joseph and sought for an adulterous relationship with him. Joseph knew that she was the one thing he was not to have the rule over in Potiphar's home. Out of anger at Joseph's rejection, Potiphar's wife falsely accused Joseph of attempted physical advances.

She was so convincing that Potiphar believed her and had Joseph thrown into prison.

What happened to Joseph when he was imprisoned? He approached life the same in prison as he did as a servant in the home of Potiphar. The results were the same: "But the LORD was with Joseph, and shewed him mercy, and gave him favour in the sight of the keeper of the prison. And the keeper of the prison committed to Joseph's hand all the prisoners that were in the prison; and whatsoever they did there, he was the doer of it. The keeper of the prison looked not to any thing that was under his hand; because the LORD was with him, and that which he did, the LORD made it to prosper" (Gen. 39:23-24).

Joseph was made the head trustee in the prison. He assigned duties and responsibilities to the other prisoners and made sure that they carried them out. It may sound hard to believe, but Joseph was right where God wanted him to be. Had not Joseph been in prison, he would have never become second in rank, only to Pharaoh, over all Egypt.

While Joseph was in prison, two of the employees of Pharaoh were imprisoned. Pharaoh had become suspecting and so angered with his chief butler and his chief steward that he had them thrown into jail (Gen. 40:1-3). Each man had an unusual dream while in prison. The characteristic of *observation* was exemplified in Joseph as the Bible says, "Joseph came in unto them in the morning, and looked upon them, and, behold, they were sad" (Gen. 40:6). Joseph was simply doing what was natural for an organizer to do. He was being an observer. As an exhorter sees a problem and is ready to offer steps of action on how to deal with it, an organizer sees something that is not right and he is ready to correct it. So Joseph then *interceded* by asking the two men, "Wherefore look ye so sadly today?" (Gen. 40:7). Joseph was able to interpret the meaning of the dream of each man. Sure enough, what Joseph predicted would happen became reality. The chief butler (steward, cupbearer) was restored back to his original position of serving Pharaoh. The chief baker was put to death, probably because he had tried to poison Pharaoh.

Two years passed after Joseph had interpreted the dreams of the chief butler and the chief steward, but it was all in God's timing. It all worked out for Joseph's good. Pharaoh had a dream, but none of his wise men could determine the meaning of it. Then the chief butler remembered how Joseph interpreted his dream while he was in prison two years earlier (Gen. 41:12), so he mentioned Joseph to Pharaoh. Pharaoh sent for Joseph. He heard the dream of Pharaoh, was able to interpret it, and gave his *evaluation* of it (Gen. 40:33). Since there were going to be seven years of great plenty in Egypt, followed by seven years of famine (Gen. 40:29-30), Joseph suggested that Pharaoh needed to set a wise and discreet man over the land of Egypt. This man was to help Egypt take advantage of the seven years of plenty in order to endure the seven years of famine. In verses 34-35 of Genesis 41, Joseph told how the plan was to be *implemented*. As the plan was implemented, the *expectation* – "that the land perish not through the famine" (Gen. 40:36) – was fulfilled. The plan needed to be *administered* by the wisest and most discreet man whom Pharaoh could find. Even Pharaoh was quick to determine about Joseph: "Can we find such a one as this is, a man in whom the Spirit of God is?" (Gen. 40:38).

Because God was with him, and he responsibly used his gift of organizational expertise, Joseph went from prison to a palace in just a matter of hours.

The first chapter of Nehemiah records that Nehemiah was informed that the wall of Jerusalem, so vital to the protection and security of the city, had been torn down for years, and no effort had been made to rebuild the wall. As a result, the remnant of Jews left in Jerusalem were in great affliction and reproach (vs. 2-3). The first reaction of Nehemiah was *intercession*:

And it came to pass, when I heard these words, that I sat down and wept, and mourned certain days, and fasted, and prayed before the God of heaven, and said, 'I beseech Thee, O LORD God of heaven, the great and terrible God, that keepeth covenant and mercy for them that love Him and observe His commandments: let thine ear now be attentive, and thine eyes open, that thou mayest hear the prayer of thy servant, which I pray before Thee now, day and night, for the children of Israel thy servants, and confess the sins of the children of Israel, which we have sinned against Thee: both I and my father's house have sinned.' (Neh. 1:4-6)

Nehemiah began to intercede for himself and his people before God. Based upon what he had been told and how he felt led by the Lord, Nehemiah decided to lead out in the rebuilding of the wall of Jerusalem. He first had to get the king's permission because he was the king's cupbearer (Neh. 1:11). Nehemiah remained in a spirit of prayer until he received permission from the king.

His *observation* and *evaluation* are recorded in chapter two. After receiving the king's permission, Nehemiah traveled to Jerusalem to begin the organizational process that was necessary to rebuild the wall of Jerusalem. He did not come to Jerusalem and announce the moment he arrived, "This is what we are going to do." When people are organized, they do not call a press conference right off and reveal elaborate dreams without a plan to reach those dreams. First, they confirm to see if a prospective project is what God really wants them to do, and they determine how God is going to make it possible. Nehemiah knew that God wanted the wall of Jerusalem rebuilt, but he also knew that there were those in Jerusalem who were opposed to it. He knew that they would be his enemies throughout the project. So Nehemiah first wanted to get everything in place. He wanted to have a plan ready to present, that he knew would work, before he announced it to anyone.

Chapter two reveals to us his first move upon arriving in Jerusalem: "I arose in the night, I and some few men with me; neither told I any man what my God had put in my heart to do at Jerusalem: neither was there any beast with me, save the beast that I rode upon" (Neh. 2:12). A "few men" is often one of the keys to the success of an organizer.

Verse thirteen informs us that he made some observations: "And I went out by night by the gate of the valley, even before the dragon well, and to the dung port, and viewed the walls of Jerusalem, which were broken down, and the gates thereof were consumed with fire." Only then was Nehemiah ready to verbally announce to the people what he thought should be done and how he proposed it could be carried out. Verses 17-18 summarize his evaluation:

> Then said I unto them, 'Ye see the distress that we are in, how Jerusalem lieth waste, and the gates thereof are burned with fire: come, and let us build up the wall of Jerusalem, that we be no more a reproach.' Then I told them of the hand of my God which was good upon me; as also the king's words that he had spoken unto me. And they said, 'Let us rise up and build.' So they strengthened their hands for this good work.

Nehemiah first interceded to God on behalf of the people of Jerusalem. Then he came and observed the situation first hand. He next interceded face to face with the Jews in Jerusalem, giving them his evaluation of how they needed to rebuild the wall of Jerusalem. He had a good plan, and he presented it well because the people responded, "Let us rise and build" (v. 18).

Chapters three and four give detailed description of how Nehemiah's plan to rebuild the wall was to be *administered* and *implemented*. In this project, Nehemiah led the effort to rebuild the wall around Jerusalem. The *expectation* of Nehemiah's plan, the completion of the rebuilding of the wall, is recorded in verse 15 of chapter six: "So the wall was finished in the twenty and fifth day of the month Elul, in fifty and two days." What happened between the time they started to rebuild the wall and completed it were not 52 easy days. It required a lot of hard work. There were some major distractions. The people feared that they were going to be attacked. But when a person with the gift of organizing comes on the scene, and the people know that the organizer is right with God, telling them what God wants them to do, people will get behind such a person with everyone participating in the process.

Personality

Organizers tend toward certain personality traits: they are dreamers, yet dependable. They are decisive, good in giving direction, able to delegate and last for the duration.

Authentic Dreamers

Joseph was called "The Dreamer" by his brothers. That is an appropriate description for an organizer. Organizers are dreamers, as we all have a tendency to be, at times, but they are *authentic dreamers*. When an organizer dreams a project in his mind, he *sees the entire picture and aspires to attain it*. Organizers can envision in their mind the whole picture, and as they do, they get motivated to do it. When Nehemiah was informed about the condition of the wall around Jerusalem, he began to authentically dream. He saw the picture in his mind of what it presently looked like. But he also saw the picture of what it could become, and he aspired to attain it. He could *see it already accomplished*. As an organizer envisions a project in his mind, he can see it completed.

When a church plans to enlarge its facilities, the authentic dreamers in the church have already seen the picture before the project has been approved and begun. The authentic dreamers may have envisioned a building project for their church five years earlier. At that time, the church may have only been filling their auditorium to half the capacity for worship services. The person with the motivational gift of organizing has seen the auditorium filled to capacity, in his mind, before it ever happens.

He has already seen a picture, in his mind, of what a new auditorium should look like. When talk begins around the church about expansion, the organizers will *seek to set it into action*. They seek to set it into motion because they see, as God has motivated them to see, an area that needs to be organized, or a project that needs to be planned and implemented. When an organizer is motivated to organize a possible project, he sees the need as authentic, because the Lord has placed it upon the heart of the organizer.

Absolutely Dependable

Organizers are *absolutely dependable*. When a person with the gift of organizing commits to a project, you can absolutely depend on him to be there and do his part, even if he is the only one who shows up.

Why is this trait a characteristic of organizers? It is because the absolute dependability of an organizer is first developed *in his will*. As an organizer delights in the Lord, his desires become the same as the Lord's. He develops a trust in the Lord where he knows that he can depend completely upon the Lord. As a result, it makes the organizer a dependable person because he knows that the Lord will accomplish His will, regardless of the difficulty of a project.

Joseph had such trust in God. When Joseph was told by the chief baker and chief butler of Pharaoh that "we have dreamed a dream, and there is no interpreter of it," Joseph replied, "Do not interpretations belong to God?" (Gen. 40:8). When he was brought from prison to stand before Pharaoh, Joseph replied in a similar fashion, "And Pharaoh said unto Joseph, 'I have dreamed a dream, and there is none that can interpret it: and I have heard say of thee, that thou canst understand a dream to interpret it.' And Joseph answered Pharaoh, saying, 'It is not in me: God shall give Pharaoh an answer of peace'" (Gen. 41:15-16). Joseph had developed such a trust in God in his will that he knew the Lord would be absolutely dependable to fulfill His will through Joseph.

Joseph developed this high level of character and communion with God because he delighted himself in the Lord. God not only gave Joseph the desires of his heart, but he gave Joseph wisdom and understanding in his heart.

As an organizer is one who is absolutely dependable, absolute dependability is *what he desires in his workers*. The organizer wants loyalty from his workers. Instead of many workers whom he does not know that he can completely trust, he prefers fewer workers than needed, if they are good, absolutely dependable workers. When an organizer feels that someone has not been loyal and dependable, he may resort to some strong measures to insure that it does not spread and lead to a breakdown in loyalty and dependability among his other workers. During the rebuilding of the wall of Jerusalem, it came to the attention of Nehemiah that some of the wealthier Jews were loaning money to their fellow Jews at unfair interest rates and difficult repayment terms. Nehemiah reprimanded those who were loaning money in such a manner. Even though they responded accordingly to Nehemiah's rebuke and agreed to his terms for being restored back to good graces, Nehemiah made them take an oath (Neh. 5:12) to pledge that they would follow the terms of restoration.

Appropriately Decisive

Organizers are also *appropriately decisive*. The organizer knows how, when, where, with whom, and to what extent his decisions need to be, especially as they affect other people. An organizer knows when he needs to be *firm*. With appropriately decisive firmness, Nehemiah corrected the wealthy Jews who were loaning money, with inappropriate interest rates and repayment terms, to their not so wealthy fellow Jews. Their act was about to cause contention during the rebuilding of the Jerusalem wall. Some of the Jews who had borrowed money could not meet the repayment guidelines and were in danger of losing their property and their homes. They were helping to rebuild the wall. If they had to move away from Jerusalem to find other jobs, the rebuilding of the wall would be greatly hindered, maybe even left unfinished. So Nehemiah acted decisively and appropriately to correct the problem.

Organizers make firm, *fair* decisions. That is how Joseph dealt with his brothers when they came to Egypt to purchase food for their father and their own families. He felt that he needed to test his brothers to see if they were repentant of selling him into slavery many years before. He first dealt firmly with his brothers, who did not recognize him. Joseph wanted to know that they had not treated their younger brother, Benjamin, as they had treated him. When Joseph saw the evidence of his brothers' sorrow and repentance for how they had treated him, and when Judah offered to be Joseph's slave in place of Benjamin, Joseph knew that there had been true repentance. It had been Judah's idea, many years before, to sell Joseph (Gen. 37:26-27). Joseph was then very fair with his brothers. He forgave them, and he provided more food and supplies than they needed. He even had all his family move to Egypt so that he could help to provide for their well-being.

The Dreamer's dreams (Gen. 37:5-9), which Joseph's brothers had greatly despised at one time, had become reality. Joseph acknowledged to his brothers that it had all been for their good:

> *Now therefore be not grieved, nor angry with yourselves, that ye sold me hither: for God did send me before you to preserve life. For these two years hath the famine been in the land: and yet there are five years, in the which there shall neither be earing nor harvest. And God sent me before you to preserve you a posterity in the earth, and to save your lives by a great deliverance. (Gen. 45:5-7)*

An organizer is appropriately decisive because his decisions will be made when they are *fitting*. An organizer knows when a decision needs to be made on the spot. Most of us have decisions of concern to us that we want to be made immediately, but it may not be appropriate and fitting to make the decision at that moment. An organizer will make immediate decisions, but if it is not absolutely necessary to decide on the spot, he will get all the facts first. He may also feel that he needs to intercede with God and receive more direction about a situation. Nehemiah would not even let anyone know what God had put in his heart to do at Jerusalem (Neh. 2:12) until he had been able to observe and evaluate firsthand the condition of the wall and the conditions surrounding the rebuilding of the wall. When he knew how he was going to do it, and he was sure that it could and must be done, he then felt that it was fitting to make his decision and intentions known to his fellow Jews. An organizer will make a decision when it is best to make it, in the right time and in the right way.

Able Direction

Organizers are able to get things done because of their ability to give **able direction**. *Authoritative in demeanor*, an organizer gives able direction. He has a presence about him in his conduct and conversation that is convincing, commanding, and influential.

Jethro had such a presence about him. When Jethro came to visit his son-in-law Moses, the spiritual leaders of Israel sought out his wisdom and advice. They made it a point to come to him and to worship with Jethro (Ex. 18:12). He was the kind of person to whom others were drawn. His presence just seemed to command respect. On another occasion, Hobab, the son of Jethro and the brother-in-law of Moses, visited with Moses (Num. 10:29-32). Jethro may have gotten too old to travel, so he sent his son to get a report on how Moses and the Israelites were getting along. Evidently, Hobab was as gifted in organizing as his father. Moses asked Hobab to remain with the Israelites throughout their journey to the Promised Land (Num. 10:29). But Hobab felt that he needed to return to his own land and his own people (v. 30). Moses respectfully and sincerely made another appeal: "And he said, 'Leave us not, I pray thee; forasmuch as thou knowest how we are to encamp in the wilderness, and thou mayest be to us instead of eyes. And it shall be, if thou go with us, yea, it shall be, that what goodness the LORD shall do unto us, the same will we do unto thee'" (Num. 10:31-32). From the previous visit of Jethro, and the organizational counsel that he gave to Moses, the Israelites had experienced firsthand the benefits and effectiveness of Jethro's administrative ability. That same ability was seen in the demeanor of Hobab. Now, they wanted him to be as their "eyes." There was an authoritative, appealing presence about Hobab, like his father, to which Moses and the people of Israel were drawn.

An organizer is adept at giving able direction because he is *attentive to details*. To be the eyes for a mobile nation of over two million people, such as the Israelites on exodus from Egypt, one would have to be able to focus on details. An organizer notices what others consider small details, but which are essential to complete a project properly. The organizer knows all the resources that are needed to keep the process flowing smoothly. The Israelites had learned that Jethro was a keen observer, and they also saw it in his son, Hobab. Both men knew what ingredients were necessary to keep the nation of Israel on the move in an orderly manner.

Another reason why organizers give able direction is because they are *alert to distractions*. The organizer anticipates that distractions will come, and he confronts them. An organizer gets up front, face to face, and deals with distractions quickly and confidently (see Neh. 4 and 6). His confidence comes because he has prayed about it and knows what God wants him to do (see Neh. 4:4-5,9,15,20; 6:9-14). The organizer is willing to endure opposition because he knows that in any project you cannot please everyone. He offsets it and strives to keep opposition and other distractions from affecting his workers.

Agreeable Delegation

The organizer knows how to exercise *agreeable delegation*. He just seems to know who is right for each assigned task. The organizer has the knack of being able to place people in the right positions.

In dealing with the demands the work requires, an organizer shows keen *discretion*. To prepare for seven years of famine following seven years of plenty, Joseph told Pharaoh to "look out a man discreet and wise, and set him over the land of Egypt" (Gen. 41:33). It would take a person who knew how to agreeably delegate responsibility to take advantage of gathering and storing food in the plentiful years in order to survive the coming years of famine. Once an organizer comes to the forefront in regards to a project that needs to be organized, it is not hard to determine who is gifted as an organizer. After listening to Joseph's evaluation, suggestions for administration, and advice on how to implement the plan for Egypt's survival during the years of famine, Pharaoh knew the man for the job. He chose Joseph. Pharaoh acknowledged to Joseph that "there is none so discreet and wise as thou art" (Gen. 41:39).

Because an organizer has keen discretion in agreeably delegating responsibilities, the *division* of assignments is made without disagreement and dissension. Organizers have an ability to break down what might appear to be impossible tasks into smaller, achievable tasks that are just right for the workers. Many felt the rebuilding of the wall around Jerusalem was an impossible task. Such feelings were due to the strongly antagonistic opponents of the Jews and the enormous difficulty of the work that lay before the Jews. But Nehemiah had discretion as to how to divide the work assignments so that the people would have extra motivation to work. For those whose homes bordered the wall, he had them repair and rebuild the part of the wall that was located next to their homes (see Neh. 3:23-24,29-30). There was extra incentive to do the work more quickly and thoroughly when the completion of their assignment had an immediate benefit in providing for their own protection, safety, and security.

Organizers are able to agreeably delegate assignments because they observe the *dexterity* of their workers. An organizer notices the skills of his workers, and he assigns tasks in those areas in which his workers are skilled. It makes the job less stressful for the workers because they know that they can do the work, and they are more confident in their work. It also helps to get the work done more quickly and with quality. The workers are not prone to make mistakes when they are doing what fits their skills.

When it was time to build the tabernacle, the perfect organizer, the Lord God, led Moses to make the right choice in choosing those who would do the work. He chose those who had the dexterity to do the tasks that were assigned to them. In Exodus 35, the Bible provides an excellent example of delegating according to dexterity:

> And Moses said unto the children of Israel, "See, the LORD hath called by name Bezaleel the son of Uri, the son of Hur, of the tribe of Judah; and he hath filled him with the spirit of God, in wisdom, in understanding, and in knowledge, and in all manner of workmanship; and to devise curious works, to work in gold, and in silver, and in brass, and in the cutting of stones, to set them, and in carving of wood, to make any manner of cunning work. And he hath put in his heart that he may teach, both he, and Aholiab, the son of Ahisamach, of the tribe of Dan. Them hath he filled with wisdom of heart, to work all manner of work, of the engraver, and of the cunning workman, and of the embroiderer, in blue, and in purple, in scarlet, and in fine linen, and of the weaver, even of them that do any work, and of those that devise cunning work." (Ex. 35:30-35)

God showed Moses how work assignments were to be delegated according to the way the work would best be done. It was best done by dividing responsibilities to fit the skills of the workers. Spirit-controlled organizers exhibit such discretion when they oversee an area of work that God has made possible for them to plan and to implement.

Accountable for the Duration

Organizers are **accountable for the duration**, believing that what they are led to organize is ordained of God. They *face a problem or a project* by first assessing the need, then accepting a project to organize once convinced that God is in it.

When an organizer responds to a prompting of God, his participation in a project is preceded by *fervent prayer*. He will continue to bathe a project in prayer after he has begun his leadership over it. Nehemiah is an outstanding example of how an organizer needs to approach all facets of a project in fervent, consistent prayer.

The organizer has a plan to follow, and he is faithful to *follow the plan prayerfully*. Some of us may get diverted away from our goals and projects because we get distracted by other things or we let discouragement by temporary setbacks or slow progress impatiently cause us to move on to brighter appearing opportunities. But not an organizer. As a project proceeds, an organizer sticks by his plan, regardless of distractions and the rate of progress. As a result, organizers know the satisfaction of a *finished product* over and over again.

Unless God moves an organizer from a project, he will not quit. An organizer will not move on before a project, which he feels called by God to organize, is finished, unless he is fired or removed from his position of leadership. Most of the sports coaches who get fired are probably organizers, especially the ones who are dismissed because their team has been in decline. In the mind of the coach who has gotten fired, he had an expectation toward which he was seeking to lead his team. Even though his team had experienced one or more disappointing seasons, each disappointing season was only a temporary setback to the coach with the gift of organizing. The coaches who are motivated as organizers believe that their plan is eventually going to work. Coaches, who have the motivational gift of organizing, are accountable for the duration, unless their superiors fire them.

Cautions for the Gift of Organizing
Misunderstandings

Because organizers are dreamers, they are sometimes misjudged as being too *idealistic*. At the funeral of Robert F. Kennedy, his brother, Senator Ted Kennedy, described Robert by this quote: "Some people see things as they are and ask, 'Why?' I dream things that never were and ask, 'Why not?'"

Almost all organizers have big dreams. When you know an organizer who has dreamed a dream that may appear too idealistic for most folks, if the organizer is one who walks and talks his faith, hear him out. He has the boldness to ask: "Why not?"

Nehemiah had his doubters, but he accomplished what they thought was too big a dream. As a result, his enemies and doubters perceived that his work was wrought of God. The Bible says, "And it came to pass, that when all our enemies heard thereof, and all the heathen that were about us saw these things, they were much cast down in their own eyes: for they perceived that this work was wrought of our God" (Neh. 6:16). One only needs to read a few more verses on into the next chapter to see why an organizer like Nehemiah should be taken seriously. After the rebuilding of the wall of Jerusalem, more organizing was still needed. As with his other dreams and ideas, Nehemiah acknowledged that God put it into his heart (Neh. 7:5).

Organizers may appear to be too *individualistic*. Because the organizer is so strongly insistent on dependability, he will be there to fulfill his responsibility even if no one else comes through. But he expects the same kind of commitment from everyone else. As we should all be reminded, even reprimanded, at times, for not fulfilling a commitment, an organizer will tend to let you know when you have neglected your responsibility. If you are not mature enough to handle deserved correction, you may misjudge a reprimanding organizer as being egotistical.

Because a project may be pressing, and an organizer allows for little slack, he may be misjudged as being *imperious*. To keep a project on schedule, an organizer sometimes has to be a little domineering and overbearing, but it is with the intent of keeping the workers with a "mind to work" (Neh. 4:6). No matter how demanding and difficult conditions may be, when people have a "mind to work," they will.

There are times when a decision must be made, even against what would be the popular tide of opinion. An organizer will often be misjudged as one who is egotistical because he often has to say, "My decision goes." The organizer responds that way because he realizes in his role as the chief administrator, "the buck stops here." A godly organizer will accept the blame, if a decision he made, that was not the choice of the majority, proves to have been the wrong decision. But as an organizer allows God to guide him in making his decisions, the organizer will make the right decisions.

An organizer may also be misunderstood as being *indolent*. Because an organizer delegates so much, and most of his work is not "hands on," a misunderstanding that some people have about an organizer is that he is not a hard worker and lazy. Those people do not see the many hours an organizer has put in prior to the beginning of a project, as well as the hours he often puts in before those participating in a project arrive for the hands on work. Often, too, after the workers have gone, an organizer can still be found on site, assessing the work of that day, planning for the next day's assignments, and working out hindrances.

There are those who feel that organizers get too *infatuated* with whatever they are organizing. Organizers do get obsessed with seeing a project come together, but they normally do it with proper balance. From reading the book of Nehemiah, it is evident that he was obsessed, but in a proper balance and perspective, with getting the wall rebuilt around Jerusalem. He knew that it was the will of God for him to lead out in organizing and implementing that project. The way in which it all came together and was successfully completed proved that God had compelled Nehemiah and that the touch of God was on his life.

Misuses

Since organizers are often in an authority position over people, the misuse of this spiritual gift has negative effects that are far reaching and are felt by many different people.

As organizers have a tendency to be dreamers in visualizing projects and concepts, in the flesh their dreams are not authentic, but *unbelievable*. Such an organizer builds "air castles" in his mind for projects that exceed what is really appropriate and needed.

I know of pastors who start building programs every time they move to another pastorate, even if there is not really a need. Usually, the pastor will convince the church that it needs to build more facilities in order to grow. He convinces the members that their present facilities are not appealing enough or big enough. He makes them believe that people are not joining the church because the facilities need to be more modern and attractive, and more spacious. So often, the church goes deep in debt in a building program. The anticipated rapid growth does not come (remember, people attract people the most, not buildings) and the church finds itself consumed in debt with limited funds for other needs. The usual result from unneeded building programs is that the pastor who got the church into such a financial mess tends to move on from the church to a new field of ministry. Unless he has learned his lesson, and he has gotten under the control of the Holy Spirit, he does the same thing in his next pastorate. Pastors who hastily lead churches into building programs probably have the gift of organizing, but they have allowed their heart to run away from their head. Instead of dreaming what is practical because it is divinely providential, they dream what is unprompted by God and impractical for their church.

Organizers can misuse their gift by becoming *unbearable*. This ties in with their characteristic of being absolutely dependable and their desiring that quality in their workers. An organizer, who is not Spirit-controlled, can be completely intolerant of disloyalty. Such an organizer needs to learn to bear some of the things that are nuisances to him because it teaches him to forgive.

One of the least enjoyable organizers to work with is one who is *unbridled*. In the flesh, an unbridled organizer can have a scorching tongue. If an organizer is in a supervisory position, who has a habit of berating his workers for their mistakes, he keeps his workers at a higher level of stress than what is normal. His workers will tend to face their work more as a job than as a calling. Unbridled organizers have a higher turnover rate among their workers than those who treat their workers more considerately and professionally.

In the flesh, an organizer may also misuse his spiritual gift by becoming *unbefitting*. An organizer, who has a faithful walk with the Lord, is appropriately decisive in making decisions that are fitting and fair. The organizer, who is unbefitting, will make decisions that are not fitting and fair, and just for spite, he may purposely make such decisions. You can imagine what such actions do for morale.

Another misuse of this spiritual gift is that an organizer can be *unbending*. As organizers know that you cannot always please everybody, and that there are times when an unpopular decision has to be made, unbending organizers want it to be their way all the time. They are not open and willing to hear or see what may be a better way to do something. Their philosophy of leadership is "my way or the highway."

An organizer may misuse his gift by becoming *unbound*. As an organizer likes dependability, he may be lenient with good workers, even though those workers may be morally weak. Paul reconfirmed what Christ taught (Matt. 16:6) that "a little leaven leaveneth the whole lump" (1

Cor. 5:6; Gal. 5:9). Even if morally weak workers are dependable workers, it is not good to allow them to work alongside those who are spiritually and morally strong. An allowance is possible if the morally weak workers follow a code of ethics, and if they are respectful and courteous in their conduct and conservation on the job. There are those who do not want to be around "trash" talk and coarse jokes and conversation. The apostle Paul also said, "Be not deceived: evil communications corrupt good manners" (1 Cor. 15:33). It is going to have a negative effect when an organizer becomes unbound in who he hires as workers and how he allows them to act on the job. It will dampen the morale of those who are not unbound, and it will further infiltrate those who are morally weak. Those who do not have moral convictions tend to make fun of those who do.

If an organizer is not spiritually motivated and guided, he may misuse his gift by becoming *unburdened* about the projects he oversees. When the organizer has a burden from God to do a project, he gets it done in an ethical manner, and he sees it through to completion. But if he gets in a state of being unburdened, he does not care how the job is carried out, as long as it gets done. He may even allow for rules and regulations to be violated, and he may allow and accept work that is inferior to what ought to be done.

Nehemiah helped to lead his people to do what their opponents said could not be done. It was because he received a burden from God, and he maintained his walk with God. If Nehemiah had not maintained that communion and fellowship with the Lord, he could have become discouraged by the distractions and obstacles they faced prior to and during the fifty-two days of hard work it took to rebuild the wall of Jerusalem. If Nehemiah had lost his burden, the wall may have never been rebuilt. We would not have the book of Nehemiah, a book that is such an encouragement concerning how to face adversity and to attempt to do what many think cannot be done.

There are many projects that were never completed and many needs that an organizer never helped to meet because he was *unbroken*. The men and women whom God can use the most effectively are those who have been broken.

What do I mean by "broken"? Unless it has happened to you, it is not easy to explain. One way to describe "brokenness" is that through God's divine discipline you have come completely to the end of yourself and what you are able to do in the power of the flesh. The end result is that your relationship with Jesus is what matters to you more than anything else.

There are times in my life that God had to reduce me to nothing so that He became my everything in order that He could do anything He wanted to do through me. I strive to stay in that state of mind. It is when I know that I have the most Christ possible in my life. It is when I decrease and He increases (John 3:30). It is when Philippians 4:13 stays current in my life because Christ is preeminent in my life (Col. 1:18). It is the state in which I do feel that I can do all things through Christ who gives me the strength to do it.

If an organizer does not have a broken spirit over the absolute need of a project, it may not ever get completed. Nehemiah was broken over the spiritual condition of his people (Neh. 1:4-9) in addition to the physical condition of Jerusalem and the social condition of his people. His brokenness led him to intercede for his people spiritually, first. That put them in a right relationship with God to follow His prompting to restore Jerusalem to its proper state.

Conclusion

What wonderful biblical examples we have of those who had the motivational gift of organizing. Their gift made them stand apart from others.

In bringing the application of this gift to our present day, those with this motivational gift often stand apart from the rest of the crowd. The nature of their position lends to their not being able to be just "one of the guys." If an organizer oversees what he has organized, and many people are involved in the project, the organizer's supervisory position calls for him to separate himself to some extent from all the others involved in the project.

All organizers, though, do not fill their role in leadership positions. Much of their work is done behind the scenes, and often, they help to make someone else look good. Usually, behind every pastor, who carries out consistently and efficiently the duties of the position, is not only a loving helpmeet wife, but there is also a secretary who helps him stay on top of his work. The same is true for other professions. A major reason for the success of one in a management position is a secretary who has the gift of organizing.

There is a key word, brought out by Nehemiah, that ought to be descriptive of every organizer, and it is of those who have the most success. An organizer not only has to learn how to rule and to be an overseer, but how wonderful it is when the term "servant" fits the organizer. Nehemiah referred to himself as "thy servant" (Neh. 1:6,11). Above all else, he was the servant of the Lord. Such organizers today will approach a project with a spirit of service that says, "I am organizing this project because it is what the Lord wants me to do, and I want to serve the Lord." In essence, when one is serving the Lord, he is also serving with and for the people whom God has led him to lead.

Let us be thankful for the organizers in the body of Christ who help to keep our churches running orderly. The wisdom of organizers is one of the reasons why our churches are able to endure year after year, decade after decade, century after century. As we all bear the burden of fulfilling the work of our church, it allows all of us to more effectively use our particular special gift of blessing. As a result, we are able to be more effective witnesses for Christ.

8

The Gift of Mercy
"In Deed and in Truth"

*Having then gifts differing according to the grace that is given to us, whether prophecy, let us prophesy according to the proportion of faith; Or ministry, let us wait on our ministering: or he that teacheth, on teaching; Or he that exhorteth, on exhortation: he that giveth, let him do it with simplicity; he that ruleth, with diligence; he that sheweth **mercy**, with cheerfulness...Rejoice with them that do rejoice, and weep with them that weep. (Rom. 12:6-8,15)*

We have come to the seventh, and final, motivational spiritual gift that is listed in our source passage from Romans 12. In a survey compiled by Don and Katie Fortune, co-authors of *Discover Your God-Given Gifts*, 30% of the respondents had the spiritual gift of mercy.[5] The next highest in percentage was the gift of serving, which was the motivational gift of 17% of the respondents. Almost a third of Christians have the gift of mercy as their major motivational spiritual gift. "Mercies" outnumber the next closest motivational gift by almost two to one. So, for about one out of three who read this chapter, your special gift of blessing will be profiled in this chapter.

The person in the Bible, other than Jesus, who best exhibited the gift of mercy was John, a disciple of Jesus and writer of the Gospel of John.

A word that stands out more in the Gospel of John than it does in any of the other Gospels is the word "love." The word "love" is found in the book of John twice as often than in any of the other three Gospel accounts. One can see the gift of mercy in John through his record of the life of Jesus. But in his three epistles, especially the book of 1 John, we really get to see the heart of one whose motivation was the spiritual gift of mercy. A passage in the third chapter of 1 John provides an excellent example of the characteristics of the gift of mercy:

> Hereby perceive we the love of God, because He laid down His life for us: and we ought to lay down our lives for the brethren. But whoso hath this world's good, and seeth his brother have need, and shutteth up his bowels of compassion from him, how dwelleth the love of God in him? My little children, let us not love in word, neither in tongue; but in deed and in truth. And hereby we know that we are of the truth, and shall assure our hearts before Him.
>
> For if our heart condemn us, God is greater than our heart, and knoweth all things. Beloved, if our heart condemn us not, then have we confidence toward God. And whatsoever we ask, we receive of Him, because we keep His commandments, and do those things that are pleasing in His sight.
>
> And this is His commandment, That we should believe on the name of His Son Jesus Christ, and love one another, as He gave us commandment. And he that keepeth His commandments dwelleth in Him, and He in him. And hereby we know that He abideth in us, by the Spirit which He hath given us. (1 John 3:16-24)

One who is motivated by the gift of mercy is going to show his mercy by actions. Mercy includes pity plus action. But there is a key element that a person with the gift of mercy must have in his life to properly fulfill his gift. It is truth. The person with the motivational gift of mercy must be cautious to stay true to the Word of God to make sure that he exhibits his gift not only in deed, but in truth. Otherwise, those with the gift of mercy will find themselves in situations that are not only harmful to them, but also harmful to the people the mercy givers are trying to help.

The passage from 1 John 3 gives a good presentation of compassion balanced with truth. Like John, the person with the motivational gift of mercy wants to encourage and uplift the spirits of other people. The mercy giver wants to show others how difficulties and hurts can be overcome. When one with the gift of mercy properly exercises his gift, he always stresses the importance of following the commandments of God as part of the process of overcoming the difficulties and hurts of life.

A Composite: The Gift of Mercy

Mercy givers (mercies) relate to and remove hindrances and hurts that others experience. They put feet to feelings of pity and passion through action.

Explanation of the Gift of Mercy

In the first chapter of Ruth, the Old Testament records that the husbands of Ruth, her mother-in-law, Naomi, and her sister-in-law, Orpah, died, leaving them as widows. Naomi felt that she should return to her home in Bethlehem-judah from the land of Moab, where she, her husband, and two sons had moved during a time of famine in Judah. Ruth, who was from the land of Moab, wanted to go with her mother-in-law. What a picture of compassion! She empathized with her mother-in-law because she, like her mother-in-law, had lost a husband through death. Naomi, though, felt that her two daughters-in-law should remain in their home-land. The Bible provides a wonderful example of mercy in action responding to the suggestion of the mother-in-law:

> *And Naomi said unto her two daughters in law, 'Go, return*
> *each to her mother's house: the LORD deal kindly with you, as*
> *ye have dealt with the dead, and with me. The LORD grant you*
> *that ye may find rest, each of you in the house of her husband.'*
> *Then she kissed them; and they lifted up their voice, and wept.*

And they said unto her, 'Surely we will return with thee unto thy people.' And Naomi said, 'Turn again, my daughters: why will ye go with me? Are there yet any more sons in my womb, that they may be your husbands? Turn again, my daughters, go your way; for I am too old to have an husband. If I should say, I have hope, if I should have an husband also to night, and should also bear sons; would ye tarry for them till they were grown? Would ye stay for them from having husbands? Nay, my daughters; for it grieveth me much for your sakes that the hand of the LORD is gone out against me.' And they lifted up their voice, and wept again: and Orpah kissed her mother in law; but Ruth clave unto her. (Ruth 1:8-14)

That is a picture of mercy. Ruth stayed with her mother-in-law. The book of Ruth is a balance of mercy and truth because she was obedient to the will of God. God wanted Ruth to leave her own people and go with Naomi to Bethlehem-judah where God had another husband for Ruth.

From the example of Ruth, we can glean that those with the motivational gift of mercy are *emotional*. In saying what they thought were their last farewells, the Bible says of Ruth and Naomi, "They lifted up their voice, and wept" (Ruth 1:9). A few minutes later, "They lifted up their voice, and wept again" (v. 14). Mercies are *embracing*. Ruth "clave unto her" (v. 14).

Mercies are also *endearing*. After Orpah left to return back to her people, Ruth said, "Entreat me not to leave thee, or to return from following after thee: for whither thou goest, I will go; and where thou lodgest, I will lodge: thy people shall be my people, and thy God my God" (Ruth 1:16). That verse is often quoted during wedding ceremonies. Ruth told Naomi, "I want to be wherever you are." She was endeared to her mother-in-law.

There was *empathy* shown on the part of Ruth toward her mother-in-law. Ruth not only sympathized with Naomi over the hurt and sadness Naomi felt, but Ruth could also empathize with Naomi because she knew the same hurt. Ruth hoped that she would be able to help Naomi overcome her sorrow.

Ruth expressed *esteem*, and she was shown esteem. She was known for her compassionate heart. Upon her first meeting with Boaz, the man who eventually became her husband, he acknowledged that he had heard about the compassion and kindness that she had given her mother-in-law (Ruth 2:11). From first hearing about Ruth and from his first meeting with her, Boaz held Ruth in high esteem.

Ruth brought *encouragement* to Naomi. When she first reported to Naomi about meeting Boaz, and how he had provided much for Ruth than she had gleaned from his field, it blessed Naomi (Ruth 2:19-20). When Boaz and Ruth were married, and she bore a son, the women of the community acknowledged and expressed to Naomi how she had been blessed by the Lord (4:14-15) because of Ruth's faithfulness to her. Ruth's mercy brought encouragement to Naomi.

One other obvious trait of those with the gift of mercy is that they are *expressive* in how they relate and communicate with others. Boaz said it so well when he told Ruth, "Blessed be thou of the LORD, my daughter: for thou hast shewed more kindness in the latter end than at the beginning, inasmuch as thou followedst not young men, whether poor or rich. And now, my daughter, fear not; I will do to thee all that thou requirest: for all the city of my people doth know that thou art a virtuous woman" (Ruth 3:10-11). Ruth "walked her talk." She expressed her mercy and kindness to others, and she was recognized for it.

Another Old Testament personality with the gift of mercy, who helps to explain the features of this gift, is Jonathan, the son of King Saul and the best friend of David. In the fourteenth chapter of 1 Samuel, the Bible records an incident where the mercy of Jonathan began to manifest itself in him. He was not aware that his father had charged the Israelite soldiers not to eat any food until the end of the day. Saul had not wanted anything to slow down the Israelites in their pursuit of their fleeing enemy. Jonathan had been used by the Lord, fighting by himself, to defeat a garrison of Philistines (1 Sam. 14:12-14), and he was famished. He saw some honey, he ate some of it, and he was physically strengthened (v. 27). When one of the other soldiers told him about the command of Saul not to eat anything until the evening, Jonathan was critical of his father.

Jonathan was angry with his father because the selfish oath of Saul denied the soldiers of something they badly needed, especially after a fierce battle. Jonathan was *emotional* about it. He said, "My father hath troubled the land: see, I pray you, how mine eyes have been enlightened, because I tasted a little of this honey. How much more, if haply the people had eaten freely to day of the spoil of their enemies which they found? For had there not been now a much greater slaughter among the Philistines?" (1 Sam. 14:29-30). Jonathan felt that allowing the soldiers to eat would not have slowed them down, but it would have provided them strength for an even greater route of the enemy. When Saul confronted Jonathan about breaking his oath, Jonathan was very emotional. He frustratingly replied, "I did but taste a little honey with the end of the rod that was in mine hand, and, lo, I must die" (14:43). His initial reply, upon learning the command that his father had given the people, showed dismay that the soldiers were not allowed to eat all day after they had won a great victory for Saul. That was his mercy manifesting itself. Those with the gift of mercy are not always the most respectful people as they go about trying to remove the hurts and unfair treatment placed upon people.

Because he was such a merciful and gracious man and leader, the people held Jonathan in high *esteem*. They saved his life. Saul had made a vow to put anyone to death who disobeyed his order not to eat before the evening. Because the people of Israel held Jonathan in such high esteem, they came to his defense. The people said to Saul, "Shall Jonathan die, who hath wrought this great salvation in Israel? God forbid: as the LORD liveth, there shall not one hair of his head fall to the ground; for he hath wrought with God this day. So the people rescued Jonathan, that he died not" (1 Sam. 14:45).

Another example of Jonathan's mercy is seen in his relationship with David. First Samuel 18:1 says that "the soul of Jonathan was knit with the soul of David, and Jonathan loved him as his own soul." Verse four says, "And Jonathan stripped himself of the robe that was upon him, and gave it to David, and his garments, even to his sword, and to his bow, and to his girdle." Those with the motivational gift of mercy are openly *expressive* in their love for others, a characteristic of Jonathan. Mercies are *endeared* to their friends. Jonathan was so endeared to his friend, David, that he had him move into the palace with the royal family (1 Sam. 18:2). Mercies completely give of themselves to another person.

Those who have the motivational gift of mercy are very emotional in their involvement with other people. A time came in the life of Jonathan when he knew that David was called by God to be the King of Israel. Jonathan was to have been the heir to the throne of his father, Saul, yet he was not jealous of David. He wanted to support his friend. When Saul turned on David and tried to kill him, Jonathan reacted emotionally on behalf of his friend. He could not stand how his father was treating David. Jonathan was willing to give his own life for the sake of his friend. His father became so angered at Jonathan because of his defense of David that "Saul cast a javelin at him to smite him: whereby Jonathan knew that it was determined of his father to slay David. So Jonathan arose from the table in fierce anger, and did eat no meat the second day of the month: for he was grieved for David, because his father had done him shame" (1 Sam. 20:33-34). Jonathan was showing *empathy* for David. He not only felt sympathy for his friend, and hurt for him, but he hurt with David and wanted to help remove the shame and sorrow that had unjustly been put upon David.

When Jonathan's intervention on behalf of David could no longer appease the jealousy and animosity of Saul toward David, the time came for David to flee for his life. It was very emotional and *embracing* as David and Jonathan said their good-byes:

> *David arose out of a place toward the south, and fell on his face to the ground, and bowed himself three times: and they kissed one another, and wept one with another, until David exceeded. And Jonathan said to David, 'Go in peace, forasmuch as we have sworn both of us in the name of the LORD, saying, The LORD be between me and thee, and between my seed and thy seed for ever.' And he arose and departed: and Jonathan went into the city. (1 Sam. 20:41-42)*

Another touching scene occurs later when David had been on the run for awhile from Saul, and he was in hiding. Jonathan was able to locate his soul brother. The Bible says, "And Jonathan Saul's son arose, and went to David into the wood, and strengthened his hand in God. And he said unto him, 'Fear not: for the hand of Saul my father shall not find thee; and thou shalt be king over Israel, and I shall be next unto thee; and that also Saul my father knoweth.' And they two made a covenant before the LORD: and David abode in the wood, and Jonathan went to his house" (1 Sam. 23:16-18).

Here was Jonathan, who could have feared for his own life again, yet he wanted to go and *encourage* his friend, David. Jonathan performed this act of friendship and mercy in the midst of potential danger to himself.

Let us now turn our attention to the New Testament and see how it explains the motivational spiritual gift of mercy. There is a Greek word "eleos" that means mercy. Similar words are translated as "pity" or "compassion." The one with the motivational gift of mercy is to show "eleos" with *cheerfulness*. Matthew gave us an example of the mercy of Jesus as he recorded in his Gospel, "But when He saw the multitudes, He was moved with compassion on them, because they fainted, and were scattered abroad, as sheep having no shepherd" (Matt. 9:36). Jesus was moved to act on behalf of the crowd in many ways.

Compassion is a strong characteristic seen in those who have the gift of mercy. On another occasion during the earthly life of our Lord, a funeral procession was passing by. The dead man was the only son of a widow. The Bible says, "And when the Lord saw her, He had compassion on her, and said unto her, 'Weep not'" (Luke 7:13).

Jesus put feet to the feelings of pity, compassion, and mercy when He brought the dead young man back to life. As He said during the time He walked upon this earth, Jesus also says to us today in this mixed up world in which we live: "These things I have spoken unto you, that in Me ye might have peace. In the world ye shall have tribulation: but be of good cheer; I have overcome the world" (John 16:33). The person with the gift of mercy wants to encourage people, lift up their spirits, and bring healing to their lives.

James, the brother of Jesus, appears to be one who had the motivational gift of mercy. One only needs to read the book of James to learn that he was a very *emotional* person (James 4:1-10 provides a representative example of his emotion). Verses 13-16 in chapter five show us how *expressive* he was:

> *Is any among you afflicted? Let him pray. Is any merry? Let him sing psalms. Is any sick among you? Let him call for the elders of the church; and let them pray over him, anointing him with oil in the name of the Lord: and the prayer of faith shall save the sick, and the Lord shall raise him up; and if he have committed sins, they shall be forgiven him. Confess your faults one to another, and pray one for another, that ye may be healed. The effectual fervent prayer of a righteous man availeth much.*

His book is not only a challenge to Christians to back up their faith with works, but it is a book to encourage and uplift Christians who may be experiencing difficulties. He shared his *esteem* for Job when he wrote, "Behold, we count them happy which endure. Ye have heard of the pa-

tience of Job, and have seen the end of the Lord; that the Lord is very
pitiful, and of tender mercy" (James 5:11). James must have been a patient man like Job. He was held in high esteem for he eventually became
the leader of the church at Jerusalem.

He exhorted his readers to help those who needed to have mercy expressed to them. James said, "Pure religion and undefiled before God
and the Father is this, To visit the fatherless and widows in their affliction, and to keep himself unspotted from the world" (James 1:27). He
certainly exhibited his *empathy* with those whom he wrote about and to
whom he exhorted others to minister.

James showed how *embracing* he was when he said to pray over the
sick, "anointing him with oil in the name of the Lord" (James 5:14). He
urged us to be *endearing* to one another by praying for and confessing
our faults to one another (5:16). As we pray for and confess our faults to
one another, and as we "speak not evil one of another" (James 4:11), we
will be *encouraging* to each other. The book of James shows us how to
exhibit mercy toward others because it was written by one who had the
motivational gift of mercy.

Examples of Mercy

Ruth, Jonathan, James and Jesus all had the gift of mercy. John, the disciple of Jesus, also had the gift of mercy.

As we can surmise from the examples above, those with the gift of
mercy are *intensely loyal, expressively loving, extraordinarily liberal in
effort*, and *extremely likable*. These traits especially stand out in mercy
givers and interact among the major characteristics of this gift.

Exhortations to Mercies

Two verses in Romans 12 give the special ***exhortations to mercies***. Those
who have the gift of mercy are exhorted to show mercy "with cheerfulness" (Rom. 12:8) and to "rejoice with them that do rejoice, and weep

with them that weep" (Rom. 12:15).

People with the gift of mercy have a tendency to empathize with other people. They are drawn more to people who have great hurts in their lives. So mercies have to be careful that they do not always just weep and empathize with those who are having it rough. The one with the gift of mercy also needs to exercise the element of his gift that uplifts and encourages the person who is hurting. He is also to exercise his gift with cheerfulness. The key of this exhortation is for those with the gift of mercy to *be encouraging*.

One with the gift of mercy is also to rejoice with them that do rejoice. A mercy giver needs to be positive as much as possible. The picture in this exhortation is that he is to *be exhilarating* with others when the occasion calls for it. When a person with the gift of mercy encounters someone who is rejoicing, the mercy giver is often more joyful than the one who has reason to rejoice. It is an exhilarating experience for the one with the gift of mercy because he is happy that God has blessed someone to whom he has been drawn.

Twice, the Bible exhorts the person with the gift of mercy to be more on the "up" side of his gift. Mercy is to be exhibited with cheerfulness and joy. You see, mercies have to work at it so that they are not always in a depressed, distressed mood because of their empathizing with hurting people. The whole purpose of this gift is to lift others up and not just to bear the burden with them.

There are occasions when one with the gift of mercy is to express the sorrowful tone of his gift. One with the gift of mercy is exhorted to weep with those who weep. The word has already been used several times in this chapter, but the key here is for the mercy giver to *be empathetic*. There are times when the most appropriate thing to do is to put an arm around someone who is in grief and just to cry with them. When one with the gift of mercy is Spirit-controlled, he knows when and how long weeping with someone is the right and best way to express his gift.

Expectation Mercies Need to Exercise Most

There are two reasons why those with the gift of mercy must be *morally cautious*. First, it protects them from improper relationships, especially in moral choices and depths of friendships with those of the opposite sex. If a mercy giver is not morally cautious, with the proper balance of mercy with truth, he will get himself in situations that will hurt him greatly as well as those to whom he ministers.

Mercies also need to be cautious about jumping in immediately to remove a hurting situation in someone's life until they know all the facts. God often brings trial as a means of discipline. Mercies can be just like servers. One with the gift of mercy may get involved in a situation too quickly to help remove a hurt or meet a need in a person's life. But God has brought the hurt or need upon that individual to teach him truth or to get his attention about an area of disobedience in his life. The involvement of the mercy giver may interfere with what God is trying to do. So those with the gift of mercy must also develop caution in their lives because it keeps them from getting ahead of God when He has brought suffering for instruction or disciplinary purposes.

Characteristics of Mercy Givers

Represent Faith by Demonstration and Desire

In verse 18 of our focal Scripture text from 1 John 3, John says, "My little children, let us not love in word, neither in tongue; but in deed and in truth."

One ought to love in word, but even more important than what one says is <u>what one does</u>. John's exhortation to Christians is to "walk your talk."

Actions are necessary to fulfill the gift of mercy. Mercies can be excellent intercessors in prayer on behalf of others. Along with feeling pity, one with the gift of mercy should put his mercy into action by reaching out visibly to someone who needs it. Mercy is to be expressed "in deed."

Those with the gift of mercy also represent faith by demonstration and desire because of the desires of their heart—their *affections*. Through these words of John, you can sense how one with the gift of mercy has a hard time understanding why other people are not as merciful as those who are mercy givers: "But whoso hath this world's good, and seeth his brother have need, and shutteth up his bowels of compassion from him, how dwelleth the love of God in him?" (1 John 3:17).

John's expressive comment exemplifies how the person with the gift of mercy feels about those of us who are not as compassionate as the mercy giver thinks we should be. For the mercy giver, the desire to demonstrate mercy comes from where affections are set. We all need to learn how to express mercy to others who need it, but the mercy giver must realize that God has given him extra motivation to show compassion and caring toward those who are in need. John was pointing out that when a Christian has the ability and means to be a mercy giver, but totally ignores an opportunity to which he should respond, he is out of fellowship with God.

In verse 19, John acknowledges that representing mercy by demonstration and desire is what *authenticates* that a mercy giver is of God and abiding in His will. He said, "And hereby we know that we are of the truth, and shall assure our hearts before Him." As one who has the gift of mercy exhibits mercy in deed and in truth, it confirms and assures the heart of the mercy giver before God and before others that the love of God dwells in him. It also serves as a witness to others that the mercy giver is a child of God.

Relate to Feelings of Delight and Despair

The Bible exhorts those with the gift of mercy to "rejoice with them that do rejoice, and weep with them that weep" (Rom. 12:15). A mercy giver can come into a room and sense the emotional climate. The mercy giver knows how to respond. Mercies are *heavy* in spirit when you are sad and down. When you are happy, they are *happy*, even happier. But regardless of the emotional state of an individual, mercies have an ability to offer *hope* for the hopeless.

My boyhood pastor, Livy L. Cope, who pastored my home church for 26 years, exemplified mercy in action. He could enter a room and relate to the emotional climate.

When my mother had major exploratory surgery for the second time, the doctors felt that she probably had pancreatic cancer. When our family was told she did not have cancer, and none of her organs showed any sign of disease, we cried tears of joy. Brother Cope happened to walk into the hospital room where we were gathered right after we had gotten the good news. He was not aware when he came in whether we had received good news or bad news. He saw us weeping, and he began to weep, too. He put his arms around my dad and said, "What's the word?" He then learned that his tears were tears of joy. Either way, the Lord had already used the mercy of Brother Cope to minister to us from the moment he walked into the hospital room.

You cannot forget that special ability about someone who is able to come into your presence, identify with your emotions, and minister to you. Brother Cope has brought comfort and reassurance to my family and me, as he has to many others, through this wonderful motivational gift that he so faithfully has manifested.

Jesus wept (John 6:35). Bible commentators and preachers speculate as to why Jesus wept. Some say He wept because of the lack of faith the people had in Him. Some believe that He wept because He was going to have bring Lazarus back from paradise when He raised him from death. It would be hard to experience a little bit of heaven and then have to come back to earth.

But I believe that part of the reason why Jesus wept was because of His compassion. Christ knew that He was going to raise Lazarus from the dead. But he still wept because he was a compassionate person. The gift of mercy manifested itself in Jesus as He saw and heard the sadness and grief because of the mourning surrounding the death of His close friend.

In 1 John 3, John offered hope even when some felt that it was not possible. He said, "For if our heart condemn us, God is greater than our heart, and knoweth all things" (1 John 3:20). What is the hope that we have, even when we are facing difficulties?

John provides an answer: "And whatsoever we ask, we receive of Him, because we keep His commandments, and do those things that are pleasing in His sight" (3:22).

If one is obeying the Lord, eventually, all things are going to work together for good (Rom. 8:28). One of the reasons that John wrote the book of 1 John was to encourage Christians to be completely hopeful. In the opening verses of this epistle, he said, "And these things write we unto you, that your joy may be full" (1 John 1:4). John wanted Christians to know that no matter what kind of situation you are in, you can have "confidence toward God" (1 John 3:21).

Remove Frustrations that Disable and Destroy

One gifted with mercy realizes when someone has a hurt in his life. However, it may be foolish actions that are frustrating and disabling a person in his Christian walk, even to the point of spiritual destruction.

The mercy giver does not approach this situation like the prophet. The prophet tends to tell the person who is doing foolish things, even though he is hurting, that "You'd better get right with God or it is going to get worse."

One with the gift of mercy does not go in and tell the hurting person his faults. The mercy giver goes into a situation with the desire to *bring healing*. It may involve the mercy giver *bearing hurts*—the hurt of the one who needs help.

One with the gift of mercy wants to seek to relieve a person of what hurts them. John said, "Hereby perceive we the love of God, because He laid down His life for us: and we ought to lay down our lives for the brethren. But whoso hath this world's good, and seeth his brother have need, and shutteth up his bowels of compassion from him, how dwelleth the love of God in him?" (1 John 3:16-17).

As revealed through those words of John, a mercy giver feels that if you have the means and ability to relieve a hurt, then you ought to meet the need or bear the hurt of a person in need of mercy, if you are right with God.

Mercies want to *banish harmful things*, to help those in the Christian life who are disabled spiritually to remove those things from their lives that are robbing them of joy. If there is a time when a mercy acts like a prophet, it is when he is motivated to remove harmful things from one to whom he is ministering. The mercy giver is ready to go in and throw out anything harmful to the person and a source of his hurting. The harmful things may be relationships or other areas that are not right in the person's life. The whole purpose, though, of the mercy giver is to bring spiritual healing and emotional healing to lives.

Respond Faithfully to Distress and Depression

As those with the gift of mercy are motivated to represent faith by demonstration and desire, to relate to feelings of delight and despair, and to remove frustrations that disable and destroy, it is natural for them to *respond faithfully to distress and depression*.

When people are happy and joyful, and when things are going their way, they do not necessarily need someone to help them. Who needs help? Those who do not know what to do and who have nowhere else to turn.

But the nature of the spiritual gift of mercy is why those with this motivational gift must be careful. Because they spend much of their time listening to what hurts other people, there are times when a mercy giver needs to make himself temporarily unavailable.

Why? To return to and study the Word of God in order to be uplifted in his own spirit, because he has been drained spiritually, emotionally, mentally, and physically by listening so much to the troubles of others.

As mercies respond faithfully to distress and depression, that is where their *attraction* is focused. Mercies just seem to be drawn to people who are distressed, depressed, or down. Although God loves us all equally, there are divine differences in regards to God's purposes for our lives and how He uses us.

The relationship of Jesus with Peter and John provides a good example of divine differences in personality. Peter was close to Christ, but John referred to himself as the disciple whom Jesus loved. It does appear that the Lord may have had a closer relationship with John than any of the other disciples. When Jesus was dying on the Cross, He asked John to take care of His mother (John 19:26-27). It was because John had the gift of mercy. Here was a woman whose son was dying before her eyes. She was in need of mercy and compassion. Peter was not the one who could best care for her. He had fallen greatly in denying Jesus. His overreaction to his plight and the death of Christ may have been to go to the other extreme. He might have wanted to seek revenge against those who had crucified the Lord. At the time when Christ was dying on the Cross, Peter was off to himself, grieving over his denial of Christ. Even though he was a broken man, he was not in a mood to give compassion. John's personality with the spiritual gift of mercy was the one that could best minister to Mary. His presence near Mary, while Jesus was on the Cross, showed his natural attraction to be where one was who was in distress and depression.

As mercies are attracted to those who are distressed and depressed, they show an *acceptance* and willingness to get involved with those to whom others will not give much time. *Availability* comes with their willingness to get involved. To mercies, actions speak louder than words. John said that the most important way to love is in deed and in truth (1 John 3:18). Mercies are there when someone needs them. They make themselves available and respond faithfully to those in distress and depression.

Restore Fellowship Where There is Discord and Disobedience

Mercies desire to **restore fellowship where there is discord and disobedience,** and they are sympathetic to criticism against others, because they are *saddened by conflict.* Those with the gift of mercy do not like to be a part of conflict and avoid it if possible.

Broken fellowship with the Lord stems from two sources: disobedience or discord, either individually or corporately.

Sometimes an individual's disobedience to God brings about broken fellowship. One with the gift of mercy senses this about a person, and seeks to restore fellowship where there has been disobedience. That is why 1 John is such a good book for those with the gift of mercy. Through the writings of John about the love of Jesus, people are encouraged and uplifted. But John also emphasized the importance of following the commandments of the Lord. Fellowship and accord are dependent upon obedience to the Lord.

When there is broken fellowship with the Lord corporately in a church, it is because people are at discord with one another due to disagreements. The result is disharmony within the fellowship of believers.

There are times, though, when a conflict in a church may be necessary if the disagreement among the members is biblical and doctrinal in nature. The broken fellowship with the Lord is among those in the body of the church who stand in support of those things that God stands against. Most of the major political issues of our day are no longer separate from our spiritual lives. Many of today's political issues deal with moral questions clearly addressed by the Bible. A person with the gift of mercy has to be careful that he is not so concerned with seeing people get back together and with bringing about a healing atmosphere that the truth of God is disregarded.

Most church splits have at their root cause theological differences. In a church conflict, prophets and teachers will side with those who want to follow what is biblically and doctrinally right. Because they can be blunt in standing up to the opposing group, prophets and teachers usually get blamed and criticized just as much as the personality upon whom the schism group has centered their discontent.

The problem, though, is enhanced the most by mercies who are not cautious to balance truth with mercy. These are the mercies who do not take the time to learn all the facts—both sides of the problem at hand—and they support the schism group because some within this group feel that they have been unfairly treated. The mercies misuse their gift, in such cases, because they take up someone else's offense. In their defense of those whom they think have been wronged, mercies keep things stirred up until the situation gets out of hand. Caution is the expectation that mercies need to exercise the most with their gift because they can actually find themselves fighting against God when they think that they are taking up the offense of someone who is fighting for God.

Another trait that helps mercy givers to restore fellowship is their ability to sense when things are not right. Mercies are *sensitive to the climate* around them. They are sensitive to the emotional and spiritual atmosphere surrounding a group or an individual. A prophet can listen to someone and determine whether the person is fake or genuine. A person with the gift of mercy can walk into a room and sense, almost immediately, if there is tension or if something is wrong. Mercies know if somebody is hurting because their spirit bears witness with those who are hurting. The mercy giver knows how to respond appropriately so that the tension is not increased but is eased.

Mercies also *strive for conversion*. They want to change the hurting and harmful situations other people are in. But the mercy giver must once again exercise caution concerning this characteristic, especially with those of the opposite sex. A Christian boy or girl might become attracted to someone of the opposite sex because their gift of mercy senses that person is hurting or is out of fellowship with God. The mercy giver may begin dating the person with the intent of spiritual conversion. But a romantic relationship is not where the gift of mercy is to manifest itself. Having served in youth ministry for eight years, too often, I have seen a mercy giver's heart run away with his or her head because the mercy giver got too romantically involved with the individual of the opposite sex whom they were striving to convert. Be so very careful, mercies, that your expression of mercy does not result in a relationship that is morally and spiritually harmful to you.

"Missionary" dating is not the method by which to lead someone to Christ. Dating is not the means by which to exercise your gift of mercy toward one who is in need of mercy. Before you ever go out on a date with someone, strive to win the person to Christ. Otherwise, you are "unequally yoked" (2 Cor. 6:14). Even if a person whom you want to date is a Christian, you will also be in a spiritually risky situation if you date someone who is a backslidden Christian.

Mercies are motivated to restore fellowship and to bring people out of situations that have caused them hurt. If it has been caused by discord, mercy givers seek to bring accord. If broken fellowship with others is because of disobedience to God, a mercy giver seeks to help the person in need of restoration to be obedient to God. The key is to restore fellowship where there has been discord and disobedience by being cautious to keep mercy in balance with the truth of the Word of God.

Require Friendships of Depth and Devotion with Discretion

Mercies *require friendships of depth and devotion*, but these friendships must be *with discretion*. John was so close to the Lord that he wanted to keep that special relationship, even in heaven. He and his brother, James, asked if they could have the seats right next to the throne of Jesus (Mark 10:35-37). The motivation behind such a request is typical of one motivated by the gift of mercy. Mercies want closeness. They want friendships that are deep, where there is devotion to one another. John was the one who referred to himself as the "disciple whom Jesus loved" (John 13:23; 19:26; 20:2; 21:7,20). John's use of that phrase was not out of a spirit of arrogance. It was the sign of a need that is common to those with the gift of mercy.

Deep friendships, with discretion, are good. Mercies need such friendships because they need someone to give them the right kind of *direction*. Mercies need affirmation, acceptance, and direction from someone whom they can trust. As mercies empathize with people, ill-intentioned individuals may try to take advantage of them, especially in moral areas. Mercy givers need someone to keep them in balance emotionally and spiritually.

Often, a mercy giver's best friend or marriage partner is a prophet. In the Bible, John (mercy) and Peter (prophecy) are often found together. It was a good relationship because they kept one another in balance. The prophet can be so harsh, at times. When he has a close mercy friend, the mercy can help to keep the prophet compassionate enough so that people will listen to him. But mercies need direction from someone, like a prophet, who will tell them, "You better be careful," or "This is not a situation in which you should be involved."

Requiring friendships of depth and devotion with discretion is not only for direction, but it also provides *protection*. As mercies especially seem to be drawn to friendships with prophets, it is good because a prophet can warn a mercy giver of unsafe involvements. Such deep friendships with the right people not only provide direction and protection for mercies, but they also give needed *correction*. You have to be exceptionally careful with a person who has the gift of mercy when you correct him. You can talk to a mercy in a nice, low-key manner, but his version of your correction is that you chewed him out. Mercies are also devastated easily, when weaknesses are pointed out or they are confronted with their mistakes. After a mercy giver has received a form of correction, his reaction to it is like the weight of the world has come down upon him. That is why one with the gift of mercy needs a close, devoted friend, who is committed to the Lord, to correct him when it is needed in his life. The person who has the gift of mercy needs a deep friendship with one whom he knows will love him and accept him even when he makes mistakes or fails at something.

Cautions for the Gift of Mercy
Misunderstandings

Mercies may inappropriately be misunderstood as being *too passionate*. In using the word "passion," the intended meaning is one who is "intensely emotional." Mercies have a boundless enthusiasm to give mercy to those who need it. Their mercy is sometimes expressed through intense feelings and emotions that appear to some as too involved and too intense. Mercy givers can be so emotional in their involvement with someone or with a cause that it appears they are controlled only by their emotions. John wrote, "We ought to lay down our lives for the brethren" (1 John 3:16). If we could hear him speak those words, it would be with the same passion that his Lord Jesus said those words when John first heard them resound in a similar fashion from the lips of Christ (John 15:13).

Mercies may also be misunderstood as being *too permissive*. As mercies want to remove hurts and bring about healing, they prefer to avoid conflict. So they may appear to be lenient theologically to keep peace.

Those with the gift of mercy may also appear to be too permissive in their mercy to those who are still unrepentant and disobedient. Mercy givers do seem to be attracted to those of the opposite sex whom others would not be involved with because of their reputations or peculiarities. This gives the appearance of being too permissive on the part of the mercy giver.

Another misunderstanding that others may have about those with the gift of mercy is that they are *too pessimistic*. This is not so out of the ordinary. It is a natural result of being involved in some of the situations in which mercies get involved. As they are around hurting so much, they tend toward the pessimistic side of their gift, instead of the positive, joyful side of it. If one with the gift of mercy has been ministering to someone who is sad or sorrowful, it has also made the mercy giver sad or sorrowful.

Mercies must strive toward the positive. Those of us who use mercies as sounding boards need to remember to do things that lift them up and encourage them so that they will also have reasons to be joyful and happy.

One other frequent misunderstanding that people have about those with the gift of mercy is that they are *too possessive*. Because they get so deep in their friendships, desiring closeness, they are sometimes misjudged as being too possessive. As I used to read about John's close friendship with the Lord, I thought that he did not give the other disciples room to become as close a friend with Jesus as he was. In coming to an understanding of the characteristics of the motivational spiritual gifts, I now realize that John's relationship with Jesus was something that occurred naturally with his gift of mercy. All of us need a best friend, but mercies do need to be careful not to be too possessive so that others are not allowed the blessing of friendship with your best friend. If someone is a friend, a helper, and a blessing to you, there are others who also need the friendship of your close friend, too.

Misuses

One of the misuses of the gift of mercy is that a mercy giver may get *predisposed*. One with the gift of mercy can become too emotional. If mercies are not walking in the Spirit, they can be prone to act solely on their emotions and never approach situations spiritually as far as the purpose of God for the person whom the mercy giver desires to help. When a mercy giver becomes predisposed, he is completely controlled by and responsive to his emotions. Most often, he does not act in accordance with the Word of God.

When a person with the gift of mercy is not in a right relationship with God, there are pages of the Bible that may as well be torn out because the mercy giver does not want to believe or apply the truth of the Scriptures on those pages. It is because their feelings, their emotions, which are out of the control of the Holy Spirit, tell them that a God of love would never say that He might punish or cause hardships for anyone. But we all have to realize that a God of love must be a just God and a correcting Father, at times. Throughout the Bible, there are ways that God has shown us how He deals with sin and how we are to deal with it. Our sins break our fellowship with God (Isa. 59:2), and our fellowship with God cannot be restored until we turn from those things that displease God (1 John 1:9).

Mercy givers misuse their gift by being *premature*. Sometimes, mercies are premature in getting involved in a situation where God has brought the hurting upon someone's life as discipline. In such cases, the mercy giver jumps in and shows mercy too quickly in a situation where God is trying to break the will of an individual and teach him a valuable lesson.

Hurting is a process God may use to bring a person to the end of himself so that he will turn to God. When mercies misuse their gift and act prematurely, they get in God's way.

For example, God allowed difficulties to come upon the prodigal son. If a server had tried to meet a need in the prodigal son's situation, or a giver had helped the young man financially, or a mercy had taken up the battle for him, the prodigal son may have remained in the far country. Things may have improved too much, and the young man may have never returned home to restored fellowship with his father, his family, and with God.

Another way mercy givers may misuse their gift is by becoming *problem-possessed*. Mercies can get to the point that they spend most of their time going from one problem to the next. As has already been stressed, those with the gift of mercy have to be very careful that they do not deal with problems all the time. They will stay defeated, depressed, and discouraged in their Christian life. When a mercy giver is problem-possessed, he is using his gift out of balance.

Mercies also misuse their gift when they become too *partial*. Their mercy is out of balance with the truth. In the flesh, mercies can become sympathetic to one side, especially in a conflict, and the side they are partial to is in violation of the will of God and the Word of God. This normally happens when those with the gift of mercy have failed to hear both sides of an issue or they have not gotten all the facts. Mercies need to make sure that they are always partial to the truth of God's Word on any issue they face or with any individual with whom they become involved.

In being too partial, mercies can become too *protective*. In the flesh, mercy givers tend to take up offenses to the extreme. A mercy giver, who misuses his gift, keeps taking up the offense, even when the person for whom he is taking up an offense has given up the fight. Through my years in ministry, I have observed situations in which individuals, who were in disagreement with one another, would get their differences resolved. What then became a greater problem were the mercy givers who would not let the situation die out because they continued to take up the offense on someone's behalf, even though that person had gotten things resolved.

One trait that I have found out about gentle mercies is that they can be very defensive when they are taking up offenses. Mercies are naturally defensive about most things, but not to the point of aggression. My wife has the motivational gift of mercy. When she returns home from the grocery store, I usually ask her how much she spent. Her first impulse is to start defending her expenditures—what she bought and why. But that is not what I asked her. I really am not concerned with the what and why of her purchases. I know that she spends money very wisely. I just want to know how much so that I know how much we have left for other things. Her response is characteristic of one with the gift of mercy. Mercies want to justify why they bought something. They do not want you to be upset with them. Such a reaction is not inappropriate. But it is, when one with the gift of mercy gets so defensive that he is defending what is not the truth and what is not right with God. Mercies misuse their gift when they become overly protective and overly defensive.

One issue of our day where we see mercy givers within the will of God taking up an offense on behalf of someone is over the abortion issue. Spirit-filled and Spirit-controlled mercies are among those who are righteously indignant in defending the right to life for unborn babies. Some are more aggressive with it than others, and maybe, too aggressive, at times. But the majority of those with the spiritual gift of mercy, who are so strongly involved in the pro-life movement, are motivated on behalf of the unborn child with the proper balance of mercy and truth. Whether it is over the abortion issue or any other issue, sweet, gentle, mercy givers can be very demanding. You would almost think that they are prophets. When mercies are demanding, in the flesh, they are not very merciful or very compassionate. Once again, caution is the key for mercies. Be cautious where and with whom you get involved. If you believe that God has called you to be a protector, such as on the line of face to face encounter in the pro-life movement, do not go beyond the boundaries that God has set, as given in His Word.

Conclusion

Praise the Lord for those who have this wonderful spiritual gift of mercy, given to almost one-third of Christians. They outnumber by a two-to-one margin the number of those who have the next closest motivational gift in size.

The fact that more Christians have the gift of mercy than any other motivational gift shows us the great need of mercy and compassion within and without the body of Christ. We should all be thankful how those with the gift of mercy minister its special healing at such crucial and needed times in all of our lives. But this blessed motivational gift is not one that should only be characteristic of only a third of Christians. Even if mercy is not our major motivational spiritual gift, it is the one gift, more than any other, that should be a natural outflow of our lives along with our special gift of blessing. Our example of one with the gift of prophecy, Peter, expressed so well why mercy ought to be exemplified by every Christian:

> Blessed be the God and Father of our Lord Jesus Christ, which according to His abundant mercy hath begotten us again unto a lively hope by the resurrection of Jesus Christ from the dead, to an inheritance incorruptible, and undefiled, and that fadeth not away, reserved in heaven for you, who are kept by the power of God through faith unto salvation ready to be revealed in the last time. (1 Peter 1:3-5)

Because of the abundant mercy of God, as expressed through Jesus, we have received the mercy of God concerning our sins. We are recipients of His mercy by not receiving the penalty of what we deserved for our sins (Rom. 6:23).

Jesus paid it all. We must make it a priority of our lives to share the mercy of God with those who have not yet known it so that they, too, can have the opportunity to receive the mercy of God unto everlasting life in heaven.

Understanding Spiritual Gifts

9

Understanding Spiritual Gifts

"For the Profit of All"

For as the body is one, and hath many members, and all the members of that one body, being many, are one body: so also is Christ. For by one Spirit are we all baptized into one body, whether we be Jews or Gentiles, whether we be bond or free; and have been all made to drink into one Spirit. For the body is not one member, but many. If the foot shall say, 'Because I am not the hand, I am not of the body, is it therefore not of the body?' And if the ear shall say, 'Because I am not the eye, I am not of the body; is it therefore not of the body?' If the whole body were an eye, where were the hearing? If the whole were hearing, where were the smelling? But now hath God set the members every one of them in the body, as it hath pleased Him. (1 Cor. 12:12-18)

"As it hath pleased Him." Isn't that a beautiful phrase? Why do you have your special motivational spiritual gift of blessing? As it has pleased the Father, He has given you your gift to be used as channel of blessing with the body of believers for the profit of all.

"And if they were all one member, where were the body? But now are they many members, yet but one body. And the eye cannot say unto the hand, I have no need of thee: nor again the head to the feet, I have no need of you." (1 Cor. 12:19-21) Isn't that a wonderful picture of the body of Christ?

At a conference a few years ago, a speaker gave a visible illustration of those verses. He held up his hands and said, "What if my fingers do not want to cooperate with one another? The second, third, and fourth finger each decide they want to go elsewhere. I want to pick up an object, but the second, third, and fourth fingers want to do something else. They are not cooperating with the other fingers and are actually working against one another and the other fingers."

His illustration was quite humorous to watch as he attempted and failed at some simple tasks with his uncooperative fingers. Our hands would not be very effective if all the fingers decided to do their own thing. You could not grab hold of an object you usually pick up with ease. You could not play a piece of music on the piano as it was meant to be played. You may not even be able to scratch where you have an itch.

I hope that you are beginning to get a visible picture of what the Holy Spirit inspired Paul to get across to the body of Christ through this passage in 1 Corinthians 12. When just one part of the body will not cooperate and fulfill its function, it has an effect on all the other parts of the body, whether you are talking about the human body or the church body.

> *Nay, much more those members of the body, which seem to be more feeble, are necessary: and those members of the body, which we think to be less honourable, upon these we bestow more abundant honour; and our uncomely parts have more abundant comeliness. For our comely parts have no need: but God hath tempered the body together, having given more abundant honour to that part which lacked: that there should be no schism in the body; but that the members should have the same care one for another. (1 Cor. 12:22-25)*

Every part of one's body is necessary in order to function at full strength. There are no weak parts of the body of Christ. When we all get to heaven, those parts of the church body that may seem more honorable to us now will be ones that do not make any greater difference for the cause of Christ in God's eyes than the less noticed, seemingly less honorable, parts of the body. Do not ever think that you have just a little part in the work of the Lord. Your little part may be what is keeping the whole process going without a hitch.

A few more verses from Romans 12 enhance our understanding of spiritual gifts. Let us pick up with verse 16, which follows the listing of the individual motivational gifts (vs. 6-8) and the exhortations for each motivational gift (vs. 9-15).

> *Be of the same mind one toward another. Mind not high things, but condescend to men of low estate. Be not wise in your own conceits. Recompense to no man evil for evil. Provide things honest in the sight of all men. If it be possible, as much as lieth in you, live peaceably with all men. Dearly beloved, avenge not yourselves, but rather give place unto wrath: for it is written, 'Vengeance is mine; I will repay', saith the Lord. Therefore if thine enemy hunger, feed him; if he thirst, give him drink: for in so doing thou shalt heap coals of fire on his head. Be not overcome of evil, but overcome evil with good. (Rom. 12:16-21)*

These verses reinforce the key phrase in 1 Corinthians 12:25, that the proper functioning of each part of the body of Christ is "that there should be no schism in the body." Wonderful advice! As the Lord spoke through Paul, what He is saying to us through the verses in Romans 12:16-21 is that each of us needs to live peaceably as much as it is in our ability to do so. There may be others who are not living peaceably, but you are to make it a point to live peaceably and do your part to keep the peace. If you have been wronged, do not avenge yourself, for "'Vengeance is mine, I will repay', saith the Lord" (Rom. 12:19).

You need to let God deal with those who have wronged you and to take care of difficulties that come into your life. God will do a better job of dealing with someone who has offended you or whose way of doing things is not according to the Word and will of God. Your main priority is to fulfill your area of responsibility where God has placed you within the body of believers through the special gift of blessing He has bestowed upon you. If each of us exercises our motivational gift in the proper manner, the body of believers functions at its greatest effectiveness.

This chapter title, **"For the Profit of All"** comes from a phrase in 1 Corinthians 12:7. Verses four, five, and six of that chapter reveal that there are motivational, ministry, and manifestation spiritual gifts.

"But the manifestation of the Spirit is given to every man **to profit withal**" (1 Cor. 12:7). As each of us is faithful to use our gift, we contribute common good for the profit of all in the body of Christ. To help us understand how all the spiritual gifts are "to profit withal," all seven motivational gifts are brought together in this chapter. We will see how they are recognized, how they are related, and how they react to one another and to different situations.

How They are Recognized

It is important for you to know what your motivational gift is, and to understand how the other gifts operate. When you have an understanding of how the other gifts function in the body of believers, then you can use your gift in a way that cooperates with your fellow members of the body.

In the first chapter, some words, beginning with the letter, "A," were used to give some practical helps on how you can discover your motivational spiritual gift and how you can help others to determine their gift:

- *Accept* Jesus Christ as your Lord and Savior. A spiritual gift is only manifested properly in the life of a Christian.

- *Acknowledge* the Lord in all that you do. If you do, He promises to direct your paths (Prov. 3:6).

- Be *Active* in serving the Lord where you are right now.

- *Admit* your need of help where there is sin in your life, and confess those sins to God.

- *Affections* can help to point you to your spiritual gift. As you concentrate on the needs of others, what motivates you to help others?

- *Affirmation* from other people can help you to recognize your spiritual gift as they see qualities of a motivational gift in you, and they let you know it.

- *Ambition* in life can give you an idea of your motivational spiritual gift. What is it that you really want to do in life? What is the goal that you are reaching for?

- *Annoyance* can point you to your special gift of blessing. Whatever irritates you can be a positive sign to pinpoint your spiritual gift. Does it annoy you when other people do not exhibit in their lives what your spiritual gift motivates you to do? Your gift should come to the forefront when there is a need that others, in your opinion, are overlooking.

As you *analyze* the different gifts, you realize that some of those characteristics are evident in your life. You also notice characteristics of the gifts in the lives of others. As you *associate* characteristics with the gift they are connected to, you discover your motivational gift. You can also assist others in determining their gift.

To discover your gift, it is important to *assimilate* into the body of Christ through a local church. Assimilation is the process by which nourishment is changed into living tissue. As you assimilate into the work of the Lord, and serve Him, there are ways in which you will feel that you are being fed. You also discover how God uses you to spiritually feed others.

To discover your motivational spiritual gift, do not neglect the most basic means by which to find your gift of blessing. *Ask* God to clearly reveal your spiritual gift to you (Matt. 7:7-8).

Those are practical ways to go about recognizing your special gift of blessing. There are also four general steps that can lead you to recognize your motivational spiritual gift: natural inclination, normal assimilation, practical elimination, and personal inspiration.

Natural Inclination

What are you naturally motivated to do? *Natural inclination* can point you toward your motivational spiritual gift. When you get saved, you may have a talent that does not have anything to do with your spiritual gift. But your talent may be a way that you manifest your spiritual gift. Although you need to be saved for your spiritual gift to be manifested as God intends it, there are natural abilities inherent in us. Even before a person is saved, there are natural characteristics, that he has already begun to exhibit, of the particular motivational gift that individual inherently possesses.

After they are saved, some people may have major changes to make in their lives from what has seemed the natural way for them to act and express themselves. But God is going to allow you to do what He has naturally inclined you to do, as it is proper and fitting within the Lord's work. It will come out with your particular spiritual gift. In considering the characteristics of the different gifts, which qualities are descriptive of what seems to motivate you? What is it that you are naturally inclined to do?

Normal Assimilation

Assimilation is the process whereby nourishment is changed into living tissue. Your spiritual gift is nourishment that is needed in the body of Christ to help keep it growing and healthy. What is your *normal assimilation*? If a church asked every member to choose, from a wide variety of ministry opportunities, one area where they would like to serve, each member would eventually **assimilate** into a project and ministry that fit their motivational spiritual gift. They would normally assimilate into the area of ministry that fit them.

That is how we ought to pray regarding positions and other responsibilities to be filled in our churches. Whether your church fills its committees and leadership positions by a nominating committee or some other process, pray, that through the selection process, normal assimilation will occur. That way, people will not be asked to fill positions or spiritual responsibilities to which God has not led them.

Where is the right place and position for you because it is how you are motivated? Where do people normally expect you to be serving the Lord within the body of Christ because it fits your abilities?

Practical Elimination

Another step that can help you to recognize your spiritual gift is through *practical elimination*. What characteristics of the other motivational gifts just practically process themselves out of your life as far as being applicable to you? Some things will be eliminated from your life because those things do not motivate you. Now there are times when you are going to have to exercise some of those characteristics that have processed out of your life. For example, church staff members who serve in ministerial positions need to have organized programs if they are going to be effective in fulfilling their areas of responsibility. Organizing may not be their motivational spiritual gift, and they know it, but it comes with the territory. If you are in any leadership position in the church, you have to develop some organizational skills. If the organizing part of your position is drudgery to you, you know that it is not your motivational gift. Even though you may have to make use of some of those qualities that process themselves out of your life, you come to know through practical elimination the qualities and characteristics that are most dominant in your life.

Personal Inspiration

A fourth step that will help you to recognize your major motivational spiritual gift is *personal inspiration*. First, what personally inspires you? What do you do in the service of the Lord that is a personal inspiration to you? That tells you what motivates you. Second, what do you do that just naturally seems to personally inspire other people? As you begin to know people, and you get to know them thoroughly, they will acknowledge the qualities of your gift that they need in their life by their response to you. Your spiritual gift ministers to them.

Why are you attracted to other people for friendships? Part of the reason is because another person has a spiritual gift that complements yours. Normally, if your closest friends are those who have the same spiritual gift as yours, you may find that you often clash on various matters, although the common perception is that you would always think alike. That does not mean that you are not to have close friends with those who share the same motivational gift. But I have observed close friendships where one has the gift of mercy, and their best friend is a prophet. They are opposite in many ways, yet they complement one another. That is the beauty of how the different motivational gifts blend together.

You can learn your spiritual gift from what personally inspires you and from the qualities in your life that inspire others because you add a dimension to their life that is missing.

How They Are Related

To help us understand the seven motivational gifts even better, let us now look at **how they are related**. From the twelfth chapter of 1 Corinthians, we have already seen the human body used as an example of how the individual spiritual gifts are related to one another. The different parts of the human body must cooperate to perform what are the simplest of tasks and functions. If you want to reach down and pick up an object from the ground, there are several parts of your body that must cooperate just to accomplish this one simple movement. As you and I do something so simple, we do not purposely think in our minds, "I want to pick up this object." Before you pick up the object, you do not begin to concentrate upon sending a message down to your arm, "Muscle, move this way, and fingers, you form yourselves in the right position so that I can grasp the object." No, to us, it is not that complicated.

There are many parts of the body that work together to carry out what is very simple and something that those of us, who have full use of our body, take for granted. It is to be the same way in the church. We need to be natural. We need to be so set at doing what we do, because it comes naturally for us, that, through our cooperation, we keep the simple tasks and functions from becoming complicated. When a person does not have the full use of all parts of his body, even those simplest of body movements can become handicapped. Likewise, when one part of the body of Christ is not functioning properly, it handicaps the rest of the body. The simplest of functions within the body of believers is made difficult to properly carry out.

To help us understand how the gifts are related, let's look at a physical illustration, a practical illustration and a Scriptural illustration to see how the seven motivational gifts are related, using the analogy that is made in 1 Corinthians 12 of the human body to the body of Christ.

A Physical Illustration

The roles of the seven motivational spiritual gifts are profoundly similar to the functions of the seven sense receptors in our bodies. This provides *a physical illustration* of how the motivational gifts are related to one another. This illustration has been gleaned from the Institute In Basic Life Principles booklet, *How To Understand Spiritual Gifts*.[6]

There are seven sense receptors in each of our bodies: heat receptors, touch receptors, balance receptors, stretch receptors, cold receptors, pressure receptors, and pain receptors. The way God reveals a spiritual truth to us will usually parallel something that is very practical in life. On several occasions, in the Bible, He has chosen to use our body to help us understand His purpose regarding an aspect of the Christian life. The function of the seven sense receptors is a way by which God has given us an illustration that shows how the motivational spiritual gifts are to affect the body of Christian believers.

Heat receptors send a warning to the brain when the body's tolerance for heat has been passed. Did you ever have to do the experiment in biology lab where a frog was placed in a pot of water that was slowly heated? Little by little, the water got hotter, but the frog was not panicked because frogs do not have heat receptors like we have in our human bodies. After a few minutes, the water heated to a boil, yet the frog did not make an effort to get out of the scalding water. Eventually, the frog boiled to death.

In our human bodies, our heat receptors send a message to the brain when our body is too hot. Your heat receptors warn you that you have gone beyond the level of heat that is safe for your body.

Who warns us in the body of Christ when one has gone beyond God's limits regarding a certain issue of one's life? The *prophet*. Prophets warn us of the judgment of God when we have let the influence of sin become strong upon our lives. It usually begins with a small influence, but like the water is slowly heated in the lab experiment with the frog, a sinful influence upon one's life increases until it very well may destroy one's life. As with the frog, there is a lack of awareness that it is happening, because it occurs subtly, until sin consumes a life. We need prophets to warn us so that we will stay out of the boiling pot of sin.

Touch receptors register the slightest touch and send a signal to the brain for a response. When you are in a crowd, you can feel it when you are touched by someone. You can even sense if it is just someone inadvertently bumping into you or someone who is trying to get something of yours, hoping that you will not notice it. Your touch receptors also help you to distinguish when a hand touches you on the back or arm in a way that you know the person wants your attention. When you are purposely touched by someone, in an nonhostile manner, it is to get your attention because that person needs something from you or he wants to get information to you. *Servers* are the ones in the church who see that needs are met as they assist where the touch is needed in responding to, assisting, and meeting the needs in the church and in the lives of others.

Balance receptors let the body know when it is getting out of balance, and they alert muscles to make the appropriate response. When I was a student at the University of Tennessee in the early seventies, the drum major for the Pride of the Southland Marching Band could bend over backwards, without falling on his back or head, farther than anybody I have ever seen. Although the crowd had come to see a football game, the stadium would roar when the band came out prior to the game with the drum major strutting out in front. Then, suddenly, he would kick his legs up and bend over so far that we thought he would fall. But he would always straighten back up, just in time, and the performance would begin. His balance receptors let him know how far he could lean backwards without getting out of balance.

When doctrine is out of balance in a church, or about to get out of balance, those who are motivated as *teachers* are alerted. They call for clarification, documentation, and correction. If teachers see some kind of error that a church is making, particularly in doctrine, they want to see it corrected. If it is in the area of a belief being taught that the teachers feel is out of line, they will ask the controversial teacher to document his teachings. The teachers will demand proof and evidence for the validity of the errant teacher's statements and teachings, then they will deal with the situation accordingly.

Stretch receptors register the amount of stretching in the skin when it is growing and in use to keep it from stretching beyond its limits. When an athlete is in training, there needs to be just the right amount of stretching and straining of the muscles and skin, if he wants to better himself. It has to be controlled just right. When the athlete is in competition, he wants those muscles to give him the strength to endure and excel on the field of competition. The muscles and skin have to be stretched and strained to make them stronger, more resistant, and more durable. But the stretching and straining must not go too far or there will be an injury to the muscles or skin that will temporarily or permanently disable one from further competition.

Exhorters stretch us in our spiritual growth with steps of progress, but not beyond our limits. They know how far we can be stretched and strained to greater maturity in the Christian faith without being spiritually, physically, and emotionally harmed.

Cold receptors give off heat from the body. When an object near the skin is colder than the skin, it draws warmth from the body to itself. Several years ago, we lived in a church pastorate where the hot water heater was located in a small pump house that was several yards behind the back of the pastorate. During one extreme cold spell, the water line from the hot water heater to the house froze. When one of the men from the church came to get our water line unfrozen and running again, he also repaired a light in the pump house that was not working. He said that if I would keep that light on, when the temperature was below freezing, it would put out enough heat to keep the exposed water line from freezing up. He was right. It did not freeze again. The water line was able to draw enough heat, from a light that was several feet away, to keep from freezing. Although this example is not one using the human body, the action of the light to the water line is the same as the heat of the body to an object near it.

A *giver* is the one in a church who is most likely to respond to the needs of a cold, hungry person. The action of the giver will be appropriate for whatever is called for in the situation of the one in need. We did not need a new water heater. It was not functioning properly because a frozen water line kept the hot and cold water from getting to our house. The warmth of a light to the water line was the action that was called for. A giver will put off enough "heat" to get a cold, hungry person in a position to support himself.

Pressure receptors are triggered when there is a deep pressure on the body. The receptor signals the body to move in order to avoid pain. Only so much pressure can be placed on a part of our body. Without adjustment, the result will be a broken bone or torn ligaments, tendons, or muscles. If you have ever watched an amateur wrestling match, one reason that there is so much movement between the two wrestlers in competition is not just to avoid being pinned. It is to also avoid pain. An opponent can concede the match when he is placed in a hold that puts too much pressure on a part of his body, making the pain too great to bear. If he is not released from the hold, he could be seriously injured.

The *organizer* recognizes when too much pressure is building up on people, especially in a program or project of the church. The organizer will delegate responsibilities to others to relieve pressure when and where it is needed in order to avoid problems. His primary purpose for relieving pressure is so that people will endure and that a project will proceed as planned.

Pain receptors signal the brain when damage is occurring to the body. Other receptors can be ignored, to some extent, but not the pain receptors. There are some individuals who do not feel pain. One may think that it would be wonderful if his body could not feel pain, but it is not really to one's benefit to be unable to feel pain when the body is being damaged or injured. For example, arthritis can cause such severe conditions on the toes and feet that results in loss of feeling. I have seen slides of a severely burned foot, soaked in scalding hot water. The pain receptors of that person had not been able to get through to the brain, due to the loss of feeling caused by arthritis, to inform the person that damage was occurring to his foot.

Pain receptors respond where there is pain because they want to help the body to do what is necessary to remove the pain. The person with the gift of *mercy* feels the emotional and spiritual pain of another and responds to that individual to help the pain to be removed or eased.

Those are the seven sense receptors in the body, and there is a very interesting parallel between their functions and those of the seven motivational spiritual gifts. All of the sense receptors are necessary in the body. If one does not respond properly, it could result in great injury or damage to the body. Damage to a person's body could also result in harm to someone else. If someone driving a car leaned over to look at something on his floorboard, and his balance receptors did not alert him if he was about to lean too far, he could fall over and his car could go out of control. It could hit another car or a pedestrian, causing injury to others.

It is important for all of the sense receptors to work properly. Most of the time, they are all working together and in cooperation with one another. Likewise, the different spiritual gifts are to operate within the body of Christ. Although there are occasions when a gift works basically alone in its function, that is not the norm. Most of the time, a gift is manifested in interrelationship with one, several, or all of the other motivational gifts. If one of us does not respond with our spiritual gift to an area where we have been alerted, it could have a negative effect upon several other areas in our church.

A Practical Illustration

Let us now turn our attention to *a practical illustration* as to how the motivational gifts are related.[7]

Imagine a new church is being organized. What would each motivational gift desire for that church? What if seven individuals, representing each motivational gift, were asked the following questions: "What do you want the reputation of this new church to be? What kind of sermons do you want the pastor to preach in the worship services? What do you think he ought to be challenging and motivating the congregation to do through his sermons?"

There are various and differing opinions, even among those with the same motivational gift, as to what the primary function of a church should be. Bible study, discipleship, education, fellowship, missions, preaching, singing, social ministries, soul winning, or worship? Let's see what each of the motivational gifts would desire if the focus was for the preaching ministry of a new church.

The prophet would want a pastor who preaches well-articulated sermons that expose sin and expound the truth of the Scriptures. He wants to hear sermons that *cut to the heart*, to expound on the Word of God so that it is "quick and powerful, and sharper than any two-edged sword, piercing even to the dividing asunder of the soul and spirit, and of the joints and marrow, and is a discerner of the thoughts and intents of the heart" (Heb. 4:12).

The server would want a pastor who preaches sermons that *compel everyone to help* in the work of the Lord. They especially want sermons to motivate those who are gifted as servers to realize that by meeting the practical needs within the church, they are assisting those who lead the church spiritually.

The server would also want a church to be organized to include practical assistance for the church members who are in leadership positions so that the leaders can be relieved of pressure that can hinder them from achieving their responsibilities. This provides opportunities for the servers to have a ministry in the new church where they can liberate those whom the server believes have the more important responsibilities. They want a church where everyone has the opportunity to be involved.

The teacher wants a pastor who preaches sermons that are *clear to the head*, understandable, and truthful, because they are based and documented upon the Scriptures. Of course, the sermons need to be doctrinally sound.

Teachers envision a program of in-depth Bible study through which one can really dig into the Word of God—where emphasis is given to the importance and specific meanings of the verses and their words. They visualize Sunday school and special Bible study teachers who study the Word of God carefully, and who bring out word meanings and other shades of the meaning of a Bible word. They will also want the church publications and the literature that the church uses to be accurate and attractive in appearance.

The exhorter wants a pastor who preaches sermons that *counsel to the heart* in pointing out what hinders and may even halt spiritual growth. They want sermons to include steps of help on how to overcome the hindrances to spiritual growth and maturity.

Exhorters also want the organization of the church to include personal counseling for those who need it, as well as practical programs available to the membership where they can apply what they are learning through the ministries and programs of the church. Exhorters like weekday/weeknight programs such as the Kay Arthur Bible studies through which the Bible is studied using practical steps of action in applying the principles learned from the Word of God. Exhorters will agree that the Sunday school can very well be the greatest evangelistic ministry of a church. But the exhorter will want other programs offered during the week, in addition to the Sunday school, that will help Christians to mature in their faith.

The giver wants a pastor who preaches sermons that challenge, motivate, and compel people to give *contributions to help* further the work of the Lord. Givers know that to effectively and continually carry on the work of the Lord there must be financial support. They will want the pastor to emphasize stewardship regularly in his sermons.

Givers also desire financial programs in the church that encourage people to give to support the work of God. The giver wants a church where there will be periodic pushes to challenge and motivate the members to give. They especially want the church to be involved in giving and supporting missions. The giver knows that a church that does not give to missions and to other worthy causes will become selfish and self-centered.

The organizer wants a pastor who preaches sermons that are *consistent in harmony* and well-organized with the points of the sermon blending harmoniously together to lead to a successful conclusion. The organizer wants a sermon so well-organized that it is understandable and he can know how the pastor came to his conclusions.

Organizers want efficiently run programs in the church. It will also need to look good on paper. They will want to see the Sunday school program organized in print so that they can have readily available before their eyes the age ranges for classes, location of classes, meeting times, and the names of the teachers. Organizers will prefer for the new church to have a printed order of worship. They like to know what lies ahead in a worship service. They will get uncomfortable if the pastor or other worship leaders deviate from the order of service except on rare occasions. The organizer likes order in the worship services, Sunday school, and other meetings of the church.

Mercies desire a pastor who preaches sermons that will show *compassion for the hopeless* and that will encourage those who are hurting. They want to hear sermons that will challenge and motivate people to be compassionate to those who are hurting, helpless, and hopeless. They can be very unmerciful with preachers whom they feel just "browbeat" and "step on people's toes." They know that such preaching is necessary sometimes, but not all of the time.

The person with the motivational gift of mercy will want the new church to reach out to hurting people, such as through an intercessory prayer ministry or through such programs as outreach to unwed mothers and the mentally handicapped. They want a church that will be involved in nursing home ministry and prison ministry. Mercies want to see people encouraged and ministered to who not only have physical needs but who also have spiritual needs.

Those are just some of the things that need to be kept in mind when starting a new church. If all the motivational gifts are not ministered to, there will be a part of the body – a spiritual sense receptor – that will not be functioning properly within the church. There are many considerations to keep in mind in order to keep the members of a church happy and content, because each of the gifts is motivated differently.

We especially need to pray for the pastors of our churches, as they seek to prepare and deliver sermons. With so many expectations on what needs to be included in a sermon in order to motivate those with each of the seven motivational spiritual gifts, it is not an easy task. It would be virtually impossible to satisfy completely every spiritual gift in every sermon. As each of us needs to develop characteristics of all the gifts, we should not have to have our particular motivational gift ministered to in every sermon.

A Scriptural Illustration

In the introduction to this chapter, a passage of Scripture was used from the twelfth chapter of 1 Corinthians to help us better understand spiritual gifts. The verses in this passage especially help us to understand how the motivational gifts relate to one another. Paul used an analogy of comparing the physical parts of the body to the various parts of the body of Christ, His church. In the analogy, Paul stressed the importance of how vital it is for the members of the body to work together and in cooperation with one another:

> But now indeed there are many members, yet one body. And the eye cannot say to the hand, 'I have no need of you'; nor again the head to the feet, 'I have no need of you.' No, much

rather, those members of the body which seem to be weaker
are necessary. And those members of the body which we think
to be less honorable, on these we bestow greater honor; and
our unpresentable parts have greater modesty, but our
presentable parts have no need. But God composed the body,
having given greater honor to that part which lacks it, that
there should be no schism in the body, but that the members
should have the same care for one another. And if one member
suffers, all the members suffer with it; or if one member is
honored, all the members rejoice with it. (1 Cor. 12:20-26
NKJV)

What a beautiful ***scriptural illustration*** of how the seven motivational gifts relate with one another in the body of Christ! Not one of the motivational gifts is more important than the other. All are necessary to keep the body of Christian believers functioning properly.

I want to take this scriptural illustration a little further than what Paul has given to us. It will help this passage to become even more meaningful in its relationship to the motivational spiritual gifts. The passage in verses 20-26 leads into the description of the ministry gifts (vs. 28-30). In verses 12-27, it is possible that Paul may have had in mind the motivational gifts in his analogy of the body. After giving the body analogy, Paul then listed the ministries through which the motivational gifts can be used.

In the twelfth chapter of Romans, before listing the seven motivational spiritual gifts, Paul also used a brief analogy that compared the parts of the physical body to the body of believers. Paul said, "For as we have many members in one body, but all the members do not have the same function, so we, being many, are one body in Christ, and individually members of one another" (Rom. 12:4-5 NKJV). He then described the seven motivational gifts (vs. 6-8). Paul emphasized that although we have differing gifts, according to the grace that is given to us, we are to "use them" (v. 6). Is it possible that Paul may have had in mind, as he was inspired through the Holy Spirit, a corresponding part of the body for each motivational gift? Paul never informed us in the Scriptures that a particular body part corresponded in its function to one of the motivational gifts, but the functions of individual motivational gifts are similar to parts of the body.

Don and Katie Fortune have suggested some thought-provoking possibilities in their book on spiritual gifts, *Discover Your God-Given Gifts*.[8] Their prayerful approach to this possibility not only has led to suggestions that follow common sense logic, but their suggestions make spiritual sense. Other than their suggestion for the corresponding body part for the server, I wholly agree with their insight into relating a body part to a motivational gift. Let's see what form each of the motivational gifts takes on in relating to a part of the physical body.

The *prophet* is the *eye* of the body. Although prophets were known in the Bible as spokesmen for God, and they were known for the prophecies that they voiced, the function of their gift is like that of the eye (see Isa. 29:10). Jesus said, "The light of the body is the eye: if therefore thine eye be single, thy whole body shall be full of light. But if thine eye be evil, thy whole body shall be full of darkness. If therefore the light that is in thee be darkness, how great is that darkness!" (Matt. 6:22-23). As the prophet keeps his spiritual eyes clear and sound, he can expose sin and expound the Scriptures. The result is that the body of Christ will see life from the perspective of how God sees it and how He wants us to live. As the church is faithful to the Word of God and following the will of God, the body of believers will be full of light, shining as a light for Christ in the world (Phil. 2:15-16; Matt. 5:16).

The *server* compares with the *feet* of the body (The Fortunes compare the server with the hands). Servers are the ones in the body of Christ who do more of the laborious kind of work. The word "server," as carried over from Greek into English, literally means "through dust." The biblical picture of serving is one stirring up dust with his feet on his way to serve someone. To the server, their feet make their way to anyone for whom they can meet a practical need or assist in order for that person to achieve greater results in the Lord's work. Several Bible verses reveal how the server can best fulfill his function as part of the body of believers. Proverbs 4:26 says, "Ponder the path of thy feet, and let all thy ways be established." Some appropriate verses from the book of Psalms say, "It is God that girdeth me with strength, and maketh my way perfect. He maketh my feet like hinds' feet, and setteth me upon my high places" (Ps. 18:32-33). Paul, quoting from the book of Nahum, said, "How beautiful are the feet of them that preach the gospel of peace, and bring glad tidings of good things" (Nahum 1:15; Rom. 10:15). The feet of servers are to go where God wants them to go. The ultimate purpose of their serving is that the gospel of peace will be proclaimed, whether it is by the server or by one whom the server has liberated so they may devote time to proclaiming the good news of Jesus.

The *mind* of the body is the *teacher*. The teacher wants to confirm, clarify, and communicate truth. They want to get all the facts, and then filter through those facts in order to give an accurate report of their findings. Teachers are thinkers. They have sharp minds. Teachers are the most gifted intellectually in the body of Christ because they use their minds in exercising their gift. A descriptive verse that shows how the mind of the teachers functions in the church is Acts 17:11: "These were more noble than those in Thessalonica, in that they received the word with all readiness of mind, and searched the scriptures daily, whether those things were so." This verse was referring to the Berean Jews. They were commended for searching the Scriptures. Teachers in the body of believers use their minds to search the Scriptures to make sure that the doctrine of the church stays pure and true to the Word of God.

The *exhorter* is the *mouth* of the body. To encourage, counsel, and guide others requires the use of the mouth and the ability to communicate to those whom the exhorter seeks to help and mature in the Christian faith. The exhorter is motivated to stimulate the spiritual progress of others. To most effectively exhort others, and use the mouth in the way God intended for it to be used, requires the mouth to be used in a way that it does not tear down others, but builds them up. The exhorter, Paul, gave Timothy sound advice on how to use one's mouth as God intended: "Hold fast the form of sound words, which thou hast heard of me, in faith and love which is in Christ Jesus" (2 Tim. 1:13). A verse that illustrates well the function of the exhorter in the body of Christ is Acts 13:15: "And after the reading of the law and the prophets the rulers of the synagogue sent unto them, saying, 'Ye men and brethren, if ye have any word of exhortation for the people, say on.'" At Antioch in Pisidia, Paul gladly stood up, when he was given the opportunity, and exhorted those who were in attendance at a synagogue meeting. What an appropriate invitation the synagogue leaders gave to the apostle Paul, our main example of an exhorter!

The *giver* takes on the form of both the *hands and arms*. The giver's giving of himself, financially and spiritually, provides what is necessary to bring ministries to life and to keep them going. The "virtuous woman," described in Proverbs 31, was one who had the motivational gift of giving. Some verses from this passage especially relate the gift of giving to the hands and the arms: "She girdeth her loins with strength, and strengtheneth her arms. She perceiveth that her merchandise is good: her candle goeth not out by night. She layeth her hands to the spindle, and her hands hold the distaff. She stretcheth out her hand to the poor; yea, she reacheth forth her hands to the needy" (Prov. 31:17-20). In essence, the givers are the arms that uphold the continuation of a ministry because financial and physical needs must be taken care of for those who lead out in the Lord's work. Givers stretch out their hands and reach forth to those who have special financial needs.

The *organizer* is best represented in the form of the *shoulders*. Organizers are motivated to conceive, coordinate, and complete projects that, for the most part, involve people working together in one accord for the Lord to reach a common goal. Such undertakings are a great responsibility to shoulder. But through the organizing of the organizer, the body of Christ is able to endure (Ex. 18:23). Organizers bear the burden with the spiritual leaders to make it easier for them (Ex. 18:22). Their organizing allows for each part of the body to fulfill its function within the church. A symbolic verse for the organizer is Isaiah 9:6: "For unto us a child is born, unto us a son is given: and the government shall be upon His shoulder." That verse describes the perfect organizer, Jesus. As organizers keep their eyes upon Jesus, they can take His yoke upon them and learn of Him, finding rest and assurance in Him, as He makes the yoke easier and the burden lighter (Matt. 10:32-33).

The *heart* of the body corresponds with the person who has the gift of *mercy*. It takes a compassionate heart to relate to and remove the hindrances and hurts that others experience, seeking to weep with those who weep and to rejoice with those who rejoice. The heart of the mercy giver bears witness with the heart of one who is hurting and in need of Christ-like compassion. Second Thessalonians 3:5 is a representative verse for those with the gift of mercy: "And the Lord direct your hearts into the love of God, and into the patient waiting for Christ." In realizing and showing the love of God to those who need His mercy and compassion, as exemplified through Christians, the Lord Jesus patiently waits to welcome them into His family or back into fellowship with the Father.

In addition to the body parts with which the motivational gifts identify, the Fortunes make another picturesque observation that distinguishes two groups within the seven motivational gifts.[9] Their observation clarifies the primary function of the motivational gifts as either being that of *speaking* or of *service*. The Fortunes believe that 1 Peter 4:11 makes such a reference to the motivational gifts. This verse follows 1 Peter 4:10, which, along with Ephesians 4:7, provides the basis for the belief that each believer receives one major motivational gift. 1 Peter 4:11 says, "If any man speak, let him speak as the oracles of God; if any man minister, let him do it as of the ability which God giveth: that God in all things may be glorified through Jesus Christ." The gifts in the body of Christ, identifying with body parts above the heart, are the teacher (the mind), the prophet (the eyes), the exhorter (the mouth), and the organizer (the shoulders). These are the gifts that depend more upon *speaking* to fulfill their functions in the church. As they do so, they are to speak as if God is speaking through them.

The second half of 1 Peter 4:11, applies to the gifts that identify with parts of the body below the shoulders. They are gifts that are less dependent on the need to speak in order to be fulfilled. They are manifested the most through acts of *service*. The word "minister" in 1 Peter 4:11, may also be translated as "serve." Within the body of believers, the one with the gift of mercy (the heart), the giver (the hand and arms), and the server (the feet) function more as serving gifts in the fulfillment of their roles in the church. These gifts are to minister and serve with the ability and strength given to them by God.

This distinction between speaking or service roles for the motivational gifts also makes common sense and spiritual sense. Those with the speaking roles may get more recognition and notice, but the passage in 1 Corinthians 12 clearly informs us that the less noticed gifts make it possible for the more noticed gifts to function. One benefit of knowing this distinction about motivational gifts is that we should not expect those who are servers, givers, and mercies to be able to verbally testify for Christ like those with the more dominant speaking roles. There are those who are not very good at speaking out for the Lord. Their service and reaching out for Christ is a greater witness. Our talk for Christ does not mean too much if we do not walk it too.

Our motivational spiritual gift is a grace gift from God. Whether it is more speaking or more serving, God has given us the grace needed to accept our gift and to exercise it (see Rom. 12:6; Eph. 4:7; 1 Peter 4:10). That is our responsibility "as good stewards of the manifold grace of God" (1 Peter 4:10). As each of us is faithful to use our gift in its proper role and function, all the parts of the body of Christ will operate in the right relationship with one another.

How They React

Each of the motivational gifts **reacts to a situation differently** according to how they deal with an issue.

To better understand why some people react differently from how you react in a particular situation, two illustrations will be the focus of this section.[10] A secular illustration allows us to see how each gift might react to a familiar situation during a meal with others. Then we will examine a spiritual illustration, which shows each gift's reaction during a hospital visit.

A Secular Illustration

For *a secular illustration*, we will get a glimpse at how each spiritual gift is motivated to react when someone spills a dessert on the floor in front of others. We will make the setting a church social at a public restaurant. Those in attendance have finished the main course of the dinner and are in the process of going to the dessert table. One individual has placed a large piece of cake, topped with ice cream, on his dessert plate. As this person is walking back to his seat, the ice cream and piece of cake fall off the plate and splatter on the floor. Everyone sees it happen. For just a few seconds, which seems an eternity to the one who had the accident, all eyes are focused on the mess that has been made. Although it is only a minor mess, it is embarrassing to the one who has dropped the dessert, especially since everyone is aware of it.

You have been there. When it happened, you know that you had a brief thought about why it happened, what needed to be done, and what if it had been you.

Each of the motivational gifts initially tends to react differently to such a situation. Now I want to be very realistic. Even the most committed Christians have thoughts come their mind that may appear blunt and not so very kind or sympathetic. Those kinds of thoughts ought to be dealt with very quickly, so that one does not dwell on them. But what we think is influenced by how we are motivated.

Here is how most of the prophets would respond, if we are really honest about it: "You clumsy thing! That's what happens when you are not careful." As one who is motivated as a prophet, I have caught myself saying that to my children – not the first phrase, but the second phrase – when one of them has spilled their milk, knocked something over, or even fallen down. My child may have needed compassion, but I initially reacted by scolding them. I am more sensitive to how I react to such situations now. Fortunately, the prophet does not always say what he thinks. A prophet's correcting someone for a mistake comes from a motivation to help a person avoid making the same mistake again. What is the motivation behind the prophet's initial thoughts to the incident of the spilled dessert? It is because the chief concern of the prophet is *caution* in such a situation. The initial reaction of the prophet is to *admonish* the person who spilled the dessert for why it happened because the prophet wants to keep it from happening again.

How would the server react? His response would be: "Let me help you clean this mess up!" The main concern of the server is *care*. The server will go right to the scene of the dropped dessert because the server is naturally caring. Servers want to *assist* the person who spilled the dessert and deal with the consequences. The server cares. He wants to help clean up the mess or assist in any way that he is needed.

The teacher would think in his mind, "You dummy! With that size piece of cake, it needed to be right in the center of the plate. And you should not have placed the ice cream on top of the cake. You should have put it to the side of the cake. It got top heavy and too far to one side, and it got out of balance." The concern of the teacher is to *clarify*. Teachers are motivated to *explain* why the accident happened.

The reaction of the exhorter is to come up with some steps of action to keep the accident from happening again. The exhorter's suggested steps might be something like this: "Next time we ought to serve dessert with the meal, on a serving tray, so that it is not necessary to go back for dessert. Or, we need to put the desserts in a less congested area. Or, we need bigger plates for the desserts. Or, we need to have the dessert evenly proportioned on the plates." Exhorters will think of something very practical that will help the process work more smoothly. They seek to *correct* the problem. They want to help *avoid* another accident.

What would the giver do? This one is not too hard to figure out. His response would be: "I'll get you another dessert." If all the desserts were gone, the giver would say, "Here, take my dessert." If you had to pay to get another dessert, the giver would say, "Here's some money. Go buy another dessert." The giver's main concern is to *compensate*. The giver wants to *offset* what happened so that no one feels left out and everyone is able to enjoy the dinner.

The organizer's immediate reaction would be something like, "I'll pick up the mess. Tom, you get a mop, and Wanda, why don't you fix another dessert." The organizer jumps into action and gets the problem taken care of right then. Why? It is because the organizer wants to *conquer* this temporary obstacle to the success of the gathering. An organizer would not want this distraction to throw a kink into the enjoyment of the dinner. The organizer seeks to *overcome* what happened so that the meal continues without further delay and the purpose of the affair is completely fulfilled.

How would the person with the gift of mercy respond to this situation? The mercy giver's reaction would be something like this: "Don't feel bad. It could have happened to anyone. As a matter of fact, it happened to me before. Let me tell you about it." The person with the gift of mercy will be the one with an arm around the person who spilled the dessert because the mercy giver's chief concern is to *comfort*. The one with the motivational gift of mercy wants to *ease* what happened for the person who was embarrassed by dropping his dessert.

Well, there we have a simple secular illustration that we may see happen. When you have seen such an accident happen, you probably had similar thoughts in your mind, according to your motivational spiritual gift. For those of you who are not prophets or teachers, you may have even found yourself initially thinking like them. And, hopefully, some prophets and teachers have found yourselves not thinking along your normal patterns of thought when such an accident has occurred. You may have had initial thoughts of compassion and sympathy.

Remember, just because you may initially think something, because it is characteristic of how you are motivated, that does not mean that you are to openly react in such a manner in every circumstance. In the case of the spilled dessert, the initial thoughts of the prophet and teacher are not the proper response to this incident. Even the thoughts of the exhorter are not what need to be heard on the spot. This secular illustration is to help us see how, depending on the situation, our motivational gift is not always the one that needs to be manifested.

In such an incident as the spilled dessert, if there were only four or five people present, who had either the gift of prophecy or teaching, the prophet or teacher needs to exercise characteristics of mercy, giving, serving, or organizing in order to properly respond to the situation. If the normal reaction of our spiritual gift is not the best response needed, either let another motivational gift take the lead or be sensitive enough to exercise the characteristics of whatever gift is needed for the moment. That is why it is important for us to have an understanding of the seven motivational gifts and to develop characteristics of all of them.

A Spiritual Illustration

In this *spiritual illustration*, a descriptive nickname is given for each gift, with actions showing what that gift really desires to accomplish during a hospital visit.

The Examinator

Our nickname for the prophet is the *Examinator*. A prophet will examine someone up one side and down the other spiritually, if he is allowed the opportunity.

The prophet comes into the hospital room, and if he knows the patient well enough, he might actually say what's on his mind. In the prophet's mind, he is thinking: "What is God trying to say to you through this sickness? Is there unconfessed sin in your life that could have caused this illness?" If the prophet actually says it, because he knows the patient well, and he feels it is appropriate for the situation, the patient might feel like another doctor has come in to *examine* him again. Sometimes, God does allow physical illness to get us to the point of dealing with spiritual illness. As a patient allows a doctor to examine him to diagnose his illness and prescribe a cure, a patient may also need a spiritual examination. A prophet, who is controlled by the Spirit, will know if and when it is appropriate to get this personal with a hospital patient. This approach should only be used as the Spirit prompts, and as the patient is open to it.

The Eliminator

The server wants to be the *Eliminator* of all pressing problems for the patient. Here is the scenario when a server walks into the hospital room to visit: "Here's a little gift I picked up for you. I brought your mail from your house. By the way, don't worry about a thing at home. I fed your dog, watered your plants, vacuumed and cleaned your house, and mowed your lawn. Is there anything else you can think of that you need done?"

The server wants to *ease* things for the patient in a practical way during his hospital stay. I do not see how some of those with the gift of serving do it. By the time the patient listens to the server's list of all the things he's done, the patient might feel led to say, "Here. You get in bed. I am going home, because if I do not get out of the hospital, you are going to need more than a bed. You are going to need a casket!"

Servers want to eliminate the load of tasks, responsibilities, and work that may pile up during one's hospital stay.

The Illuminator

Our nickname for the teacher is the *Illuminator*. The teacher will do some preparation before making his hospital visit. When he gets to the patient's room, he will want to share his information with the patient: "I did some research on your sickness, and here is what I found out about it." Hopefully, what the teacher has learned does not go like this: "You know, most people have never heard of your disease before. It is very rare." Or, "I have some good news and bad news for you. The good news is that I have found out everything you need to know about your illness. The bad news is, 'Do you have a burial policy?'" The patient may or may not want to hear what the teacher has found out. The teacher wants to *enlighten* the patient more about what his sickness may be, especially if it is not a serious one, and the learning of the teacher can bring some relief for the patient.

The Escalator

We will use the nickname *Escalator* for the exhorter. An exhorter wants to take others to a higher level in their faith, but not straight up, fast, like an elevator. An exhorter seeks to take others to a higher level spiritually like an escalator, at a slower, but ascending pace that allows one to walk up the steps at a quicker pace, if he wants to and is ready for it.

The exhorter wants to come in and encourage the patient. He desires for his visit to build up the patient and to help the hospital stay make the patient a more mature Christian. The exhorter will also try to use the patient's hospital stay to be of benefit to other Christians. An exhorter will think of saying something to the patient like, "Listen, you ought to feel honored that God has allowed you to be sick." But, the exhorter will be more diplomatic than that. If I was a hospital patient, and not feeling well, if someone began talking to me like that, he might get a fluffy bed slipper in his mouth. As I got to feeling better, though, I might not be so hostile to the exhorter when he said something like this: "How can we use your sickness to help others? Here are some suggestions that I learned, when I was in a similar situation, that can help you to better yourself from this experience." The exhorter wants to *edify* the one who is in the hospital.

The Emancipator

The nickname for the giver is *Emancipator*. The giver wants the patient to be free from financial bondage due to the hospital confinement or because an outside financial burden could help add further to the patient's problems.

The giver will most likely bring the patient a gift of some kind. The conversation will be pleasant, but the giver will be interested in how the patient has been treated. Has he gotten good treatment and attention? Is the room adequate? What about the rest of the facility? Is it equipped for the tests and treatment the patient needs? Eventually the conversation will turn to finances. The giver will ask, "What kind of bill is this hospital stay going to run you? Do you have enough insurance to cover it?" The giver's concern is one of *economics*. The giver may even feel that God has sent him to that patient to help meet a financial need the patient may have because of the hospital stay, whether it is for medical expenses or some other financial need.

The Estimator

Our nickname for the organizer is the *Estimator*, because he is able to estimate exactly what needs to be done, spreading out the work among several individuals so that the strain is not too great on anyone. The organizer's properly estimating what needs to be done is a pressure reliever for the patient and his coworkers.

In this case, we will make the visiting organizer the committed Christian boss of the patient. The organizer will brighten the patient's day by informing him, "I have delegated your job to three other people while you are in the hospital." A good organizer will spread the work out between three others so that the extra work will not be too much of a burden to them and their normal workload. The organizer wants to make things easier for one who is in the hospital. He wants the patient to be able to *endure* his hospital stay while he is away from his job and other responsibilities. The organizer also desires for others to be able to endure the extra workload placed on them because their fellow worker is in the hospital.

The Exterminator

Our nickname for the person with the motivational gift of mercy is the *Exterminator*. The mercy giver wants to completely remove all the hurts and burdens of the patient through sympathizing, empathizing, and identifying with the present condition of the patient. How would the person with the motivational gift of mercy approach a visit to a patient in the hospital?

The initial conversation that the mercy giver has with the patient will probably sound like this: "I feel so bad for you. I can't get you off of my mind. How are you feeling today?" If the patient is not feeling good, by the time the mercy giver gets through being merciful, the patient may even find himself trying to cheer up and encourage his visitor. A few minutes into a visit by a mercy giver will already find the patient feeling mentally better. One with the gift of mercy will come in and *empathize* with the patient. A visit by a Spirit-controlled mercy giver will be comforting and encouraging for the patient.

I hope that these illustrations have helped you to see how the different motivational spiritual gifts react to varying situations. Hopefully, it will cause you to be more patient when someone's reaction to a situation is different from yours. Like you, they are reacting, if they are a Spirit-controlled Christian, as it is natural, appropriate, and willed for their gift to react. The situation and the circumstances involved will determine which gift is more dominant in responding to the situation. It may also mean that you need to exhibit qualities of a gift other than your special gift of blessing in order to respond as needed to a particular situation.

Conclusion

The proper use of spiritual gifts is what makes it possible to reach the world for Christ. We have learned how to recognize our motivational gift and how to relate to one another with our spiritual gift. The way each of our motivational gifts is to relate and react to the other gifts is to be for the good of all. The living out of our motivational gift is "to profit withal." I have taken five verses that particularly stand out regarding spiritual gifts to make one summary statement about how we have received our special gift of blessing, what we are to do with it, and why. Here is a Bible explanation, using Scriptures only, that reveals why you have a spiritual gift and what you are to do with it:

> As every man hath received the gift (1 Peter 4:10), as God hath dealt to every man the measure of faith (Rom. 12:3), as it hath pleased Him (1 Cor. 12:18), even so minister the same (the

gift) one to another, as good stewards of the manifold grace of God (1 Peter 4:10), to profit withal (1 Cor. 12:7), that there should be no schism in the body (1 Cor. 12:25).

Every Christian has been given one motivational spiritual gift to use within the body of Christ for the common good of all. The proper use of the gifts keeps conflict and discord out of the family of faith. There are many areas of service (ministries) through which you can employ your gift. Its effect (manifestation) will be exhibited in many different ways.

You are to develop qualities of all the motivational gifts, so you need to be able to recognize characteristics of all the gifts. To keep your church in one accord, you need to have an understanding of how all the motivational gifts relate to one another. God considers them all equally important, and they are all necessary for the body (church) to function and operate to its greatest efficiency and effect. You also need to have an understanding as to how each gift reacts to various situations. The reason that there is so much conflict in the church today is because we do not understand why others react differently from us. We tend to feel that other people ought to think, act, and react like we do. If that was the case, there would be many needs and situations, that come up within a church, that would not be met or dealt with.

How can we more effectively use our spiritual gifts to make a positive difference for Christ in the world?

First, *recognize what inspires* others (their motivation), and use your gift to *complement* theirs. Do not act like you are in competition with other Christians, even sister churches, who are trying to reach others for Christ and bring into their church families some of the same people whom you are trying to reach. Learn to compliment and complement one another, even when someone you had hoped would join your church ends up joining another church. Be thankful that the person whom you had sought to reach for Christ has been reached spiritually and is involved in a church. Regarding prospects for our churches, an overused, but truthful cliché states, "There are plenty of fish in the pond for all of us." You have to go fishing to catch fish. Those who catch the most fish are the ones who go fishing the most.

Second, *realize what irritates* others and learn how to use your gift to *cooperate* with them. There are times that we may not be in complete agreement with other Christians on certain matters, but we can learn how to give in a little bit in those areas that are not "essentials" of our faith. We can cooperate with one another so that our gifts will complement, and not resist and counteract one another.

Third, *receive illumination* from the gifts of others that will help you with decisions and circumstances in your life by *communicating* with those who are motivated differently from you. The dictionary refers to the word "illumination" as being a religious term. I like that! Although the word has secular meanings, one of its meanings is spiritual in nature. In this sense, it is like the light comes on where you have not clearly seen something of spiritual significance. You receive illumination from the other gifts by communicating with them.

In a church, it is wonderful to get involved in friendships with people who have different spiritual gifts from yours. Your friendship with them is a spiritual friendship. Your reason for being with them is not always social, but it is spiritual in its benefit to you and to them. In such friendships, you learn that you can go out with people and not have to feel like you need to be entertained. You find your conversation with these special friends centers around spiritual matters.

Those spiritual friends, who have a different motivational gift from you, can point out blind spots in your life that you are not aware of. It will help you to further develop your own spiritual gift. You will be a greater witness for the Lord.

You can learn some of the blind spots in your life from those who have a different spiritual gift than yours. That is illumination! Sight is brought to a place in your life where there has been blindness. It is not the easiest illumination to receive. It appears that this kind of illumination is one that many Christians are not receiving, or they simply are not heeding it when it is received.

What is the result of the three steps that have just been suggested? The result is that we (the church) will *impact* those within and without the church, and we will *change* the world around us more significantly, more noticeably, and more positively for Christ. Isn't that a wonderful thought? We can have these different spiritual gifts, but do you know how we are going to change the world and how we are going to reach our world the way God meant for us to do so? It will be when we start acting like the church ought to act, and when we start living every day like Christians ought to live.

God has given you your special gift of blessing to use as He intended, to become a channel of blessing within the body of believers. The blending together of all parts of the body of believers, who are all properly fulfilling their function within the body, results in a channel of blessing that flows mightily throughout the world, penetrating the world with the love of Christ. We have learned about the other spiritual gifts, and their characteristics and cautions. We have seen what the Word of God has to say about them. Hopefully, by now, you recognize your special gift of blessing. Let me remind you again, that we are to develop characteristics of all the motivational gifts in each of our lives. At different times, you are to manifest qualities of the other gifts in your life. The question of the moment, though, is, "What about right now?" Most of you probably have a good idea of what you believe to be your major motivational gift. The question for you to consider right now is this: "What am I doing, at this point in my life, with my special gift of blessing?"

Father, I thank You for this manifold gift of grace that You have given to each of us. Lord, I pray that right now all who have read this book will use their special gift of blessing in a way that will impact this world, at least, the world around us, and that will change this world for Christ. Thank you, Father, for the greatest gift of all, the forgiveness of our sins and the gift of eternal life in heaven through Jesus Christ our Lord and Savior, in whose name I pray. Amen.

1. Words and tune, EUCLID, Harper G. Smyth, 1903.

2. Oswald Chambers, *Approved Unto God* (Bristol, Great Britain: Oswald Chambers Publications Association and Marshall Pickering, 1987), 65.

3. Ibid., 68.

4. James H. Smith, *You Have A Grace Gift* (Memphis: Baptist Brotherhood Commission of the Southern Baptist Convention, 1987), 83-84.

5. Don and Katie Fortune, *Discover Your God-Given Gifts* (Tarryton, New York: Fleming H. Revell's Chosen Books, 1987), 26.

6. *How To Understand Spiritual Gifts* (Oak Brook, Illinois: Institute in Basic Youth Conflicts, 1986), 57.

7. Adapted from *How To Understand Spiritual Gifts*, 85.

8. Fortune, *Discover Your God-Given Gifts,* 28-32.

9. Ibid., 31-32.

10. The idea for these illustrations came from *How To Understand Spiritual Gifts*, 80, 82.

Spiritual Gifts Inventory

Identifying Your Spiritual Gift

Part 1. Personal Choice

Check the circles that identify you. This sentence characterizes me:

Usually	Sometimes	Rarely	
☼	☼	☼	1. I have the need to express thoughts and ideas verbally, especially regarding right and wrong.
☼	☼	☼	2. I have an ability to see practical needs and am motivated to meet them.
☼	☼	☼	3. I have the motivation to check out and verify statements which have been made by others.
☼	☼	☼	4. I am motivated to urge people to their full spiritual maturity in Christ.
☼	☼	☼	5. I have a keen ability to discern wise investments in order to have more money available to give.
☼	☼	☼	6. I have an ability to visualize the final goal of a major undertaking.
☼	☼	☼	7. I have the ability to sense the atmosphere of joy and distress in an individual or group.
☼	☼	☼	8. I have the tendency to make immediate evaluations on what is seen and heard and to speak up quickly.
☼	☼	☼	9. I find joy in serving when it frees others to do more important things.

Usually Sometimes Rarely

Usually	Sometimes	Rarely	
✧	✧	✧	10. I have a tendency to evaluate all new truth I hear from what I already understand from Scripture.
✧	✧	✧	11. I have an ability to discern where a person is in the process of spiritual growth and to help them grow more.
✧	✧	✧	12. I have a desire to give quietly without public notice.
✧	✧	✧	13. I have an ability to break down major goals into smaller achievable tasks.
✧	✧	✧	14. I have a tendency to attract people who are experiencing mental and emotional distress.
✧	✧	✧	15. I have an amazing ability to sense when someone or something is not what it appears to be and I respond firmly to dishonesty and deception.
✧	✧	✧	16. I have a tendency to disregard personal health and comfort in serving others.
✧	✧	✧	17. I have a desire for others to know I am competent when I teach and I may share how I became qualified to teach the subject.
✧	✧	✧	18. I have a desire to give precise steps of action in urging people toward spiritual maturity.

Usually Sometimes Rarely

☼   ☼   ☼   19. I am motivated to give as unto the Lord at His promptings, not at man's appeals.

☼   ☼   ☼   20. I have an ability to know what resources are available and needed to reach a goal.

☼   ☼   ☼   21. I desire to remove hurts and bring emotional healing to others rather than to look for the benefits from problems.

☼   ☼   ☼   22. I desire to see God's discipline brought to those who offend, so that justice may be done and others will be warned.

☼   ☼   ☼   23. I have a difficulty in saying "no," resulting in a variety of involvements and a tendency to get over-involved.

☼   ☼   ☼   24. I have a desire to present truth in a systematic sequence.

☼   ☼   ☼   25. I am motivated to explain truth with logical reasoning in order to make it understood and accepted.

☼   ☼   ☼   26. I have a desire to give financial gifts that I know will be used in such a way as to bring glory to God.

☼   ☼   ☼   27. I have a tendency to remove myself from distracting details in order to focus on the ultimate goal.

Usually   **Sometimes**   **Rarely**

○   ○   ○   28. I have a greater concern for the mental distress of people than for their physical needs.

○   ○   ○   29. I have an openness about my personal faults and failures and an honesty about myself before others.

○   ○   ○   30. I enjoy providing for the physical needs and comforts of others.

○   ○   ○   31. I find delight in researching and reporting as many facts on a subject as possible.

○   ○   ○   32. I have an ability to visualize spiritual achievement for people and to use this to motivate them to action.

○   ○   ○   33. I have an ability to test others' faithfulness and wisdom by how they handle money.

○   ○   ○   34. I have a willingness to endure reaction from insiders and outsiders in order to reach an ultimate goal.

○   ○   ○   35. I have a tendency to avoid firmness with others unless I see it will eliminate greater hurts.

○   ○   ○   36. I have a tendency to be impulsive in actions and to be wholeheartedly involved in whatever is done.

Usually Sometimes Rarely

⚙   ⚙   ⚙   37. I have a genuine need for appreciation to confirm that service is necessary and satisfactory.

⚙   ⚙   ⚙   38. I emphasize the importance and accuracy of reporting facts.

⚙   ⚙   ⚙   39. I have a desire for face-to-face discussion in order to determine and ensure a proper response.

⚙   ⚙   ⚙   40. I have a tendency to practice personal frugality and have an ability to be content with the basic necessities of life.

⚙   ⚙   ⚙   41. I have a need for loyalty and confidence from those who are being directed and served.

⚙   ⚙   ⚙   42. I have a sensitivity to words and actions which will hurt other people.

⚙   ⚙   ⚙   43. I have a tendency to be painfully direct when correcting friends.

⚙   ⚙   ⚙   44. I have a strong desire to be with others, thus providing more servicing opportunities.

⚙   ⚙   ⚙   45. I am alert to factual details which are not noticed or mentioned by others.

⚙   ⚙   ⚙   46. I have an ability to identify with people of different types and backgrounds in order to minister more effectively.

Usually   Sometimes   Rarely

☼   ☼   ☼   47. I have an alertness to how other people use their money.

☼   ☼   ☼   48. I have an ability to know what I should and should not delegate to others.

☼   ☼   ☼   49. I have an ability to discern love in other people.

☼   ☼   ☼   50. I desire to give open evidence of loyalty and commitment.

☼   ☼   ☼   51. I enjoy short-range projects and have a tendency to become frustrated with long-range responsibilities.

☼   ☼   ☼   52. I have a tendency to remain silent until information has been heard, observed, and discussed.

☼   ☼   ☼   53. I have a motivation to bring harmony between diverse groups of Christians and an awareness that harmony is basic to spiritual maturity.

☼   ☼   ☼   54. I have an ability to see financial needs which others tend to overlook.

☼   ☼   ☼   55. I have an ability to inspire and encourage workers by cheerfulness, approval, praise, and challenges.

☼   ☼   ☼   56. I have an enjoyment and unity with those who are sensitive to the needs and feelings of others.

Usually	Sometimes	Rarely	
✿	✿	✿	57. I am willing to suffer for doing what is right, no matter what the cost.
✿	✿	✿	58. I often have a tendency to feel inadequate and unqualified for spiritual leadership; I would rather do practical service.
✿	✿	✿	59. I tend to exercise diligence and endurance in completing responsibilities.
✿	✿	✿	60. I have an ability to welcome personal tribulation as a chief motivator of spiritual growth.
✿	✿	✿	61. I have a desire to use giving as a way to motivate others.
✿	✿	✿	62. I have a joy and fulfillment in seeing all the parts come together in a finished product.
✿	✿	✿	63. I have a tendency to close my spirit to those who are insincere or insensitive.
✿	✿	✿	64. I have an ability to be very persuasive in defining what is right and wrong.
✿	✿	✿	65. I have the desire to complete a job with evidence of unexpected extra service.
✿	✿	✿	66. I place an emphasis on the precise meaning of words.
✿	✿	✿	67. I desire to see outward evidences which demonstrate inward conviction.

Part 2. Multiple Choice

Circle the answer that is true about you.

68. When I am asked to teach a lesson, I enjoy more
    a. doing research for the lesson.
    b. presenting the lesson.
    c. I don't like doing research.

69. I enjoy research in order to
    a. present what I have studied.
    b. clarify the subject for myself.
    c. I don't enjoy research.

70. I enjoy more speaking to
    a. a group.
    b. an individual.
    c. I don't enjoy speaking.

71. When speaking to a group, I receive greater joy from
    a. seeing an immediate response of commitment.
    b. having an opportunity to counsel as a result of speaking.
    c. I don't enjoy speaking.

72. I enjoy personal follow-up in order to
    a. encourage spiritual growth.
    b. confirm and strengthen the commitment the person has made.
    c. I don't enjoy much follow-up.

73. I am more comfortable in helping to meet
    a. the practical needs of others.
    b. the mental and emotional needs of others.
    c. neither a nor b

74. In a worship service, I'm more concerned with
    a. the atmosphere of the service.
    b. the scriptural pattern of the service.
    c. neither a nor b

75. Given the responsibility to organize for an activity, I prefer to
    a. delegate to others.
    b. perform most of the responsibilities myself.
    c. I'm not given to organizing activities.

76. I enjoy most
    a. short-range projects.
    b. long-range projects.
    c. I'm not involved in many short or long-range projects.

77. I enjoy counseling individuals in order to
    a. give them steps of action to follow.
    b. discern what their practical needs are and find out how to meet their needs.
    c. neither a nor b

78. In helping persons with problems, I am more comfortable in
    a. counseling them.
    b. meeting a practical need.
    c. I don't do enough counseling to know.

79. I enjoy teaching
    a. in order to communicate truth.
    b. as an opportunity to counsel others.
    c. I don't teach.

80. In finding solutions to human problems, I usually begin with
    a. Scripture and relate it to human experiences.
    b. human experiences and relate them to Scripture.
    c. I don't know.

81. If I were responsible for an organization where conflicts were caused by an employee, I would
    a. have the tendency to change the employer's responsibilities and position to eliminate the problem.
    b. work with the employees to gain benefit from solving the conflict.
    c. I don't deal with others' conflicts enough to know.

82. I receive greater joy in giving to

    a. meet the practical needs of an individual.

    b. a person who is involved in a specific ministry to others.

    c. Neither brings a greater joy.

83. I am interested in solving problems so that

    a. unnecessary suffering can be prevented.

    b. I may challenge the person on to spiritual maturity.

    c. I'm not involved in helping others solve problems.

84. I am interested in spiritual growth primarily for the sake of

    a. growing to maturity.

    b. eliminating suffering and disharmony caused by wrong responses to problems.

    c. Neither reflects my interest in spiritual growth.

85. When I am being helped by someone, it is more important to me to

    a. sense a genuine concern and interest in the person helping me.

    b. be given steps of action in solving a problem.

    c. Neither is important to me.

86. I desire harmony in an organization

    a. so that it may run smoothly and effectively accomplish its goal.

    b. because of the joy and fellowship which results.

    c. I desire harmony for reasons other than these.

87. I receive greater joy in

    a. being able to discuss a problem openly and freely.

    b. designing steps to solve the problem.

    c. I'm not significantly involved in solving others' problems.

88. I am motivated to do research in order to

    a. establish correct doctrine.

    b. understand doctrinal differences among Christians and how to bring harmony and oneness.

    c. I don't enjoy research.

Tally Sheet for Spiritual Gifts Survey

Instructions:

1. Using the Survey you filled out, give yourself the following points:
   Questions 1-67
   > 2 points for Usually; 1 point for Sometimes; 0 points for Rarely
   Questions 68-88
   > 2 points for letter (a or b) checked

Prophecy	Serving	Teaching	Exhorting	Giving	Organizing	Mercy
1	2	3	4	5	6	7
8	9	10	11	12	13	14
15	16	17	18	19	20	21
22	23	24	25	26	27	28
29	30	31	32	33	34	35
36	37	38	39	40	41	42
43	44	45	46	47	48	49
50	51	52	53	54	55	56
57	58	59	60	61	62	63
64	65	66	67	82b	75a	84a
68b	73a	68a	70b		76b	85a
69a	75b	69b	71b		81a	86b
70a	76a	74b	72b		86a	87a
71a	77b	79a	77a		87b	88b
72b	78b	80a	78a			
	82a	88a	79b			
			80b			
			81b			
			83b			
			84b			
			85b			

% Total

2. Add up the points in each column. This is the "raw score."
3. Convert your total points to percentile, using the table on the next page.
4. Enter total and percentile in the boxes at the top of the graph on the last page.
5. Make a dot on the graph in each area using your percentile scores, then draw a line between the dots. This will visually indicate your stronger motivational gift(s).

Table for Converting Raw Scores to Percentile

Raw Score	Prophecy	Serving	Teaching	Exhorting	Giving	Organizing	Mercy	Raw Score
0	1	1	1	1	1	1	1	0
1	3	3	3	3	5	4	4	1
2	6	6	6	5	10	7	7	2
3	9	9	9	8	15	11	11	3
4	13	13	13	10	20	14	14	4
5	16	16	16	13	25	18	18	5
6	19	19	19	15	30	21	21	6
7	22	22	22	18	35	25	25	7
8	25	25	25	20	40	28	28	8
9	28	28	28	23	45	32	32	9
10	31	31	31	25	50	35	35	10
11	34	34	34	28	55	39	39	11
12	38	38	38	30	60	43	43	12
13	41	41	41	33	65	46	46	13
14	44	44	44	35	70	50	50	14
15	47	47	47	38	75	53	53	15
16	50	50	50	40	80	57	57	16
17	53	53	53	43	85	60	60	17
18	56	56	56	45	90	64	64	18
19	59	59	59	48	95	67	67	19
20	63	63	63	50	99	71	71	20
21	66	66	66	53	99	75	75	21
22	69	69	69	56	99	78	78	22
23	72	72	72	58	99	82	83	23
24	75	75	75	60	99	86	86	24
25	78	78	78	63	99	89	89	25
26	81	81	81	65	99	93	93	26
27	84	84	84	68	99	96	96	27
28	88	88	88	70	99	99	99	28
29	91	91	91	73	99	99	99	29
30	94	94	94	75	99	99	99	30
31	97	97	97	78	99	99	99	31
32	99	99	99	80	99	99	99	32
33	99	99	99	83	99	99	99	33
34	99	99	99	85	99	99	99	34
35	99	99	99	88	99	99	99	35
36	99	99	99	90	99	99	99	36
37	99	99	99	93	99	99	99	37
38	99	99	99	95	99	99	99	38
39	99	99	99	98	99	99	99	39
40	99	99	99	99	99	99	99	40
Raw Score	Prophecy	Serving	Teaching	Exhorting	Giving	Organizing	Mercy	Raw Score

Table for Identifying Your Spiritual Gift

	Prophecy	Serving	Teaching	Exhorting	Giving	Organizing	Mercy	
Total								Total
%								%
95								95
90								90
85								85
80								80
75								75
70								70
65								65
60								60
55								55
50								50
45								45
40								40
35								35
30								30
25								25
20								20
15								15
10								10
5								5
	Prophecy	Serving	Teaching	Exhorting	Giving	Organizing	Mercy	